CAN'T STOP THE GRRRLS

CAN'T STOP THE GRRRLS

Confronting Sexist Labels in Pop Music from Ariana Grande to Yoko Ono

Lily E. Hirsch

ROWMAN & LITTLEFIELD

Lanham • Boulder • New York • London

Published by Rowman & Littlefield
An imprint of The Rowman & Littlefield Publishing Group, Inc.
4501 Forbes Boulevard, Suite 200, Lanham, Maryland 20706
www.rowman.com

86-90 Paul Street, London EC2A 4NE, United Kingdom

British Library Cataloguing in Publication Information Available

Library of Congress Cataloging-in-Publication Data

Names: Hirsch, Lily E., 1979- author.
Title: Can't stop the grrrls : confronting sexist labels in pop music from Ariana Grande to Yoko Ono / Lily E. Hirsch.
Other titles: Can't stop the girls
Description: Lanham : Rowman & Littlefield, 2023. | Includes bibliographical references and index. | Summary: "From stars like Britney Spears and Mariah Carey to classic icons like Yoko Ono, female musicians have long been the target of toxic labels in the media and popular culture: liar, crazy, snake, diva, and so on. This book takes a candid look at the full range of sexist labeling and inspires us to think about these remarkable women on their own terms" —Provided by publisher.
Identifiers: LCCN 2022033657 (print) | LCCN 2022033658 (ebook) | ISBN 9781538169063 (cloth) | ISBN 9781538169070 (epub)
Subjects: LCSH: Sexism in music. | Women musicians. | Women in popular culture.
Classification: LCC ML82 .H57 2023 (print) | LCC ML82 (ebook) | DDC 780.82—dc23/eng/20220718
LC record available at https://lccn.loc.gov/2022033657
LC ebook record available at https://lccn.loc.gov/2022033658

CONTENTS

AUTHOR'S NOTE

Words can be wrong. Words can do wrong. How do I discuss that wrong while using those words? How do I discuss that wrong while using any words?

My goal in writing this book is to examine how toxic labeling happens over and over again in the music industry and media, and how it affects female musicians and audiences more generally. By spotlighting the consequences as well as the pervasiveness of this labeling, I hope to create a certain awareness and, in the end, real change—both in the words we use and the assumptions we make about women in music. However, in order to out this labeling, I have to platform the related toxic attacks—ones often both misogynistic and racist. To make matters worse, the female musicians under discussion in this book have already experienced extraordinary public pile on and hate. It is not my intention to add to that bullying. There are then clearly several moral issues to consider.

In this regard, I've been thinking lately, too, about the recent documentaries focused on the mistreatment and abuse of female celebrities, which seem to have come out as I was working on this book in some sort of zeitgeist alignment fed by collective rage. In fact, several documentaries have focused on Britney Spears and Janet Jackson, among others. But there was also the Hulu series *Pam & Tommy* (2022). The project purported to have noble goals of education, like the documentaries. And yet, the show re-created parts of the infamous sex tape that was stolen from Pamela Anderson and Tommy Lee. In so doing, it arguably exploited the trauma of Anderson's past as entertainment, with lots of skin and even a talking penis. Though Anderson herself refused to participate, the show's creators still felt justified in creating the series, hiding behind inconsistent notions of gender discrimination and moral betterment. Although this approach to the crimes of the past clearly seems wrong, what is the right way to confront and challenge abuse when it involves someone else's trauma?

In the presentation of this book's material, ethical considerations revolve around readers' potential reactions. I cannot presume to know how this book will affect individual readers—what triggers one person may not trigger another. And, as the *New Yorker* has pointed out ("What If Trigger Warnings Don't Work?"), marking a text up front as somehow traumatizing might work against the writer's aims or even the psychological health of individual readers. I'm certainly well aware of the negative emotions this book might inspire—as I myself was furious as I researched and wrote many parts of this book. But again, what is the best way to combat past injustice without offending or inadvertently traumatizing or retraumatizing readers?

I don't have answers to all of these questions. I do, however, want to note these issues openly and up front. And I want to promise you, the reader, as well as the women highlighted throughout the book, that I was aware of each concern in every part of the writing process. I have tried to quote only minimally the worst of the attacks. The toxic labels and slurs I do cite are only included to make broader points around their wrong. Though I have sought to write accessible prose, I have no hidden agenda around entertainment, and I do not include speaking roles for anatomical parts. That intended writing style—comprehensible and user-friendly—is meant to help make my arguments sharp and effective. I hope these objectives are clear throughout, and that, in the end, this book can be the start or continuation of significant reevaluation and ultimately revolution in the language we use to frame women and their achievements in music.

ACKNOWLEDGMENTS

Several wonderful individuals helped shape this project. I want to high-light and thank two of my favorite scholars in music—Robert Fink and Ellie Hisama—for supportive conversation and communication along the way. A similar thanks to my fellow panelists and chair Robin James at the 2021 national conference of the American Musicological Society (AMS), at which I presented the paper "The Yoko Effect—From Alma Mahler to Ariana Grande." The whole experience was hugely motivating and uplift-ing, and AMS has continued to help, through its new Cusick Fund, a unique resource for independent scholars. I'm truly honored to be part of the inaugural grantee group. I also want to express my gratitude to Shelly Peiken for allowing me to interview her for the final chapter, by phone, on February 28, 2022.

Michael Tan deserves an especially loud tribute. In some ways, he's been more than an editor; he's been a collaborator. With our overlapping vision and similar sensibilities (as well as his kindness), it's been a true pleasure working with him on this project. I also want to thank the whole team at Rowman & Littlefield. This book is my second project with R&L and for good reason: it's a joy to work with a publisher I can count on and trust.

For useful information about and insight into K-pop, I want to acknowl-edge Lillian Yang. I also want to recognize the many strong women I have known in music—all of whom have helped me see the truth about gender bias and toxic labeling. Some of them I am lucky to call friends: Melanie Vartabedian, Cori Shechter, Carrie Mallonée, Tasha Jahn, and Amy Wlodarski, to name a few. One, in particular, deserves special mention, Joy Willow. She introduced me to music as my piano teacher when I began taking lessons at age seven. But she quickly became my confidante and friend, as well as a personal role model. Now, I consider her family.

For more general conversation and inspiration, I would like to thank my partner in vibes, Sybil Halloran, as well as my partner in life, Austin Roelofs. While I was researching and writing this book, Austin was constantly on the lookout for material related to the topic, sending links to news articles and fresh stories. But, practical help aside, I want to acknowledge him because he always gives me hope. Some men, like Austin, are strong enough to support the women around them unconditionally.

This book, in so many ways, is for my children, Grant and Elliana. It is heartening to see how readily they accept difference—their own and others'—and react with tolerance. More than anything, I want this book to be part of a conversation that will ultimately benefit them while helping us all match their promise.

FOREWORD

Meshell Ndegeocello

I was nurtured in a way that music not only held the potential for spiritual glory, or a change in one's circumstance, or as a legitimate livelihood, all of which were rare enough in the homes and families of other people I knew. Music was also taught to me as a way to communicate my selfhood authentically, as a tool for my wielding and an aid to others in understanding me. Music was a foundation for interaction, connection, and friendship. Music could make or break a party, be a vehicle to convey information, change the energy in a room, make you cry, be the audible spark for the inner fire you need for your workout, it entertains and enlivens. Music is in the realm of magic to me. That magic comes in many forms and one of the most powerful incarnations is when it is allowed to flourish and encapsulate the vibration of the feminine. Women are not only the subject and object of song but all through history women were often a child's first introduction to its power, to lull, to soothe, to teach, and to embody and transmit love.

I was lucky someone taught me about music, showed me its power, revered it even more than the social myths about women. It's not to extol the virtues of that person, my father was morally uneven, ethically compromised, frequently seduced by the trappings of class, dazzled by the sparkles of the music industry. But his love of music was pure, his command of it was natural, his humanity most evident and transparent when he played. He was a singular musical force trapped inside a common man. His instruction was often harsh, dogmatic, unjust, and unyielding but his lessons were lifesaving. I too could be a singular musical force. I too was trapped in a corporeal shell. I thought this made us equal. But I quickly learned that my shell was valued less than his. Nothing taught me that more than the music industry.

As an androgynous woman, clear about her queerness and unwilling to commodify it, the industry faced an uphill battle. They tried hard to spin my identity into something socially acceptable or something exoticized and hypersexual. I cared little enough about marketing to allow that during the time after I was signed, when I was still just happy to be there. But when it came to making music, once I explored outside the bounds of the image they'd defined, I was uncooperative and difficult. The complicated nature of my womanhood was entwined with an equally offensive idea of my race. "Black music" to the White executives at my record label was something they were more qualified to judge than I. What Black, female emotion should sound like was their area of expertise. When I made an album called "Bitter," it was left to wither without the usual machine of marketing and support behind it. If I didn't dance the dance they knew, or god forbid I didn't dance at all, I was no longer valuable.

Finding a way to be myself in the music industry has required a mutual adjustment of expectations, lowered on both sides. It has cost me relationships, fame, budgets, access, stature. The industry simply lost my interest, their credibility, any power to enthrall or make me believe. The losses surely hurt them less. But the wins—making the music I felt in my heart, making music about subjects outside of love and sex, not putting my image on every cover, not towing a carefully drawn PR line in interviews, protecting my privacy, feeling proud of myself—were all greater than anything I'd earned before.

When I see Madison Cunningham, St. Vincent, Moor Mother, Matana Roberts, H.E.R., Zoh Amba, U.S. GIRLS, Brandee Younger, and Joan as Police Woman, or Toshi Reagan, Terri Lynn Carrington and all the immensely talented women who have dedicated their life to their instruments, I am able to see how the change is flourishing. As in so many industries and communities, women are weaving and constructing new worlds in which to thrive, paths of their own, innovative ways to exist within and outside, to participate while transforming a male created, dominated, perpetuated infrastructure that is fickle and narrow and prescribed. The work stands tall no matter the gender of the person who has created it, but the work of women stands tallest because it was often not meant to stand at all. My belief is that we must create it, record it, promote it, perform it for ourselves, of ourselves, and they will come. It is a terrible gift, the requirement to make the space ourselves for ourselves but it is the only way the space will come, and it is the only way it will be ours.

INTRODUCTION

On January 21, 2022, singer Ari Lennox announced that she was through with the music industry. She wanted to be dropped from her label. After a disgusting interview on the *Podcast and Chill* show, she needed to be "free." The host, MacGyver Mukwevho, had asked her, "And where are we at right now? Is someone f*cking you good right now?" It was the final straw; she didn't want to deal with any more abusive attention. On Twitter, she explained her decision, insisting that anyone who was judging her for her decision "wouldn't last a day as a signed artist."

Just over two months later, the rapper Doja Cat similarly announced her retirement after a frustrating experience performing in South America, with fans upset about her performance and her no-show for pictures. She posted, "[I]'m a f***ing fool for ever thinking [I] was made for this." In light of the media's radical history of treating musicians in toxic ways, many people *would* struggle as signed artists, as Lennox insisted, possibly opting for an early out or at least a brief hiatus. But it's no coincidence that both Lennox and Doja Cat are women. Let's be clear: the toxic treatment of musicians isn't the same for all genders, and women are clearly pushed and exploited in ways that other artists aren't.

Sadly, it's taken me a while to recognize this truth. In 2004, I remember watching the Super Bowl and missing the scandalous reveal of Janet

Jackson's breast. But I couldn't avoid the aftermath, as a confusing narrative emerged. She had supposedly done this on purpose. She was oversexed and scandalous, some said. And it didn't matter that Justin Timberlake had wrongly ripped her clothing. She alone was to blame. Then, in 2007 and 2008, I followed the latest Britney-be-damned takes as Spears in rapid succession shaved her head and was hauled off to the hospital. She was "crazy," I thought, nodding along with the headlines.

As a student of classical music, I had studied "crazy" composers who were nonetheless respected, such as electronic music pioneer Karlheinz Stockhausen, who believed that he came from a planet near the star Sirius. But they were men, so their "crazy" was a sign of genius. I must have internalized that message. Whereas his "crazy" was good, Spears was just "crazy," with no redemptive spin. If I made a false move, I might be considered that kind of "crazy," too, and, as I learned from the messaging around Jackson, I would have no one else to blame, no matter who else was involved.

I didn't even need to read anything specific about Yoko Ono. I knew, or believed I knew, that she broke up the Beatles. And I wasn't alone. In a 2015 *Vulture* article, "Yoko Ono and the Myth That Deserves to Die," journalist Lindsay Zoladz wrote, "I bought the Yoko Myth wholesale . . . I thought I knew about Yoko Ono. I had a lot to learn." When I started dating a guy in a band, I held my tongue, aware of the warning. Eventually, I lied: "The music is great! Yes, even that part with the cowbell."

Of all the tales we've been told about women in music, the popular version of Ono's history is one of the most pervasive and powerful. It has become myth, defined here as an "oppressive belief" with the ability to standardize certain cultural values.[1] The name "Yoko" has also transformed into a label of sorts, affecting more than just Ono, even in hindsight. For example, legendary musician Alice Coltrane is still understood by some as the "Yoko Ono of jazz," blamed for her husband's late shift in style and punished for replacing McCoy Tyner on the piano in the John Coltrane Quartet.[2] There are also, of course, many "modern-day Yokos," dubbed as such in the press and in public opinion. The list extends from Courtney Love and L'Wren Scott to Taylor Swift and Meghan Markle, Jessica Simpson and FKA twigs to Ariana Grande and Perrie Edwards, among others.

The press coverage of each of these women contains parallels, especially in regard to their love lives or the troubles of their partners. But in some cases, the media also explicitly branded these women "Yoko," drawing them into an ill-defined category of objectionable women. In the *New York Daily News*, December 10, 2012, the headline: "The New Yoko? Taylor Swift Blasted as the 'Yoko Ono' of One Direction." On *News Break*, "Is Meghan Markle the Modern-Day Yoko Ono?" Courtney Love was forced to address the label, in *Rolling Stone* (April 6, 2014), "Courtney Love Rejects Yoko Ono Comparisons." And in other examples, journalists themselves have countered the attack, as in the case of Ariana Grande (in the *Rolling Stone* article, September 10, 2018, "'You Did This to Him': Ariana Grande, Mac Miller and the Demonization of Women in Toxic Relationships").

The "Yoko" tag is then one of many words in a vast overlapping network of toxic labels and slurs routinely attached to women in music. These labels include gold digger, bitch, witch, jezebel, liar, crazy, snake, diva, and slut, among others. And many of the "modern-day Yokos" have been branded with these words as well. Swift is supposedly a snake; Grande a diva; and FKA twigs a gold digger. But, as this book makes clear, all of these gendered labels perpetuate a double standard in the treatment of women in music, a "miss-treatment" of women in pop music.

Not only are the words often female-specific, but the attached stigma is, too. "Crazy" is a word of condemnation in Spears's case but a sign of genius for men. The labels mark a woman when she supposedly makes a misstep, though that same action, performed by a man, can be positively explained away. Mariah Carey, for example, has been called the ultimate diva, with rumors of her supposed wild backstage demands, including a supply of blue M&M's (a rumor she has denied). At the same time, Van Halen admits to a similar demand—for M&Ms with all the brown ones removed—and, according to *Insider*, there's "a brilliant reason." The all-male band members just want to make sure concert promoters are reading their concert rider, including details of the stage setup. It's "shrewd business."[3]

The double standards and the related toxic labeling of women vary by individual, and racism has a significant impact in certain cases. But this abuse, whether deployed as insult or disguised as a joke, in all cases works to enforce certain norms of behavior expected of women—in Kate Manne's words, a "logic of misogyny."[4] And by women, I refer here and throughout the book to anyone who identifies as such. With a celebrity platform, the labels punish women so labeled but also all of us, as we receive or process the intended message and act or don't act accordingly. At times, it's confusing, as it was for me after the 2004 Super Bowl. At other times, it's worse, when a person needs help but is afraid to reach out because she doesn't want to be labeled "crazy." Then, it's dangerous or even deadly.

In these ways, the labeling plays a role in a collective gaslighting, mobilizing "gender-based stereotypes" against "victims to erode their realities."[5] We question what we thought we knew or understood as well as what we desperately need. The popular expression "sticks and stones may break your bones, but words can never hurt you" is, then, wildly wrong. Words can hurt us. And the wounds are everywhere, for the women specifically targeted as well as everyone else.[6]

To understand this treatment and its effects, we have to go back to the beginning, and on a biblical scale, with Eve, Adam's early scapegoat. Although evolving in the details of its application, or even the labels themselves, the blaming and shaming of women is clearly far from new. But this example also highlights a significant ingredient in the labeling of women— a woman's relationship to another person. In some ways, it then makes a twisted kind of sense that music has become a hotbed of gendered putdowns. After all, making music is relational in nature, with people working together, negotiating sound, and interacting with each other as they do so. The creation of music also requires the support of other people, often family members or partners.[7] All of these people are potential fodder for twisted myths, invented stories, and toxic labels.

Still, romantic relationships with men seem to feature significantly in the toxic labeling of women. Obviously, other types of romantic relationships existed and exist. But they haven't always received the same attention for a variety of reasons around cultural conditioning, prejudice, and patriarchal standards. In some cases, musicians and their handlers also actively sought to hide same-sex couplings, as in the career of Whitney Houston or the promotion of the all-female band Fanny.[8] This attention to men has helped twist the telling of women's history since the beginning, with double standards that certainly don't match the reality of relational possibilities or gender fluidity. Despite the flawed setup, the messaging and repercussions have been all too real—both seen and unseen but always experienced or felt by someone.

During the Romantic era, it was the relationship between the composer Gustav Mahler and his legendary wife, Alma, that became the basis for Yoko-adjacent labeling. Alma supported the much older Gustav while suppressing her own career as a composer—at his request. But she was terribly unhappy living for and through him and eventually had an affair. With their marriage in trouble, Gustav finally helped her publish some of her music. After Gustav's death, she married other high-profile artists, including architect Walter Gropius and writer Franz Werfel—inspiring parodist Tom Lehrer's song "Alma" (1965). The chorus:

Alma, tell us:
All modern women are jealous
Which of your magical wands
Got you Gustav and Walter and Franz?

As a woman in music, she stood out. Her reward? In her biography, author Oliver Hilmes calls her the "malevolent muse." And not just anywhere—in the title, *Malevolent Muse: The Life of Alma Mahler*. Alma may not have been perfect, but men in music, like the notoriously difficult Ludwig van Beethoven or even the anti-Semitic Richard Wagner, have never been treated comparably in the writing of classical music's history.

Another early point of comparison is French novelist George Sand (real name, Amantine Lucile Aurore Dupin), a woman who dispensed with the norms of her day and had a love affair with Romantic composer Frédéric Chopin. He promptly died after their breakup. In the book *Chopin's Funeral*, Benita Eisler records accusations that Sand, in part, caused his death. Mahler biographer Henry-Louis de La Grange made comparable claims, blaming Gustav's death on Alma: did her affair "hasten his death?"[9] With a pattern coming into focus, I wonder now: were women connected to male artists supposed to support their men quietly, without complaint, and out of the spotlight (like J. S. Bach's wife, Anna Magdalena, who it seems wrote some of his music, though you certainly wouldn't have heard that from her)? And if they didn't, were they then punished, censored, and maligned?

The notion of the male musical genius plays a role here. This figure is expected to work alone, a solitary creature suffering for his art. How do we even talk about the women who certainly helped this "genius," whether transcribing his music, writing the music, or simply preparing his meals? Is there room for anyone else, or does the ideal of genius and our commitment to that ideal erase the truth? Here the notion of the lone genius also collides with Western values around success, achievement measured by tangible results—art, music, writing—what Alan Henry called in 2019 "glamour work," rather than less tangible work, including cooking and cleaning.[10] How do we define the achievements, the worth, of any woman who supports a man or a family, making it possible for others to shine in a more established and visible sense? Where is the book chronicling the women who fed famous artists or tidied up after well-known writers? And is there room here for discussion of the female geniuses who certainly existed, too?

Another clear issue is the nature of fandom. Romantic pianist and composer Franz Liszt was one of the earliest star-musicians to capture the hearts of women in droves, driving them to overheated distraction. The Beatles were, of course, a group similarly pursued, with their every move chronicled, summed up in a new term: Beatlemania. In *Larger than Life: A History of Boy Bands from NKOTB to BTS*, Maria Sherman connects the screaming throngs of female Beatles' fans to the times: "Their underwear-throwing, red-in-the-face, teary-eyed hollers for John, Paul, George, and Ringo were an extension of the 1960s sexual revolution, a real rebellion of gendered oppression."

But this positive investment had its costs. Audiences took ownership of their favorite musicians—and still do. Any girlfriend or romantic partner could be seen as an unwelcome reality check, threatening the fantasy of some imagined amatory connection. As Sherman writes, addressing the love lives of the members of the boy band One Direction, "It's high time the girlfriends of yore get the respect they deserve for making it out alive, because the hate they received was unjust." With this in mind, the rule (once written into contracts) in K-pop, the South Korean pop music phenomenon, is that members can't date. The rule is draconian, but it has a sound basis in marketability—eliminating fan upset or distracting personal drama. In the *New York Times* article "We're Dating, K-Pop Stars Declare. You're Fired, Their Label Says," music critic Kim Zakka maintained, "Since the business worked based on the fantasy of the fan having a pseudo-relationship with the idol, the idol dating in real life breaks the business model." The musicians themselves, however, address the issue more diplomatically. In an interview with *Insider*, Donghwi, of the boy band Great Guys, explained, "We agreed not to have a girl in our lives, so we can focus more on our mission. We love our fans, that's enough for us."[11]

In addition to these partnership problems, the mistreatment of women in pop music has firm foundations in a long history of discounting and even punishing women in music, whether or not they're connected to a man. Early operatic singers were thought to be dangerous, less than ideally feminine, and loose morally. Composition has likewise been viewed as at odds with perceived feminine virtue. And publishing music or playing it publicly only made matters worse. Although playing an instrument was part of "good breeding" in private spaces, women who dared to take the stage as instrumentalists were not always tolerated during the eighteenth and nineteenth centuries. The problem was apparently contagious. Jean-Jacques Rousseau claimed that watching these women perform could have an effeminizing effect: "Unable to turn themselves into men, women turn us into women."[12] As public musicians, women apparently threatened men. That thinking echoes in a 1971 *New York Times* headline: "Fanny, a Four-Girl Rock Group, Poses a Challenge to Male Ego."

In popular music, negative attitudes toward women who made music publicly melded with notions that women were not commercially viable. In 1996, singer Sarah McLachlan organized an all-women concert tour, Lilith Fair, in order to counter the criticism she heard over and over from radio programmers—"we can't play two women back to back"—as well as similar statements from labels and concert promoters.[13] Somehow, men were the accepted default in music. Whereas women in music were a risk, men were presumed consumer-friendly. The very label "woman" was and is a problem.

In music criticism, there were not enough women to counter such illogical conclusions and practices, if indeed they could have or would have. During the nineteenth century, women struggled for a variety of reasons to become accepted public writers. But music criticism, which gradually emerged during the eighteenth century and early nineteenth century, was an even greater slog.[14] This state of affairs has had amazing resilience, and men early on dominated rock criticism.[15] The effect on how we have listened to and thought about popular music and music more generally cannot be overstated. Not only that, the system is self-perpetuating. Women have not always felt comfortable in such a male-dominated realm and, if they did, for acceptance, they may not have wanted to break with tradition, talking about music in new ways (women can, of course, be misogynists, too).[16]

While male rock critics disparaged certain men in music with "feminine" descriptors—"soft, weak, light, wimpy"—gendered values impacted critical treatment of female musicians more directly. They were mocked as "girl groups" or ignored entirely.[17] If they were discussed at all, critics often downplayed the music, focusing instead on the female musicians' body or appearance. Along these lines, in a story about the history of the Pretenders, Scott Cohen of *Spin* found it necessary to reveal that founding member Chrissie Hynde "prefers stockings to panty hose because she doesn't like to wear panties."[18] As Nicola Puckey wrote in the introduction to *Misogyny, Toxic Masculinity, and Heteronormativity in Port 2000 Popular Music*, "[P]opular culture and popular music are complicit in reinforcing and normalizing misogynistic actions and attitudes." And it certainly hasn't helped that the production of popular music has been and continues to be a predominantly male enterprise, with men traditionally working as recording engineers and producers—supported by gendered stereotypes around technology more generally. Of course, there have been and are important female figures who work in gear-heavy fields of music, especially electronic music, such as Suzanne Ciani, Laurie Spiegel, and Wendy Carlos. But again, the perception of that male control matters, reinforcing the status quo and contributing "to women's avoidance of and exclusion from music technology-related careers."[19]

In all of these ways, music seems overwhelmingly stacked against women. At the same time, music fans in recent years have supported reassessment of certain female music icons, exposing their mistreatment as a possible first step toward a more fair-minded engagement with their work and music as a whole. The 1990s and early 2000s in particular have become points of fresh consideration, related to the fan-led #FreeBritney movement. With that turn have come reevaluations of the media coverage of female celebrities, including Spears, Lindsay Lohan, and Janet Jackson, among others (see Jessica Bennett, "Speaking of Britney . . . What about All Those Other Women?" *New York Times*, February 27, 2021, as well as the 2021 documentary *Framing Britney Spears* and *Malfunction: The Dressing Down of Janet Jackson*).

This activity must also be connected to the #MeToo movement, recent contentious political battles around gender, as well as new developments in digital media, which have given celebrities a direct platform, allowing them to speak for themselves (e.g., on Twitter and Instagram). In light of this activity, the conversation around gender bias seems especially wide open in this particular moment. People are both receptive to rethinking past prejudice and pushing hard to keep those walls in place. In either case, and every case in between, it is significant that the discussion is happening. And this book is meant as a contribution to it and perhaps the start of new, related conversations, too.

With this goal in mind, *Can't Stop the Grrrls* confronts the past as well as ongoing wrongs in the treatment of women in music. However, rather than solely recounting each wrong, this book outs the labels that have negatively affected these women: "Yoko" first, and then "crazy," "gold digger," "snake," "liar," "diva," "slut," and "bitch." In particular, I focus on female musicians Yoko Ono, Courtney Love, Britney Spears, FKA twigs, Taylor Swift, Kesha, Mariah Carey, and Ariana Grande. In no way, then, is this book exhaustive. For that, I would need the late composer and conductor Nicolas Slonimsky to update and refocus his 1953 encyclopedia of insult (his *Lexicon of Musical Invective: Critical Assaults on Composers Since Beethoven's Time*). Instead, this book presents particular attacks as high-profile examples, examples we all know, or at least thought we knew. With that shared history in its various versions, I target a fundamental aspect of misogyny's power: language! After all, the words in these examples condition our view of the world, the ways we behave within it, and the way others treat us. Those words also help classify, often in terms of who has power and who doesn't.[20] And those words can become action, too, as they did for Courtney Love, Britney Spears, and Kesha, sometimes with serious legal ramifications.[21]

The impact of words in these ways may be amplified by celebrity. Words around stars—accessed in print, online media, or televised—have built-in amplification, built-in weight. Even something as seemingly trivial and light as celebrity gossip can affect how we view ourselves and those around us.[22] The toxic labeling of female pop icons, then, has serious repercussions for all of us. Are these labels a general warning or threat—telling other women to stand back, stand aside, or stand accused? Throughout this book, I will point out how toxic labels insidiously and subtly direct what women in music can and cannot do while limiting our general definitions of success and achievement, especially for women. The wider lessons impact women but also the very notion of woman, a category always in flux. As Judith Butler famously argued in *Gender Trouble*, gender is performative.

I hope, with awareness of these labels and their operation, this book can offer a path forward. After all, as Amanda Montell makes clear in the book *Wordslut*, it's not language itself that is misogynistic; it's how we use language that's the problem. And it's a problem we can solve. By tracing the range of misogynistic labeling in the coverage and consumption of several highly visible and influential pop icons, as well as its effects on women more generally, this book asks readers to forget what they thought they knew about women in music. Instead, it's time to learn about these remarkable women on their own terms, as they were and wanted to be, so that other women may be themselves, too.

1

THEY'RE GONNA CRUCIFY HER

In May 1970, the Beatles released their final album, *Let It Be*, just after the group's official breakup. The year before, on March 20, 1969, Yoko Ono and John Lennon married. During their honeymoon, Lennon wrote the song "The Ballad of John and Yoko," narrating in song their marriage in Gibraltar and honeymoon trip, including a stop by the Seine. In the chorus, recorded with Paul McCartney, Lennon sang, "The way things are going / They're gonna crucify me." Me?

"Me" was an easy rhyme with the final word in the preceding lines: "Christ you know it ain't easy / You know how hard it can be." I suppose "my wife," "Yoko," or even "her" simply wouldn't have worked. At the very least, it wouldn't have worked as well as "me": They're gonna crucify *her*. In reality, however, it was always Ono on the cross.

In December 1970, *Esquire* magazine infamously published Charles McCarry's racist Yoko takedown, titled "John Rennon's Excrusive Gloupie." The accompanying picture depicted Ono as a yellow-skinned giant, covered in overwhelming black hair, with Lennon, below her, as a little beetle. The image has striking similarities to an illustration by Erich Schilling published in Germany in 1935. Reproduced on the cover of the book *Yellow Peril! An Archive of Anti-Asian Fear*, it's a drawing of a huge yellow octopus with slanted eyes, enveloping the world with a devilish smile. McCarry's article matched the racist taunts fans outside the Beatles' Apple Corps headquarters, at 3 Savile Row, would shout at Ono when she went into or out of the building. And the hate mail was just as bad, with letter writers blaming Ono for everything big and small, even World War II itself.[1] Well-known critic Lester Bangs summed up the widespread verdict in *Rolling Stone* in March 1971, describing Ono as the person who had "led poor John astray and been credited by more than one Insider with 'breaking up the Beatles.'"

Lennon told comedian and talk show host Dick Cavett in a sit-down that aired on September 21, 1971, that the Beatles "were drifting apart on their own." But it was only much, much later, in 2012, that a presumably more objective Beatle spoke up, when Paul McCartney stated in an interview with Sir David Frost, "She certainly didn't break the group up."[2] As photographer Bob Gruen, a friend of Lennon and Ono's during the 1970s, said, "Their manager [Brian Epstein] had died, they were beginning to drift into different kinds of music, and didn't feel the need to work together to make more Beatles music."[3] In Gruen's words, "The Beatles broke up the Beatles."

Peter Jackson's 2021 three-part docuseries, *Get Back*, backs up Gruen's testimony, with unseen footage of the Beatles working together in late 1969. In it, George Harrison quits the band with little fanfare but is convinced shortly thereafter to rejoin the group. Later, he talks about making his own solo album. In one scene, McCartney jokes about people fifty years later believing that Ono broke up the Beatles because she "sat on an amp." The disintegration of the group was clearly in the air, though the band members often made light of the situation, with their humor and friendship delightfully on display in the Jackson epic (run time, 468 minutes). After Harrison quits, someone asks about the group's next move. Lennon lightly quips, "We split George's instruments."

Still, the Ono hate has certainly endured, even in supposed spaces of levity and laughter. In a YouTube video posted by Hammertime Media (and many others), comedian Bill Burr narrates a 1974 recording of John Lennon, Chuck Berry, and Yoko Ono making music together. In the clip, produced by Burr circa 2013, Burr explains that he is absolutely "infuriated" that Lennon didn't get Ono "in line," stop her from singing with the group. He insists he would have "dressed her down," saying, "If you ever f**king do that again I will slap you so f**king hard in the head your eyes are going to look like mine." The bit itself is beyond offensive, and "just kidding" is no cover. In a single "joke," Burr manages to work in racism, misogyny, and support of overt domestic abuse. The humor, if that's what you want to call it, is basically at the level of a dumb blonde joke coupled with the offense of a hate crime.

Of course, this hatred hit hard and early, and not just in the British press, which the couple sought to escape in part by moving to New York City in 1971. The Beatles' popularity had already crossed the Atlantic, and the American press was clocking the group's every move, though rock criticism itself was really still emerging.[4] Even among respected journalists, the trajectory of Ono's reception was clear from the start. In the *Los Angeles Times* and other newspapers informing American pop culture, such as the *New York Times*, a thread emerged, sometimes subtle, sometimes not: Yoko was different, Yoko was to blame. Tracing the coverage, we see the emergence of the main elements of the Yoko myth, crystallized and supported by standard ideals of appearance, assumptions of race, tropes of an ancient Eve and villainous Dragon Lady, as well as gender conventions and misogyny—all with an illogical logic all their own.

THE YOKO FACTOR

On June 25, 1968, the *Los Angeles Times* broadcast the beginning of Lennon and Ono's relationship: "Lennon was reported in Ireland with Japanese film artist Yoko Ono, who has been his frequent companion while his attractive blonde wife has been on holiday in Italy."[5] Although Lennon was, indeed, stepping out on his wife, indiscretion in celebrity culture was certainly not a deal breaker in public reception, at least for a male star. But this article made it clear that Ono was also a cheater, noting later in the article that she was "married to American film director Anthony Cox." More than that, the article included telling description of Ono, noting her "Japanese" descent, and ultimately comparing her to Lennon's first wife, Cynthia, "attractive" and "blond," conventional and accepted.

When Lennon's divorce was announced a few months later, the same sort of attention to detail remained: "Japanese-born."[6] Across the Atlantic, the racial reference was the same but heavily slurred: the headline in the *Yorkshire Evening Post* (Leeds, England), "Jap Girl Named in Lennon Divorce Suit" (August 22, 1968). Even when the *Los Angeles Times* reported that Ono had had a miscarriage on November 22, 1969, she was described as "Beatle John Lennon's Japanese mistress."

Once Lennon and Ono were married, papers hammered home Ono's Otherness, with her Japanese background included in the announcement of their nuptials on March 20, 1969, in the *New York Times*. And the *Los Angeles Times* once again compared Ono to the other Beatle wives, in an article of December 7, 1969, by Norman Moss, accompanied by pictures of Patti Harrison, noted as a "model"; Linda McCartney, the then "newest Mrs. Beatle"; Maureen Starr, a "Beatle fan as soon as there were any"; and Ono, quoted in the article aligning herself with the other wives: "We're all married to the same phenomenon. We all have a million girls trying to get at our husbands." While Moss revealed that the other wives weren't surprised by Lennon's break with his first wife, described as "a good-looking, dark-haired girl (now a blond) with sparkling eyes and a ready wit." The two had grown apart, Moss maintained, but he continued, "They were surprised by Yoko," whom he defined as "Japanese" with "a certain notoriety in the art world," achieved "by such stunts as a film in which the only images on the screen were people's rear ends."

Though the article here admits her success in the world of art, that achievement was quickly summed up by a single work, her 1966 film *No. 4*, commonly known and ridiculed as *Bottoms*. In a 2022 profile of Ono in the *New Yorker*, Louis Menand insists that the work is "not just a joke"; it "mocks self-importance." No one can stand out or attract celebrity attention "from the rear." Moss, however, didn't highlight the work's intent. In the end, he only really noted the film to isolate Ono further as different. We will see that same sort of dismissal and comparison in the coverage of FKA twigs more than forty years later. She was weird or Other, as was her artistic output, in both cases.

In truth, the attention to Ono's background—not to mention the related slurs—hid the complexities of Ono's background. As a young girl, she had emigrated from Japan to the United States, when she was sent to live with her father who was already working at a bank in San Francisco. She returned to Tokyo in 1937 but moved again to the United States, to New York in 1940, where her father was then working. She was forced to return a second time to Japan because of World War II and rising resentment, a "very anti-Oriental" attitude Yoko experienced even before the war.[7]

During the U.S. bombings that destroyed Tokyo in 1945, she and her family had to flee the city, struggling to survive in a farming village near Karuizawa, where Ono in her own words became "fashionably thin." There, she was harassed by local children who said she smelled "like butter," too American, too urban. After the war, she was accepted into the prestigious Gakushuin University, the first woman admitted into its philosophy program, but left after two semesters, moving with her family again to New York, where she attended Sarah Lawrence College. In an interview with journalist Joan Crowder, in 1994, Ono recalled, "I remember when I was very young in America, trying to explain to friends that the Japanese were not all bad. Then when I was in Japan, I was saying that not all Americans are bad."[8]

Still, it was her Otherness, her Japanese origin, that was the point of interest in the papers, ignoring her full history and her self-identification after the war as "an amalgam," not fully Japanese and not fully American.[9] And make no mistake, this interest was hardly neutral: *John Rennon's Excrusive Gloupie.* Though Asian Americans are often thought of today as the "model minority," the United States has a long history of sanctioned discrimination targeting Asian groups, including the internment of Japanese Americans during World War II. Though congressional investigations conducted at the time made it clear that Japanese Americans were not really a credible threat, Lieutenant General John L. DeWitt was unmoved, insisting "A Jap is a Jap."[10]

Unofficial oppression, subtle and not so subtle, has also affected the daily lives of Asian Americans for decades. Before World War II, cruel Japanese caricatures captured the American imagination as villains appeared on screen often with extremely slanted eyes, buckteeth, or long, needlelike nails. A systemic fear of "the East" was set as ideology; and "yellow perilism," in the words of authors John Kuo Wei Tchen and Dylan Yeats, was "hardwired into the formulation of Western Civilization itself."[11] Even in the "model minority" myth, a seeming positive take, Asian Americans are thought of as different, labeled high achievers, "nerds," or "misfits," still segregated from accepted whites.[12]

This racist history has perhaps become more visible in recent years, with unsanctioned violence directed at Asians and Asian Americans during the COVID-19 pandemic, including a shooting targeting Asian American women in Atlanta on March 16, 2021. The COVID blame was eerily prefigured by pop culture, with the 2011 movie *Contagion* following the main character, played by actress Gwyneth Paltrow, as she brings a deadly disease to the Midwest after dining at a restaurant in Hong Kong. Within this history, as Sheridan Prasso writes in the book *The Asian Mystique*, Asian women may have had an even harder row to hoe. Generally, they have been taken less seriously in Western culture, pulled down in part by the many fantasies around them, including the image of the subservient geisha and exotic sex goddess. Against this background, Ono was an easy target. The media had plenty of culturally prepared ways to blame Ono when the public didn't want to blame the men, in this case the Beatles, for their own actions.

THE ORIGINAL SIN

Within that gendered and racist attack, it wasn't just Ono's appearance and background that were the primary issues of contention. It was also what she did with that appearance. And when she posed naked alongside Lennon on the cover of their new album *Unfinished Music No. 1: Two Virgins* (1968), recorded on their first night together, writers were ready. In the *Los Angeles Times* of December 13, 1968, journalist Charles Champlin ruminated at length on the image, describing his perception of the ugliness of the cover: "They are a sore sight for eyes, to understate the case fairly drastically." Of course, Ono bore the brunt of the criticism. To close the article, titled "Pushing Limits of Freedom of Nudity," he creepily wrote, "Last night I dreamed I saw Miss Ono in a Maidenform bra. It seemed a useful beginning."

The cover's rebuke at the time is somewhat misleading because women had posed nude before. But, in this case, Ono posed nude with Lennon, and casually. Sexiness, the male gaze, was not the point. The cover was meant to showcase a reality: the naturalness of a naked man and a naked woman.[13] And that was, indeed, different.

It might not have helped, too, that Lennon responded in the October 18 article by bringing up Adam and Eve: "Frankly, we see nothing wrong with the cover. Has anyone ever taken offense at Adam and Eve?" The short answer is, of course, "Yes." In *Enticed by Eden*, Linda S. Schearing and Valerie H. Ziegler insist that Eve is seen as the "temptress" in

Western culture and can "stand for more than simply the 'first female.'" In the authors' words, she is "frequently understood to be the prototype/ template of *all* women." Lennon in this way opened an uncalled-for door, inviting in the Eve trope, Western culture's original female sin. When *Rolling Stone* broke with other publications that refused to reproduce the cover, the magazine did so with a related quote from the Bible: "And they were both naked, the man and his wife, and were not ashamed." The comparison no doubt prompted related questions: Was Ono, like Eve, to blame? Did Ono, like Eve, lead Lennon/Adam astray? With her supposed existing penchant for "bare bottoms," who was really behind this controversial cover?

Just a day later, the paper noted Lennon's arrest on a drug charge: "Beatle John Lennon was arrested Friday with his Japanese girlfriend, Yoko Ono, on a drug charge. It was the first arrest to mar the image of the Beatles." No information was provided about Ono's history or lack thereof with drug abuse (she has said she hadn't even smoked a cigarette, let alone done drugs, until she met Lennon). It went unsaid: Lennon had never been involved with drugs before, but then, with Ono, he was. There would be a similar framing of Kurt Cobain's drug use, with Courtney Love implicated as the problem's source. And again, in this narrative around Lennon's self-medication, Ono was "his Japanese girlfriend," a transgressive Eve, especially at the time when interracial marriage had only just been legalized in the United States, in 1967.

But these moments were just a warm-up for the main event: the announcement of the Beatles' breakup on April 11, 1970. With his new solo album, McCartney included a "self-interview," in which he responded to the question "Is your break with the Beatles temporary or permanent, due to personal differences or musical ones?" His answer: "Personal differences, business differences, musical differences, but most of all because I have a better time with my family. Temporary or permanent? I don't know."

With his Q&A tagged, the *Daily Mirror* famously announced the breakup with the headline "Paul Quits the Beatles." In the *Los Angeles Times*, the headline similarly declared, "McCartney Quits the Beatles." And, yes, the ensuing article mentioned Ono: "One of the factors in McCartney's decision to go it alone was his drifting apart from 20-year-old John Lennon who, since his marriage to Yoko Ono, producer of a film starring bare backsides, has been concentrating on a campaign for world peace." The article managed to a make a desire for peace sound ridiculous by mentioning it alongside the media's favorite example of Ono's artistic work.

In a *Rolling Stone* article, Jann S. Wenner maintained that McCartney might have announced the end of the Beatles, but the dissolution was well underway before that, quoting Lennon, "we were long gone, a long time ago."[14] And Lennon reportedly was miffed that McCartney had announced the split before he could. In an article of July 18, 1971, writer Joan Hanauer not only confirmed that McCartney was not alone in his decision to leave the band but also highlighted Ono's support of the breakup: "Yoko Ono also believes her husband, John Lennon, did the artistic thing by 'putting a stop to the Beatles before the Beatles deteriorated'" ("Yoko Squirts Self-Help Our Way in 'Grapefruit,'" *Los Angeles Times*). The sentiment surely did not endear Ono to fans. But as viewers watched the *Let It Be* film (1970), documenting the creation of the Beatles' final album, with its iconic scene of the band playing one last time on the rooftop of their Apple headquarters, longtime Beatlemaniacs found new, more damning ways to blame Ono.

"DRAGON LADY"

On January 23, 1972, in the article "Beatles' Story Can Now Be Told," writers Dan Carlinsky and Edwin Goodgold in the *Los Angeles Times* reviewed continued fan disappointment and upset over the breakup. Many were utterly bereft: "The world has not yet recovered from the disintegration of the most important musical group of the 1960s—the Beatles." And to many, the question remained, "Why did they do it?"

From implied fault, Carlinsky and Goodgold then confirmed the rumors, blaming Ono explicitly. Citing a "secret source," they conjured a more complete explanation, recycling racist images of Ono, seemingly "demure" but instead magically manipulative: "It all started with Yoko Ono, a demure, charming girl—or so everyone thought. But shortly after she married John Lennon, Yoko began to display a mysterious, hypnotic power apparently acquired in the Orient." The racist reasoning was hardly disguised, with Ono's supposed Svengali-like hold on Lennon credited to her perceived exotic origins. This anonymous source further assigned Ono dialogue: "You're the star," she supposedly would say to Lennon, "why don't you take the billing you deserve? Call the group Yoko's Husband and His Three

Sidemen." Interestingly, these two male writers did later in the article manage to give another woman, McCartney's new wife, "American-born" Linda Eastman, some of the blame, explaining that McCartney had become too "Americanized."

The same reference to stereotypes of the mysterious woman from "the Orient" emerged again in renewed scrutiny surrounding Ono after Lennon was murdered, shot to death by Mark David Chapman on December 8, 1980. Two days after the gruesome killing, the *Los Angeles Times* ran the article "Ono: Dragon Lady or Love Goddess?" The article managed to highlight more of Ono's artistic work, apart from the regular mention of butts, but again worked in multiple racist and misogynist tropes. Reviewing Ono's love affair with Lennon and the response, the author concentrated on her reputation "as an emasculating female, a dabbler in art and music, more concerned with her own self-expression than with Lennon's musical development."

That supposed emasculation was part of the headline's "Dragon Lady" tag, which references a real figure, the empress Tzu Hsi, who was demonized as powerful, sexually depraved, and cruel. Her history, like the history of so many women, was itself an invention, distorted to serve Western fears and desires.[15] According to SooJin Lee's "The Art of Artists' Personae," the "Dragon Lady" branding "demonizes powerful, publicly conspicuous Asian women as mysterious, vicious, and dangerous Oriental femme fatale."[16] It's an approximation of a transgressive, threatening woman—a character— thrust upon a real person. And that character is designed and deployed, like misogyny as a whole, to curb the influence of any woman who breaks with traditions meant to support the man-on-top standard.[17]

Ono had no protection. Not even her grief was reason enough for the media to rethink or adjust its criticism. In fact, Lennon's death was for some a starting point—an opening and invitation for even more abuse. Ariana Grande would experience a similar pile on in the aftermath of her ex-boyfriend rapper Mac Miller's deadly drug overdose. In both cases, the man, while alive and active creatively, is solely credited with this success. But, for the very worst of his actions or a devastating end, the woman is liable. And her truth never seems to matter. She was and is judged according to his life as well as his death.

"CUT PIECE"

To be clear, this treatment, in Ono's case, hid Lennon's reality as well as hers. And her reality certainly didn't deserve the designation "dabbler" or related dismissive reference to her artistic work. Although the December 10 article mentioned her study at Sarah Lawrence, it did not highlight the fact that she had studied both music composition and art. Far from mere hobbyist, during her time in New York in the 1950s, Ono was a part of avant-garde compositional and artistic circles that included famous male composers John Cage and La Monte Young.

She produced powerful art, such as her violent *Cut Piece* (1964), performed several times in the 1960s, including a showing at the Carnegie Recital Hall on March 21, 1965. It is in many ways one of her most well-known pieces, an event that invites the audience to cut pieces of her clothes while she sits vulnerable to attack and exploitation, as she would be her entire life. But she also wrote music, such as her early composition *Secret Piece* (1953), which included natural sounds from the site of the performance. The piece incorporated new thinking around breaking boundaries in music, underscoring the artificial divide between music and noise, art and everyday life. She also contributed to the artistic work of Fluxus, associated with "happenings," experimental performances that put process and improvisation above the fixed, final work.

The "Ono: Dragon Lady or Love Goddess?" article specifically referenced her performances at Carnegie Recital Hall and the Village Gate in the early 1960s, with a composition that included the sound of the restroom's flushing toilet. But, again, the author omitted significant detail, furthering the "dabbler" narrative. For example, in one of these Carnegie concerts, on November 24, 1961, Ono collaborated with George Brecht, George Masiunas, and La Monte Young, and featured her piece *AOS—to David Tudor* (1961), an "opera without instruments," with performers reading newspapers in different languages against a French lesson, all of which transforms into a terrifying overlay of speeches by Hitler and his one-time ally Hirohito. A powerful visual performance accompanied the sound, hands and legs moving and bound. To conclude the piece, Ono included vocalizations, "amplified sighs, breathing, gasping, retching screaming." The sound "avoided self-conscious subjective expression in favor of 'real' sound."[18]

Yoko Ono. Photofest

That program of vocal disruption says a lot about Ono's controversial
singing—the sound that inspired Burr's "joke." In all aspects of her art, she
purposely questioned accepted norms—norms of music, norms of singing,
alongside and with norms of conventional womanhood. Today, college-
level music appreciation classes continue to take seriously John Cage and
his piece 4'33", a composition without a single traditional note, focused as
it is instead on ambient noise. And academic composition still seems to
value innovation and theoretical philosophy, often over traditional musical
sound. Ono, like Cage, challenged definitions of traditional art in similar
ways. Ono, like Cage, produced art as statement and boundary transgression. Within ivory musical towers or avant-garde circles at the time, Ono's
program made sense (though she has not been fully embraced or integrated
into music curriculum, as Cage has been). And yet, within the context of
the Beatles, for many, her work didn't. She didn't. Ono's music was then
dismissed and she was called a "Dragon Lady" two days after her husband
was murdered.[19]

EXPLAINING WITHOUT EXPLAINING AWAY

The many omissions and wholesale public condemnation of Ono—in the media and elsewhere—represent, in part, the extreme side of fandom. In *The Beatles and Fandom: Sex, Death, and Progressive Nostalgia*, author Richard Mills observes, "It is a deep inflexibility and unreconstructed bigotry and conservatism that leads to a refusal to accept change. The sexist and racist treatment of Yoko Ono by fans demonstrates this dark side of fandom." But it wasn't just change within the Beatles, her presence, and then their split. It was Ono's program of change, her break with societal traditions, especially established patriarchal standards, underlined by comparisons to the other Beatles women. Ono didn't conform to accepted Western ideas of the ideal woman or even seemingly positive images of a nice Japanese woman, the "geisha," "good housewife," or "wise mother."[20] She deigned to create, she deigned to be different, she deigned to be herself. And, for that, she was punished.

The cause at its core was bound up with misogyny. In *Down Girl: The Logic of Misogyny*, Kate Manne defines misogyny as the policing of women. It's not about a general hatred of women. It's about enforcing expected norms of female behavior, norms of giving to and supporting men. Women, in the logic of misogyny, are meant to serve men; and if they don't, they are viewed as a threat. The treatment of Ono was meant to call out her perceived transgressions as a way of putting her back in her supposed place and as a warning to other women: mind your manners, mind your men. This twisted logic is certainly not actively organized. But power rarely is. It's a collection of individual reactions that take on a certain reason within a wider social system of thought, and no one's officially in charge in the end. And yet, through that loosely organized system, gender norms hold sway, and racial stereotypes are never far from the conversation.

The harshness of Ono's treatment might seem both absurd and criminal. But, for many, her actions and very being felt personal as an attack on a man's privileged place in the world. Men, as well as participating women, responded in kind. By standing out, in terms of gender and race (misogyny, indeed, overlapping racism, as it often does), she violated her assigned societal rank and usurped a system of male dominance. And no power move was available in response. Any attempt to decry the disparity, the inequality, or the unfairness potentially could make matters worse. Calling out misogyny, as Manne writes, "is liable to give rise to more of it." It's "a catch-22 situation."[21]

Nonetheless, Ono did wage her own particular battle on behalf of women and herself, just as other musical icons would (e.g., Sarah McLachlan with the Lilith Fair; Missy Elliott as an early source of female power in rap; or Lady Gaga, who has consistently challenged prejudices around gender identification). With Lennon, Ono put out the 1972 single "Woman Is the N°gger of the World"—the song's title, of course, offending many (and rightly so) in language and the comparison of the plight of Black people and women. Lennon would apologize for any offense while insisting that the song does, indeed, reflect the status of women. Ono would also publish in the *New York Times* the article "The Feminization of Society" (February 23, 1972), musing in it, "Most of us women hope that we can achieve our freedom within the existing social set-up, thinking that, somewhere, there must be a happy Medium for men and women to share freedom and responsibility." But, she argued, real change needs revolution, and part of that is "the use of feminine tendencies as a positive force to change the world."

Ono and Lennon would model some of that change; Lennon took over domestic duties and Ono focused on her art after their brief split in 1973 and the birth of their son, Sean, in 1975. In a 1980 interview with David Sheff for *Playboy*, Ono explained the motivation for the couple's time apart, insight, too, into their new living arrangement: "I think I really needed some space because I was used to being an artist and free and all that, and when I got together with John, because we're always in the public eye, I lost the freedom. . . . And the pressure was particularly strong on me because of being the one who stole John Lennon from the public or something . . . and I think my artwork suffered." Ono performed then with the mixed reception and booing you might expect (in the *Los Angeles Times* coverage of a Yoko performance in 1973 without Lennon in San Diego, Yoko is quoted as saying, "Yes, I know some people still think I'm a joke, but what am I supposed to do?"). Meanwhile, Lennon took primary responsibility for the care of their son. In a *New York Times* article of November 9, 1980, Lennon told writer Robert Palmer, "In a way, we're involved in a kind of experiment. Could the family be the inspiration for art, instead of drinking or drugs or whatever? I'm interested in finding that out."

When Lennon was murdered, the news coverage made it clear that Lennon's decision to carry out typical domestic duties was part of Ono's likability problem. In the *Los Angeles Times* article "Beatle John Lennon Slain" (December 9, 1980), journalist John Goldman reviewed Lennon's biography, including his role as "a house-husband." "This change," Goldman maintained, "only gave added intensity to the rumors that it had been Ono who had been somehow responsible for the 1970 break-up of the group." Whatever Lennon and Ono did together, at this point, was entirely Ono's fault. But, remarkably, one of the biggest issues in her reception was and is her very presence. She was there in the hallowed Beatles space. No action required. To many, she simply didn't belong.

LET HER BE

A month after "Ono: Dragon Lady or Love Goddess?," another article hit the primary beats in Ono's reception history, threads that would stretch through the next decades, uncut still. In the article "The Breaking Up of the Beatles; A Delicate Balance Ends When Yoko Ono Moves into the Studio" (January 1, 1981) in the *Boston Globe*, Geoffrey Stokes again highlighted her difference from the other Beatles' wives, who "were decidedly domestic." He also insisted there was an irony in the group recording "The Ballad of John and Yoko," "since there is a case to be made that John's love for Yoko effectively ended the Beatles." But he brought up another significant issue—one that we have avoided so far: the other Beatles' dislike of Ono, including her oft-cited presence during recording sessions: "Though she was arrogantly sure of her genius, she was a square peg in no hole as far as they were concerned. They didn't particularly like her at a distance; as a constant comrade following John into the men's room so they could continue their conversations, they found her unbearable. And when he tried to impose her musical suggestions on their work, they found her a threat."

The mention of "her genius" was a pointed barb, because genius in its Latin origins referred to a "divine aspect of maleness."[22] As Christine Battersby writes in *Gender and Genius*, "The genius can be *all* sorts of men; but he is always a 'Hero,' and never a heroine. He cannot be a woman." Being there, in recording sessions, was yet another violation of norms, in society and among the Beatles. In *Shout! The Beatles in Their Generation*, author Philip Norman writes, "The Beatles first became aware of Yoko at Abbey Road studios. They could hardly do otherwise. She did not stay, as was proper—as was womanly—in the control room. She came down onto the sacred floor of the studio, where none but Beatles and their closest male aides were allowed, and settled herself down at John's side." Norman made the double standard transparent—this woman was not proper. And the other Beatles apparently agreed, at least at times. On *The Dick Cavett Show*, Cavett teased Harrison, there as a guest, by pointing at the chair Harrison sat in, "Yoko sat in that very chair." Harrison jumped up, a seeming joke but, of course, something else entirely.

Clearly, Ono's very presence was a concern—a supposed threat to the Beatles. And with that idea, there would always be doubt that she could have helped the group. Even her collaboration with Lennon, her role in the lyrics and concept of the song "Imagine," went uncredited and unacknowledged on the official record for forty-six years. In a 1980 interview with BBC Radio 1, Lennon tried to credit Ono, and she brushed aside the acknowledgment. But he continued, explaining directly to Ono that "if it had been Bowie, I would have put Lennon-Bowie. See, if you had been male."

I don't suspect Jackson's 2021 *Get Back* will change the standard notion of Ono as an unwelcome meddler, though it's a real glimpse into Ono's activities in that sanctified Beatles space. In the series, Ono is quiet and rather unobtrusive. She is reliably there, often knitting, eating, or reading the paper. If the iPhone had existed, she may have been filmed quietly scrolling, occupying time like we do now. And Lennon and Ono, only recently married, were clearly in love and unwilling to be apart. Still, in response to the docuseries, the same sort of complaints resurfaced, as journalists and social media users debated her very right to be there.

One Twitter account, that of Ian McNabb, posted a comment from his mother: "Why didn't Yoko make the f*ckin' tea? Not exactly busy was she?" Here again was that courtesan image, with Ono failing to live up to the stereotype by bringing the men their tea, even though, in the series, viewers see a young man clearly assigned to do just that. Even the *New York Times* saw fit to print journalist Amanda Hess's mixed take on Ono in the documentary, in the article "The Sublime Spectacle of Yoko Ono Disrupting the Beatles": "At first I found Ono's omnipresence in the documentary bizarre, even unnerving," though the author ultimately viewed her "stamina" in remaining there as an impressive and provocative "performance." When I first saw Hess's review, I was relieved to read any positive perspective. But, even with some sympathy for Ono's presence, why is there this effort to explain it as a "performance"? Why is there this need to justify Ono, when other non-Beatles were there, too? Why is her very existence an issue in the Beatles-verse?

Yoko Ono, throughout her life, has played with prejudice artistically, even in *Cut Piece* to a certain extent. Her film collaboration *Rape* (1969) is part of a similar response, with its disturbing pursuit of a woman as she walks through London. And she has joked about her negative reception and even powerfully reclaimed it, as she did in a concert on December 11, 1968, released on film in 1996. At the event, the performers, including the Rolling Stones, the Who, and Eric Clapton, were all in costume; Ono wore a witch costume, an image she would again play up in her 1974 song "Yes, I'm a Witch": "Yes, I'm a witch, I'm a bitch. I don't care what you say."

Ono embraced her Dragon Lady persona, too. In 2002, she said, "Well the press referred to me as the Dragon Lady and for a long time I was not very happy about it. But at a certain point I said, look, the Dragon Lady is a beautiful concept because it symbolizes power and mystery." Her strength in this reclamation is remarkable, as is her perseverance in the face of historical tragedy and public hate. In some ways, that hate would only intensify in response to her strength. As she wrote in "Feeling the Space" in 1973: "[S]ome of his [Lennon's] closest friends told me that probably I should stay in the background, I should shut up, I should give up my work and that way I'll be happy. . . . Because . . . the whole society wished me dead" (*New York Times*). It was her candid recognition of Manne's catch-22.

Other female singers at the time, such as folk singer Marianne Faithfull, who performed in the 1960s and dated famous Rolling Stone Mick Jagger, did not experience the same level of backlash. Faithfull was certainly not exempt from the sexism of the music industry at the time, with record companies led by men, as well as male-heavy management and production, an issue still today. Stones' manager Andrew Loog Oldham, who discovered Faithfull, described her as "an angel with big tits." And she was treated accordingly, as she put it, in an interview with Alexis Petridis, for the *Guardian*, "as somebody who not only can't even sing, but doesn't really write or anything, just something you can make into something . . . I was just cheesecake really, terribly depressing." The movement for women's liberation hadn't quite found a place within the politics of counterculture. As Sheila Whiteley observes in *Women and Popular Music*, "the lifestyle and the musical ethos of the period undermined the role of women, positioning them as either romanticized fantasy figures, subservient earth mothers or easy lays." But by 1969, it didn't seem to matter. Faithfull's singing career had been replaced by the job of being Jagger's girlfriend, a muse, which she called "a shit thing to be." To Petridis, she said, "It's a terrible job. You don't get any male muses, do you? Can you think of one? No." But she was white and blonde, and she performed this "shit" job without public complaint then. As Tanya Pearson writes in *Why Marianne Faithfull Matters*, "It's not that Mick Jagger asked her to stop working, insisting that she follow his band around instead, but that Marianne had been under the assumption that her career was trivial from the beginning." Perhaps that, in part, exempted her from treatment comparable to Ono's (though she would be punished with a chocolate-related rumor, which we will cover in chapter 9).

Other female singers at the time, even those connected to famous musical men, just didn't have the same convergence of factors as Ono, propelling the hate to the level of myth: misogyny, racism, Beatles fandom, and a misunderstood, independent artistic program. Ono also didn't "shut up," silent in the background, except, of course, when she did. Maybe that was a fundamental distinction between Ono and a musician such as Faithfull, who wasn't subjected to the same level of misogynistic hate. Standing out is one thing, but speaking out apparently is unforgivable. And Ono did both. In an interview with history professor Gordon H. Chang at Stanford University on January 14, 2009, Ono recognized the no-win situation: "You can't really stand up for yourself, because then people say, 'How dare you!' and if you're silent, then they will think there's something really creepy about it."[23]

The accepted animosity directed at Ono would filter into pop cultural representations as well as later public opinion and media attention. Even in 2013, in an article titled "The 5 Most-Hated Rock and Roll Wives," Ono comes in at #1, right before Courtney Love (at #2, a dubious distinction to which we will return): "The obvious top choice for this list is John Lennon's wife Yoko Ono, who is widely credited with breaking up the Beatles." It's certainly not the case that women since Ono haven't experienced similar public abuse. But Ono has become the standard to which other musical women are often compared. Yoko has become a sort of pejorative tag, like "Dragon Lady" or "jezebel." She is herself a pattern of subversion, the model "witch." Her name has also been canonized as insult—an insult used against women in music and women more generally.

Her pop culture depictions reflect the standard Ono narrative but also support it, ensuring her continued use as yardstick for the evaluation and related oppression of other women. In the next chapter, I will highlight several of the most infamous appearances of this pop standard, first in the film *This Is Spinal Tap*, just four years after Lennon's death, and then on *The Simpsons*, a cartoon, or "kid stuff"—"just kidding"—that almost disguises the harsh message and its potential effect on viewers, especially women. Entertainment is then a message and teaching moment, and that lesson can be a warning sometimes hidden in humor.

2

"YOKO OH NO"

The Yoko myth is trotted out and rehashed perennially in pop culture. One week in December 2020, thanks to questionable leisure decisions mid-pandemic, I couldn't get away from the myth in popular entertainment. Watching episode 4 of the 1994 teen drama *My So-Called Life*, I was surprised to hear series mom Patty Chase muse of Yoko, "Why do you think people give her such a hard time? Is it just because she can't sing?" Two days after that, reading the 2020 Sophie Kinsella chick-lit confection *Christmas Shopaholic*, main character Becky tells her best friend Suze why she broke up with her college boyfriend, who was in a band. "Because of the band," Suze guesses. "Because they all thought you were Yoko." "Kind of," Becky responds. In the 2017 Netflix special *Oh, Hello on Broadway*, which I watched a month later, Yoko even made an appearance of sorts as a raccoon, coming between two friends, Gil Faizon and George St. Geegland (played by Nick Kroll and John Mulaney).

The myth rears its head again and again, each time uncontested. The rehashing of the myth might spotlight one aspect of the myth over another: focusing on gendered stereotypes or "Dragon Lady" racism, or simply making fun of a woman's independent artistic efforts. But the general theme endures. She was in the wrong. She did something wrong.

This chapter explores the media messaging in three specific Ono references in pop culture: in the movie *This Is Spinal Tap*, on the television show *The Simpsons*, and on the HBO series *Flight of the Conchords*. The number of other on-screen Yoko plot points is staggering—on *Just Shoot Me!* (1997–2003), *That '70s Show* (1998–2006), *Freaks and Geeks* (1999), *The Big Bang Theory* (2007–2019), *Buffy the Vampire Slayer* (1997–2003), *The Middle* (2009–2018), and the animated shows *Metalocalypse* (2006–2013) and *King of the Hill* (1997–2010), to name a few. But the representations on *The Simpsons* and *This Is Spinal Tap* are iconic. And in this discussion, *Flight of the Conchords* is an especially useful contrasting example.

The site TV Tropes (tvtropes.org) lists the specifics of many of these Ono appearances under the heading "Yoko Oh No," described as pop culture representations of "a musician's girlfriend whose antics or presence cause the band to break up." In its sheer repetition, this girlfriend character's constant appearance qualifies as a readily identifiable "trope," defined by the site as "a storytelling device or convention." But it only works as a "convention" because the myth of Yoko Ono—her reputation as the person in the wrong—has been so well-established in the public imagination. As the site maintains, a "trope" is "a shortcut for describing situations the storyteller can reasonably assume the audience will recognize." Though a trope depends on shared knowledge, in its repetition the trope also helps maintain that shared idea. The use of "Yoko Oh No" as a shortcut, then, depends on audience recognition of Yoko's blame while supporting recognition and related acceptance of Ono's supposed fault in the future. It becomes a way to perpetually punish Ono and other women who do not conform.

The entire process potentially teaches women what they should and should not do. And that lesson is based on the customs of a patriarchal and racist system. As studies show, media, including television and film, reflect and influence cultural and social norms as well as shared beliefs.[1] Those standards further shape people's behaviors—how they conduct themselves and interact with others. It's peer pressure as entertainment. A person might even modify previous patterns of behavior in order to conform to perceived social customs.[2] Widely consumed cultural representations of the "Oh No" trope can then influence how people treat women as well as the decisions women themselves make. This connection—between media viewing and behavior—also applies to the many funny appearances of the "Yoko Oh No" trope, though comedy can work toward cross-purposes, too.

Through humor, comedians can upend or even challenge the Yoko myth. But comedic send-ups can also be dicey, making way for a conflicted laugh. Are we laughing at the myth or at Yoko? Or both? When parody comes into play, the audience has even more room for interpretation, given the intertextual possibilities in a parody's reliance on a preexisting work or idea—whether as tribute, criticism, or both—all with a fresh twist or perspective. Although *This Is Spinal Tap* and *The Simpsons* may reinforce the standard narrative despite the humor, *Flight of the Conchords* plays more fully in an ambiguous comedic space, supporting and disrupting convention. And yet, I still wonder: does the mere appearance of the "Yoko Oh No" trope keep it alive? Can a joke dependent on the idea of Yoko's blame ever make right the label's wrong?

TAPPING INTO THE YOKO TROPE

One of the most iconic (and perhaps earliest) iterations of the "Yoko Oh No" trope is in the cult classic film *This Is Spinal Tap*, released March 2, 1984. The movie plays with clichés of rock to make musician jokes of the highest quality, all supported by the set-up: a pseudo-documentary of the fictional British band Spinal Tap, which made its first appearance on the ABC television show *The T.V. Show*.

The movie follows the band as it embarks on a doomed tour of the United States, all documented by filmmaker Marty DeBergi, played by the film's actual director Rob Reiner. We are meant to laugh at these once rock gods, especially the group's two lead guitarists (that's right, two leads) David St. Hubbins (Michael McKean) and Nigel Tufnel (Christopher Guest), with flashbacks recalling the band's better days, when they performed as a sort of imitation Beatles band powered sometimes by psychedelic flowers. Their subsequent embrace of rock-ready masculinity appears ridiculous with over-the-top songs such as "Big Bottom" and an upcoming album titled *Smell the Glove*, originally featuring a since-censored cover showing a naked woman positioned like a dog on all fours and controlled with a leash. Publicist Bobbi Flekman, played by Fran Drescher, has to explain the cover's offense to the band's clueless manager Ian Faith, who weirdly relies on his beloved cricket stick in his management of the band. In the film, the stick is one of many phallic points of humor.

Harry Shearer, Christopher Guest, and Michael McKean in This Is Spinal Tap *(1984), directed by Rob Reiner. Embassy Pictures/Photofest*

The sheer loudness of rock is the basis for perhaps the film's best-known joke, when Tufnel proudly claims his amplifier goes past the normal ten, all the way to eleven. But a core and recurring reference revolves around the Yoko myth, with St. Hubbins dating Jeanine Pettibone, played by June Chadwick. Guest, McKean, and Harry Shearer, another actor and creator of the film, all call the relationship "the Yoko plot."[3] Interestingly, the actress playing Pettibone, Chadwick, didn't note the Yoko angle until later, explaining in an interview, "I didn't start to see anything until I had the tenth person say, 'Oh, it's a Yoko Ono character,' and I thought, *Oh, maybe it is.*"[4]

The first mention of Jeanine comes in a phone conversation, with Jeanine out of view and David in a hotel room happily talking to her as Nigel looks on with a blank expression. After he ends the call, David enthusiastically tells Nigel, "Jeanine is going to come meet us." "To drop some stuff off," Nigel deadpans. But, of course, she's coming to stay, making her first in-person appearance during rehearsal, the group on stage playing in Milwaukee. The film's viewers hear her before seeing her, a big "hello, darling" literally interrupting the band as it jams. The audience then sees her, a pretty white blonde with blue eyes and big red lips, sitting dangerously close to the sound engineer.

After Jeanine and David happily reunite, manager Ian excitedly joins the group on stage, showing them the reimagined cover for *Smell the Glove*, all black, a parody of the Beatles' famous *White Album*. With no identifying text, however, David is concerned, insisting that it "looks like death." Ian argues that that's a good thing: "death sells." When David looks to Jeanine for guidance, she shakes her head, also disagreeing with Ian. His opinion confirmed, David continues to argue against the new cover. The audience quickly recognizes the power Jeanine wields over David and its potential effect on Spinal Tap.

In an interview cut, director Marty speaks with David, who explains that Jeanine has had a rich influence on his spiritual life, helping him sort out his personal philosophies. "I wonder if you have as much influence over his musical expression," Marty says to Jeanine. She offers an easy "yeah," explaining that she listens to his playing as well as his experimenting and tells him whether it's good or bad. "Yes, she's very honest," David adds. The Yoko parallel is obvious when Marty follows up: "How does that go over with the other band members?"

We soon see the hinted at and ever-growing rift when Jeanine participates directly in the group's musical plans, perhaps the biggest source of strain. At a diner, the group sits together around a table, talking about their new album, which David suspects is cursed by its macabre blackness. Jeanine comments that a better sound mix might have helped the album succeed. Nigel shoots back, "How do you know?" He makes it clear that she does not belong in the group's discussion of musical matters: "It's like me saying you're using the wrong conditioner for your hair," he condescendingly explains. When she continues, talking about the mix, she incorrectly uses sound terminology, "doubly" instead of "Dolby." Nigel laughs at her.

This laugh plays on an enduring notion of women's place in rock, a limited space that men control. As artist-producer Paula Wolfe writes, "Men have historically occupied senior positions within the music industry and this has resulted in a situation whereby such positions of power are associated with men."⁵ The male domination includes music's production—the control of music's recorded sound. That thinking relates to the godlike status of the producer, a sort of ruling magician, as well as the idea that women can't understand or deal with technology.⁶ Despite the ramifications of this idea, the "doubly" moment is beloved by fans—a moment Chadwick credits to Guest: "That line was given to me by Chris Guest, and I thank him profusely for it each time I see him."⁷ In the film's narrative arc, it's also crucial.

Up to that point, the tension between David, Nigel, and Jeanine had been somewhat open-ended. It's a funny plot point: fodder for hilarious deadpan looks, courtesy of Nigel, and a way to poke fun at David's insecurities and put-on hypermasculinity as he sings "Heavy Duty"—"I don't need no wife"—while very clearly depending on Jeanine. Jeanine, as the acknowledged Yoko character, does not at first appear sinister, at least to me. Perhaps she knows what she's doing; perhaps she has something to offer. Perhaps, through comedy and parody in particular, *This Is Spinal Tap* might undercut the typical Yoko narrative, casting Yoko and the Yoko label in a new light. But when Jeanine utters the word "doubly," the narrative seems to pick a side, a side based in flawed assumptions about women. The scene makes it clear that this Yoko character doesn't know what she's doing. She is in the wrong. Again.

After the "doubly" comment, Jeanine continues to insert herself, proposing a new band look based on each band member's zodiac sign. Nigel responds, "Is this a joke?" Laughing, he adds, "Mine would look better in doubly." With her intrusions, manager Ian eventually quits, and Jeanine assumes management duties. Her rise to power is mirrored in her scene positioning, often above David. He sits in a chair, she sits higher, next to him on the arm of his chair—both connected to him and in control. In another scene, he sits in a chair while she rests atop a table beside him, again elevated. In a climactic fight, Nigel quits the band, yelling at David and explicitly blaming Jeanine for the group's issues. Backed up by her placement on high, he calls her "some fucking angel hanging over your head."

At a concert in Stockton, California, the group performs with Jeanine onstage playing the tambourine. The central conflict of the movie is Jeanine and the rupture she causes as she takes over the band, then becomes a part of the group once Nigel is out. She is everything the press feared in Yoko—a woman with the supposed power to control and ruin a beloved music group—though in this case, the racist element is disguised by Jeanine's whiteness. Garden-variety misogyny takes center stage. Though the film has comedic punchlines galore, the Jeanine character supplies its emotional weight as the true villain of the movie. Overall, the portrayal of her as the bad gal does not seem to be a "just-kidding, she's awesome" kind of joke. Absent, in the end, is any subtext that Jeanine—and by extension, Yoko—may, in fact, be capable or talented. And the film's end only makes matters worse.

To conclude the film, Nigel returns, delivering the news that the group's controversial album, *Smell the Glove*, thanks in part to manager Ian, is a big success, at least in Japan (an interesting geographical choice, to say the least). In the final scene, the reunited Spinal Tap plays in Japan in front of throngs of screaming fans. Ian is there triumphant, smugly looking down on an unhappy Jeanine, evidently stripped of her power and this time positioned lower in the frame. The scene seems to suggest that she is back in her rightful place, below the men. And in that last scene, Ian is, in fact, also holding his favorite cricket stick as if he's ready to strike. It's a supposed happy ending at Jeanine's expense.

I have long loved *This Is Spinal Tap*, with its insider, music-specific humor, but with newfound knowledge of the violent response to Ono, I felt deeply unsettled while rewatching this final scene more recently. In a *New York Times* review of the film dated March 2, 1984, critic Janet Maslin decides that the "mock-documentary" is not "mean-spirited at all." "It's much too affectionate for that." And I agree; that is absolutely true of the film's depiction of its sometimes-clueless band members who get stuck in stage props, find themselves lost on the way to the stage, and have trouble harmonizing while honoring Elvis. But there is in the depiction of Jeanine something a bit darker and less "affectionate." As I look at Ian holding that cricket stick, Bill Burr's "joke" about slapping Ono blurs in my mind.

There is also an offensive lesson. In "We've Been Getting the 'Yoko' Thing Wrong for 50 Years" (*Mel Magazine*, August 16, 2019), writer Tracy Moore reflects on her relationship with a male musician and the times she herself has been dubbed a "Yoko" through no fault of her own. She writes, "I should have known from the mockumentary *Spinal Tap*, which demonstrated with Yoko stand-in Jeanine, girlfriend of singer/guitarist David St.

Hubbins, that an overbearing girlfriend/manager was Kryptonite to male creative morale." She "should have known" that by being in a relationship with a male musician, she might eventually be blamed, like Jeanine, and like Ono.

For those who missed that lesson in Ono's real-life treatment, *This Is Spinal Tap* filled the gap, pushing forward the same message of warning and threat. And the film's now legendary status—dubbed in 2003 the "number one rock-and-roll movie of all time" by *Rolling Stone* magazine—only further cements the underlying message's resonance, augmenting and extending its reach.

BARTMANIA

Other examples of the deployment of the "Yoko Oh No" trope differ in their detail, some supporting the Yoko myth with little reflection on the events of the past and others flipping the narrative entirely. But the same overall effect potentially remains in the very maintenance of the trope. That is especially true of the iconic 1993 *Simpsons'* episode, the cartoon wildly popular among a diverse audience and named by *Time* magazine in 1999 the best television show of all time. The series, which began in 1989, is based on a comic strip by Matt Groening, but a changing team of writers and producers wrote the show's eventual episodes. One of those early writers, Conan O'Brien, reflected on the series's cultural impact in *Vanity Fair's* "Simpson Family Values" (August 2007): "I think long after my *Late Night* show is gone, I feel like the *Simpsons* episodes I worked on will always be in the ether. People will be watching them on some space station, like, 200 years from now." The impact of the *Simpsons'* Yoko treatment, given the show's platform and cultural impact, is clearly significant, as author Moritz Fink confirms in the book *The Simpsons: A Cultural History*, describing the long-running series as "universal" and "an epitome of a global media culture." Comparing the fandom around the show to Beatlemania, he calls the early 1990s a time of "Bartmania."

Throughout its history, *The Simpsons* put their own twist on pop music and its history. Its take on Yoko fit that pattern. In the 1993 "Homer's Barbershop Quartet," episode 1, season 5, which focuses specifically on Yoko as an artist, the lesson is less ambiguous than in *This Is Spinal Tap*, at least at the start. In the episode's setup, the Simpson family visits a swap meet, and the kids find an old record with Homer on the cover—*Meet the Be Sharps*—a parody of the Beatles' album *Meet the Beatles*. To a surprised Bart and Lisa, Homer explains that in the summer of 1985, he was in a famous barbershop quartet, with Apu, Barney, and Principal Skinner, the latter voiced by Harry Shearer of *This Is Spinal Tap*. The choice of barbershop is a clever one, with boy bands, such as the Beatles, indebted to barbershop's close harmony singing.[8]

In a flashback, the group's English manager advises Homer to keep his marriage a secret, to appeal to the female fans, and has Apu change his last name to disguise his Indian descent, avoiding the peril of yellow perilism. Marge is in tears when she learns that she cannot be a part of Homer's public life. But she, ever the dutiful wife and muse, goes along with the scheme and still manages to inspire the group's big hit, "Baby on Board." The entry of the Yoko character is, in part, prepared by Marge, in her dress and beaded necklace, a contrasting woman, the right kind of woman. But it is also primed by ample direct reference to the Beatles: first at the Grammy Awards, when the Be Sharps win in the category of "Outstanding Soul, Spoken Word or Barbershop Album of the Year" and Homer meets George Harrison, voiced by Harrison himself, though Homer is more excited about the party food; and then when Homer describes to the kids the group's downfall. Referencing a Lennon quote from 1966 ("We're more popular than Jesus now"), Bart asks, "What happened? Did you screw up like the Beatles and say you were bigger than Jesus?" The group absolutely did, Homer tells Bart. They even used the line as the title of their second album, *Bigger than Jesus*. But the real trouble wasn't arrogance or blasphemy. No, the group struggled when golden-voiced Barney got a new girlfriend.

Set again in the past, Homer, during a recording session, asks, "Where's Barney?" Skinner answers, "He's with his new girlfriend, the Japanese conceptual artist." As in *This Is Spinal Tap*, we hear about her before we see her. The episode had already established that difference is a problem for the group, with Apu hiding his ethnicity. The mention of the girlfriend's ancestry is then significant in the episode and in keeping with Yoko's real-life treatment in the press. With that introduction, Barney enters with his Yoko, both all in black, except for their skin—Barney's coloration Simpsons yellow (the show's default "white") and his girlfriend noticeably paler.

The two have new ideas for the group, taking barbershop, in Barney's words, "to strange new places." They play a recording of an alternating iteration of the would-be Yoko saying "number eight" and the trademark Barney burp, on loop. Rather than ignorant and meddling, as in *This Is Spinal Tap*, the butt of the *Simpsons'* joke is Yoko's experimental art. And audiences are meant to laugh at her from the start. Later, at Moe's Tavern, Barney orders a beer, and his new girlfriend chooses "a single plum floating in perfume, served in a man's hat." Interestingly, though Barney articulates the couple's aims in the episode, audiences quickly associated the unwelcome noise with the Yoko figure. In a review of the episode in the *Baltimore Sun* (September 30, 1993), critic David Zurawik summarized: "We see [the quartet's] triumphs and, sadly, their demise when one member falls 'under the spell of a Japanese conceptual artist' who believes she can take barbershop music to 'strange, new places.'" *She believes*, it's assumed, based on the Yoko narrative. And Barney is merely her vessel.

As in *This Is Spinal Tap*, there is a "happy" ending, with the Yoko character in her supposed rightful place—in this case, gone. At the end of the *Simpsons* episode, the Be Sharps reunite in the present, singing together on top of Moe's, like the Beatles' final rooftop performance. George Harrison drives past in a limo, rolls down his window, and comments, "It's been done." The men are back together, and Yoko is no more, or at least out of sight.

FLIPPING THE YOKO SCRIPT

On the other end of the spectrum, several examples of the "Yoko Oh No" trope upend the Yoko myth to a certain extent, as *This Is Spinal Tap* and "Homer's Barbershop Quartet" could have but didn't. However, the question remains: how successful are these comedic flips, given the recycling of the trope? Does reference to "Yoko Oh No" maintain the myth even when aspects of it are challenged through humor?

On the show *30 Rock*, the star of the show within the show, Jenna, played by Jane Krakowski, identifies a certain power in getting a musician to leave his band for her. In season 6, episode 16, "Meet the Woggels!," she specifies "like Yoko Ono and the Beatles, or Lance Drake Mandrell and Wilson Phillips." The Yoko narrative remains intact, but the reference at least ascribes to Yoko a certain admirable power: a power Jenna wants. The reference to Lance is also a fun gender flip, with Lance a character on the show played by Billy Baldwin, married in real life to Chynna Phillips from the '90s girl group Wilson Phillips.

The Barenaked Ladies song "Be My Yoko Ono," first a demo in 1989, offers another perspective, again identifying something admirable in Ono's impact, specifically her devotion to Lennon: "Isn't it beautiful to see two people so much in love?" The Canadian group even takes on Ono's blame, to some extent, singing in the up-tempo hit, "But I don't like all these people / slagging her for breaking up the Beatles." They don't explicitly explain that the blame is wrong but, instead, insist that they "don't like" it. After all, apparently, they would give up "musical genius" to have their own "personal Venus."[9]

A more evident sendup, however, appears courtesy of Flight of the Conchords, in episode 4, season 1, of the HBO show *Flight of the Conchords*, titled "Yoko" (2007). Like *This Is Spinal Tap* and *The Simpsons* to some extent, this show's premise is a great context for music-related references as well as fantastical breaks in song: two guys from New Zealand trying to make it as musicians in New York, starring real-life musicians from New Zealand Jemaine Clement and Bret McKenzie. In the episode, those guys, bandmates and best friends, adjust to new developments in Bret's romantic life, specifically his new girlfriend, Coco, the name an obvious Yoko reference. In the episode, however, rather than the expected joke at Coco's expense, it's Jemaine who's the problem. During a date at Coco's apartment, Coco and Bret nervously compliment each other: "I like your eyes" (her) / "The eggs were really nice like your lips" (him). In the scene, they are about to kiss when Jemaine, up to that point off-camera, interrupts, "Are we going to watch a DVD or what?" The camera pans to Jemaine, who we learn is also on the date. Coco sweetly wonders if it's a bit too late for the movie, and Jemaine agrees, saying, "We should probably get home." But Bret wants to stay. When Coco asks Bret if he would like to spend the night, Jemaine cluelessly jumps in, insisting again that it's time for them to go, as if Coco wanted him to stay, too. Eventually, Jemaine reluctantly agrees to the sleepover, still oblivious.

On their next date, Bret sings Coco a song, and again Jemaine makes a surprise appearance, both physically and musically, with his deep voice sonically sticking out in Bret's song. When Bret concludes his serenade,

Jemaine interjects, "What are we going to do now?" "We were going to go cycling," Bret responds, the "we" seemingly referring to Coco and Bret. But, in the next cut, Bret and Jemaine are riding together on a tandem bicycle, while Coco follows on foot holding their stuff. Who is the episode's "Yoko," Coco or Jemaine? Coco has done nothing to disrupt the band. Jemaine, in contrast, has done everything to disturb a budding romantic relationship that is not his own, unless the audience invests in the possible homosexual connection between Bret and Jemaine. Not only that, Coco is white, whereas the two guys are the outsiders in New York; Jemaine, in fact, is part Maori, an indigenous people in New Zealand—a reference point in the show's episode 8 of season 2, "New Zealand Town."

But Bret's about to take a stand. After a week of Jemaine tagging along on Coco and Bret's dates, Bret's finally had it: "You're always there," he tells Jemaine, who reasonably responds, "So are you." But Bret insists, enough is enough. Only then, with his feelings hurt, does Jemaine begin to think Coco might be a "Yoko." During the next band meeting with band manager Murray, Jemaine petulantly and passive-aggressively complains about Coco, who Bret insists is "nothing like Yoko." Fueling Jemaine's fire is Coco herself, who appears with sandwiches for everyone and a new, quite impressive poster for the group, which Jemaine insists they don't need, pointing to a pathetic scrawled poster he himself created for the band.

The episode in this way does not explicitly rebuke the common take on Yoko's negative reception. But it does shift the blame away from Yoko and toward the man, with Jemaine here the real problem. Her contribution to the group actually appears worthy, especially compared to Jemaine's pitiful doodle. When Bret refuses to link Coco with Yoko, Jemaine childishly replies, "Ono, she isn't." Murray comments, "Jemaine, you're putting 'oh no' together to sound like 'Ono.'" "Ono, I didn't," says Jemaine. "You did it again," Murray observes. Jemaine continues, "Ono, did I?" Bret astutely gets to the heart of the matter, identifying Jemaine's new insistence that Coco is a Yoko as a manifestation of his hurt feelings, because he can no longer come on the couple's dates. He's "projecting his feelings, making it about the band." With Jemaine still unwilling to admit the truth, Bret quits the group. But it's not Coco's/Yoko's fault. It's Jemaine's.

The episode as a whole offers an alternate reading of the Yoko label—a way for a man to disguise his feelings, his love for a bandmate, by blaming the woman. But this treatment does not necessarily rehabilitate Yoko in reception or attempt to counter the Yoko myth in full: she's "nothing like Yoko," Bret says. And in making that clear, the character Coco herself never takes a stand. She, for example, does not insist in her own voice that Jemaine stop coming on dates or argue that her poster is much, much better than Jemaine's picture, which it is. When she seems open to breaking up with Bret, as Jemaine wants, Bret cuts her off. The comedic context allows us to laugh at Jemaine and the Yoko myth simultaneously. But the episode turns the myth on its head while supporting it to some extent. Though the Yoko myth lives on in the episode, the guys of Flight of the Conchords still manage to cast it in a new light, as a product of a man's own personal issues. And, in so doing, the episode goes further than *The Simpsons'* episode or *This Is Spinal Tap*, both of which go nowhere in confronting the misogyny of Yoko's public treatment.

I admire the Flight of the Conchords' upending of various aspects of the narrative but, at the same time, remain concerned that reference to the myth at this point gives the myth the oxygen it needs to keep breathing, whether we're laughing at the trope or with it. In the end, Ono is still in the wrong—a wrong reinforced and publicized over and over again. The "Yoko Oh No" trope cycles on loop, a misogynistic machine operating on its own and maintaining Ono's guilt, with seemingly no end in sight. That operation has repercussions, solidifying a certain shared belief and promoting related norms of behavior.

Yoko herself reveals awareness of her negative labeling and reputation, responding to it and even incorporating it into her art. In 2016, an art exhibit in her honor at the Reykjavik Art Museum in Iceland included a hat holding an unusual liquid-solid combo, a reference to her animated *Simpsons* character and the ordering of a "single plum, floating in perfume, served in a man's hat." She has said, "Those hate vibes, they're like love vibes, they are very strong. It kept me going. When you're hated so much, you live. Hate was feeding me." But what about the other women? To be sure, the lessons of Ono's treatment resonate deeply, in more ways than I can account for or quantify.

In an interview with Lily Troia, a band manager, in the *Star Tribune* (August 17, 2012), journalist Jahna Peloquin asked about Troia's relationship with Adam Levy, a member of the band Honeydogs: "Does it ever get complicated managing the band of someone you're in a relationship with?" Troia responds, "No one wants to be a Yoko." And outside of music, on a

site devoted to female tattooers, longtime tattoo artist Kate "Shanghai" Hel-
lenbrand recounts her reluctance initially to break into the male-dominated
world of tattoo art: "I said I didn't want to be a Yoko Ono. I didn't want
to bust up the boys' club." Novelist Alice Elliott Dark, in the article "Oh
Yoko! 20 Ways of Looking at an Art-World Icon," recognized the negative
effect: how Ono's treatment in this way acts as a warning. For her, the hate
directed at Yoko was "frightening": "She was the type of person I most
wanted to be—yet she was hated. I found this very discouraging."

Women in real life get the message and, if they don't, the media is there
to call them out, shaming them and shunning them, especially if they are
involved in music, connected romantically to a musician, or perceived as
different already. Just as the many "Yoko Oh No" iterations appear over
and over again, so do the many real-life takedowns of women in music—
women condemned in the press as "Yokos" for being themselves. These
callouts may not curb the supposed missteps of these women but, like the
cultural representations of the Yoko myth, they can act as another means of
reinforcing customs and customary conduct, curbing the self-expression of
other women. One of the earliest musical figures fed into this misogynistic
machine was Courtney Love, the subject of the next chapter. Born Courtney Harrison, she might have chosen the name Love for herself. But, for
many fans and members of the media, it was all hate.

3

"YOKO LOVE"

"Just call me Yoko Love," Courtney Love told journalist Lynn Hirschberg. She had just received a call from Nirvana's drummer, Dave Grohl, and then handed the phone to the band's lead singer Kurt Cobain, Love's husband. "They all hate me," she explained, "Everyone just f°cking hates my guts." In the published heading, the interview was hyped in part with the following: "For *Vanity Fair*'s September 1992 issue, Lynn Hirschberg set out to find out if the pair were the grunge John and Yoko?"

Many in the media and public had already decided, as Love clearly knew. And the answer was a resounding "Yes." Nirvana manager Danny Goldberg wrote in his book *Serving the Servant: Remembering Kurt Cobain* (2019), "Almost immediately there were people who referred to her as 'Yoko.'" And the comparison continued, even amid tragedy. Seven months after Love's husband killed himself on April 5, 1994, *Chicago Tribune* writer Greg Kott called her "the most famous rock widow since Yoko Ono."

When Love appeared on the public stage and as media abuse mounted in the press and among Nirvana fans, Love's treatment in the press hit several of the key points in Ono's own reception. As in the *Vanity Fair* article, the focus was most often on Love's influence over Cobain, especially in terms of drug use. And if Love's own music was mentioned, it was rarely in words fully flattering. As Hirschberg noted, "Courtney's singing is a mix of shouting, screeching, and rasping," though she admitted Love's songwriting "is powerful."

The media would turn Love into her own particular caricature, laughing at her distress as they would at the serious struggles of other young female celebrities later in the 1990s, such as Britney Spears and Lindsay Lohan. A year after Cobain's suicide, which left Love to raise their baby daughter alone, comedian Molly Shannon impersonated Love on *Saturday Night Live*. She continued to do so, seven times in total, between 1995 and 1998. In one appearance on May 11, 1996, Shannon as Love stumbles onto the stage, apparently impaired in a drugged-out haze and hosting a David Letterman-like late-night talk show. When a stagehand enters to help her, she shouts, "Get off me!" But after she demands a cigarette, and the stagehand gives her one, she pounces on him, forcing him into a sloppy, full-body make-out session. The joke, I guess, is that she wants it but pretends she doesn't. Also, ha ha (sarcastic laugh), she's hilariously intoxicated. Rather than Letterman's typical "Top Ten List," Shannon's Love shows the audience the "Top Ten Bruises on My Body." The evidence of her pain—her hurt—is a literal punchline.

There were also those who accused Love herself of killing Cobain, directly or indirectly, through her own drug habit. Amazingly, that camp included Love's father, Hank Harrison, the former manager of the Grateful Dead.[1] As the years went on, to some she was Yoko-like but even worse. In the *Guardian* article "Black Widow" (October 25, 2002), Colin Paterson wrote, "It is unfair to say that Courtney Love is to Nirvana what Yoko Ono is to the Beatles—unfair to Yoko, that is." Paterson broadcast the bent of his attack in the title, recycling the worn-out image of the femme fatale as a "black widow," the erotic woman who mates, then murders—yet another label as weapon in the misogynists' arsenal.

Love has often taken on the media prejudice, as well as the misogyny she faced more generally. In the now infamous Hirschberg interview, Love described her meetings with male record executives interested in signing her band, Hole, formed in 1989, and the difference between her treatment and her husband's: "Now Kurt is able to go into Capitol, go into a meeting, decide he doesn't like it halfway through, walk out on the guys mid-sentence, and everyone goes, 'There goes Kurt. He's so moody. Nirvana's great.' But I go in and spend three hours with Jeff Ayeroff [at Virgin] and tell him more about punk rock than he ever knew. I give him quality time, but, I'm sorry, I don't want to be on his label and he gets a boner about it and calls me a bitch."

Her recognition of gender bias and courage in calling it out, however, wavered somewhat when she addressed her Yoko reputation. In a 2014 *Rolling Stone* interview, Love told Miriam Coleman, "I don't think the Yoko comparison is fair, I never sat in on rehearsals." She spoke out on her own behalf but did nothing to invalidate the unfairness in Ono's reception. Given her mistreatment, her reaction to the Yoko tag may be understandable. No matter the truth, it would surely be hard to welcome another label meant as a pejorative. Love also may have unknowingly consumed the Yoko myth's message, like so many of us. Broadcast in Ono's own press coverage and in appearances of the "Yoko Oh No" trope as entertainment, Love was, in some ways, conditioned to accept the popular conception of Yoko and heed its powerful warning.

Love generally stood up for herself and for women. She was herself. But when it came to Yoko, she may not have been able to see the full picture, at least initially. After all, it's been warped and twisted by a misogynistic system of enforcement crucial to the maintenance of a patriarchal standard. In the 1990s, Love, during the height of her fame, was then stuck in an incomplete moment of rebellion, something she herself would acknowledge. She pushed against norms expected of women in music, but her revolt, with online media on the ascent, could only go so far.

FROM HOLE TO HALF

Early in her media coverage, Courtney Love was singled out as transgressive, someone who challenged accepted notions of a woman's place in rock. And she absolutely did. In the article "Belting Out That Most Unfeminine Emotion" (February 9, 1992), Simon Reynolds, writing for the *New York Times*, describes Courtney Love's music with her band, Hole, in the negative: "abrasive," "tortuous sound," and "punishing." In the interview, Love insisted she could only dole out that punishment and still succeed because she was pretty: "When women get angry, they are regarded as shrill or hysterical. In the mid-80s there was a great all-female hard-core band called Frightwig. But because they were ugly, they were easy to dismiss as uptight feminists. One way around that, for me, is bleaching my hair and looking good."

At the time, Love was aware of the contradiction. She explained to Reynolds: "It's bad that I have to do that to get my anger accepted. But then I'm part of an evolutionary process. I'm not the fully evolved end." In her published diary excerpts (*Dirty Blonde*, 2006), she reveals a similar ambivalence toward traditional femininity—an ambivalence related to her experience and the traditions of the time. When she was twenty years old, she wrote, "I am not a Beautiful youth. Adolescent Boy. This Experiment in Boyishness has Failed. I am a woman . . . MAYBE . . . I depend upon Artifice as I have been taught."

In her career, she would similarly stand up for herself while replicating, sometimes ironically, aspects of the established feminine norm. She bowed to the apparent necessity of hotness but railed against other expectations of women in music. She also took to task those musical women who seemed to kowtow completely. In the same interview with Reynolds, she said of women singers, "Why don't they pick up a guitar?" She believed at the time that women weren't putting in the work—learning how to play instruments. They accepted their plight as decoration and stopped there. They didn't fulfill the expectation as she did—only as a means to an end, a means of rocking. But, in making her point, she also dismissed female singers—recycling long-held ideas that singing is "natural" and, therefore, not necessarily a special talent.[2]

This ambiguity is everywhere in Love's statements at the time and in her music. In the Reynolds article, it's easy to recognize that mixed messaging, with Love and her ideas center stage, along with other women in rock—"a new batch of female rockers." But this particular coverage, spotlighting Love's ideas about music, would be somewhat unique, especially as Love's relationship with Cobain began to overshadow her own musical accomplishments, at least in the press. Just a month after Reynolds's article, newspapers across the country announced Love's marriage to Cobain in a quiet ceremony in Hawaii. In *USA Today*'s "Union Made in Nirvana" (March 17, 1992), journalist Edna Gunderson described their wedding, noting Cobain as "press-shy" and Love as "garrulous."

With Nirvana a revelation at the time, at the center of a new grunge sensibility and zeitgeist, and Love already an outspoken female musician, the coming together of Love and Cobain had certain ready-made similarities to the relationship between Ono and Lennon. Just ten days after the wedding announcement, Patrick MacDonald published in the *Seattle Times* "Will

Kurt Cobain Become the Next John Lennon?" It's easy to wonder now if that analogy was all about Cobain's musical achievement and fame, with Nirvana a pop phenomenon like the Beatles. Or was his marriage to Love also a factor in the Lennon parallel?

Later in 1992, the somewhat benign coverage of the two lovebirds took a darker turn, thanks in part to Hirschberg's *Vanity Fair* piece. In that article, Hirschberg focuses initially on Love, then pregnant, as a person—rudely "late," with lots of makeup almost hiding her acne and seemingly too much to say, her speaking style described as "verbal pyrotechnics." When Hirschberg outlines Love's background, she does so snidely, sure as she was that Love lies: "She says she was born in San Francisco in 1966 (that date seems off—she is probably older than twenty-six, although not much)." I don't forgive Hirschberg for the article's tone, but, fine, the date was off.

Love was born in 1965, moving from place to place after her hippie parents divorced. She lived with relatives and even had a stint staying at a juvenile facility in Salem, Oregon, before she left school and moved to England. There she got involved in the punk scene. She would also work as a stripper and try her hand at acting, in the movie *Sid and Nancy* (1986), about drug addicts Sid Vicious of the English punk group Sex Pistols and his girlfriend, Nancy Spungen, supposedly a groupie, prostitute, and drug dealer. Posthumously, Spungen would become another partner in the musical world used to disparage Love.

The Hirschberg article supported the Yoko comparison throughout, underscoring Love's blame in a tense relationship between her and the other members of Nirvana: "Since Courtney and Kurt's courtship began last year, she has reportedly antagonized [Dave] Grohl and [Krist] Chris Novoselic, the other two members of Nirvana." Hirschberg quotes an unnamed source: "Courtney always has a hidden agenda. And Kurt doesn't. He's definitely being led." Part of that storyline, with reference, too, to Spungen, was description of the couple's drug use and Love's own admission that the couple indulged in "a lot of drugs" during a trip to New York, when Nirvana performed on *Saturday Night Live* at the start of the year. Another unnamed source is quoted: "Courtney was pregnant and she was shooting up." Not only that, Hirschberg suggests, just as journalists did with Yoko, that Love was to blame for Cobain's habit: "Courtney has a long history with drugs. . . . Reportedly, Kurt didn't do much more than drink until he met Courtney."

Like Ono, Love has claimed the opposite. In the film *Cobain: Montage to Heck* (2015), Love insists that she was not doing anything illicit when she met Cobain, who by the fall of 1991 was a heroin addict. Love herself had struggled, especially during the summer of 1989, but she had found a way out of her addiction. Novoselic confirms, in the Cobain biography *Heavier than Heaven*, "People blame Courtney, that Courtney turned him on to heroin, but that's not true. He did it before he even met Courtney. Courtney did not get Kurt on drugs." If anything, Love's relationship with Cobain was, in part, to blame for her own sobriety lapse. As biographer Charles Cross writes, "She chose Kurt and, in doing so, chose drugs."[3]

WORDS BECOME DEED

The *Vanity Fair* take, however, established a certain agenda—a tone and focus in Love's general press coverage. No surprise, then, that Love and Cobain would remain wary of the press thereafter (or that the article's author would find herself in hot water with other musicians later in her career: "M.I.A. Takes Revenge on *New York Times* Writer Lynn Hirschberg," *Pitchfork*, May 27, 2010). Several newspapers picked out and picked up the article's revelations about Love's drug dependence. Reporting focused in particular on Love's habit while pregnant, incited, in part, by the controversial cover of *Vanity Fair*'s September issue—Love pregnant and in a see-through negligee, the picture retouched to remove a lit cigarette from her hand.

Love was not pleased with the public backlash or her depiction by the media. To many, she was an unfit mother already. And two days after she gave birth, to Frances Bean Cobain on August 18, 1992, a social worker from the Los Angeles County Department of Children's Services arrived at the hospital with a copy of Hirschberg's article. Now a part of a complex legal system, Love would not be allowed unsupervised time with her daughter for more than seven months.[4]

The backlash, Love mused in an interview with Jonathan Gold for the *Los Angeles Times* (August 16, 1992), fit a certain pattern: "I have this thing about me, this catalyst, that brings out hate in people, and I wonder about it." She described a performance in 1991, in front of a rowdy audience, that took a turn when she fearlessly dove into the crowd. Some among the wolfish pack groped her and assaulted her; when she returned to the stage, she had no clothes on—an uninvited *Cut Piece*. This experience, in part, inspired her song "Asking for It," released on her album *Live through This* (1994). In the chorus, she asks, resigned, "Was she asking for it? / Was she asking nice?" The song has also been released with Cobain performing backing vocals on the bridge: "If you live through this with me / I swear that I will die for you." After the bridge, the chorus's questioning becomes more urgent, the guitars no longer a light strum. When it's repeated again, Love's voice jumps in register as she yells, demanding answers she'll never get.

Cobain was less philosophical about his wife's treatment and the related public response to his personal life. When he accepted an MTV Video Award for best new artist, he pointedly said into the camera, "It's really hard to believe everything you read." In another performance, in 1992, shown in the film *Montage of Heck*, Cobain riffs on the rumors, arriving on stage in a wheelchair wearing a hospital gown. He tells the crowd that Love "thinks everyone hates her" and asks the audience to yell "Courtney, we love you." Still, in "Cobain to Fans" (September 21, 1992), an interview with the *Los Angeles Times* and writer Robert Hilburn, Cobain admitted to using heroin but insisted he only experiments. The interview had been arranged by Nirvana's manager, Goldberg, who wrote in his book, "Since the Department of Public Social services process had been triggered by a magazine article, I thought that a positive story might lower the temperature."

In the article, Cobain claimed that any canceled shows or failed appearances were rooted in a mysterious stomach problem, not addiction. He also addressed the media speculation directly, telling Hilburn, "It didn't bother me at first (when people started talking or writing about possible drug use) because I've always admired Keith Richards and all these other rock stars who were associated with heroin. There had been some type of glamour element to it." But the speculation about his habit, he said, had exceeded even his comfort level: "The biggest thing that affected me was all the insane rumors, the heroin rumors . . . all this speculation going on. I felt totally violated. I never realized that my private life would be such an issue."

He felt bullied, too, a callback to his own difficulties as a child. And that invasion had him already thinking about walking away from the band, though the music always brought him back: "I guess I must have quit the band about 10 different times in the last year." I wonder now, would that speculation have become so intense if Cobain was not linked with Love?

As Cobain knew, he had a certain luxury with drugs. As an addict, he could seem authentic and cool, a rebel. But Love, a woman, could not, or at least not in the same way. But, with his connection to Love, her drug problem was now his problem, too, at least in his public reception.

Whitney Houston's reception is a striking example of this double standard. She famously addressed her drug use in a 2002 interview with Diane Sawyer: "Crack is cheap. I make too much for me to ever smoke crack . . . I don't do that. Crack is whack." Those last three words, in Gerrick Kennedy's telling (*Didn't We Almost Have It All: In Defense of Whitney Houston*), forever altered "the way we look at Whitney." Unlike the drug use of male musicians, her addiction became "a punchline." Even after her tragic death in 2012 (she drowned in a bathtub with cocaine in her system), some in the public were still laughing. In 2019, comedian Chris Rock complained about a long meeting that could have been an e-mail by posting a meme of Houston looking terribly bored. He added the note: "Hurry up I got crack to smoke." In media coverage, Houston's drug use was anything but Cobain's hoped-for cool. And, for Houston, both gender and race impacted the distinction.

As with Houston, Love had no way to avoid the condemnation or jokes. Not only was she blasted for her abuse of drugs, but she was also blamed for Cobain's heroin use, supposedly corrupting him and failing as a mother before she even gave birth. With Cobain admitting to the possibility of a Nirvana breakup as well as the drug use and media criticism, it's no wonder the Yoko tag continued to plague Love—so much so, in fact, that she started to develop a certain "feeling" for Ono.[5] For this reason, she even wrote an "ode" to Ono, "Twenty Years in the Dakota," released as a Hole single the following month. Cobain had brought up the Dakota Hotel in New York, where Lennon and Ono stayed after the Beatles' breakup, when Love was in labor: "Twenty years stuck inside The Dakota, I won't let that happen to you."[6]

In the song, almost monotone, Love narrates Ono's past without naming her: "She spent twenty years in the Dakota"; "She spent twenty years like a virus." The pitch sinks at the end of the word virus, gritty and raw, just as it does on the word Dakota. But Love also makes the connection that everyone else had made already, linking herself with that unnamed "she": "They want to burn the witches inside us." *Us*. Defiant, she also sings, "Well, I know you haven't sank me / And you haven't sank her yet." But the weight was real. In the final section, the music slows, as Love wistfully croons, "Hey Jude, hey Jude," along with a "na-na-na" refrain, both a direct reference to the Beatles and their hit "Hey Jude" (1968), a serious song meant to comfort Lennon's son, Julian, dealing then with his father's new relationship with Ono. The allusion signals the heaviness in both songs. In Love's song, the burden and threat are external; they're "coming for" her. And then she asks, "Judy, Judy, are they coming soon?"

A GOLD DIGGER, OH NO!

But no song could turn the tide, especially given the negative speculation around Love's musical success. In a profile for *The Times* (London), "No Love Lost" (March 28, 1993), writer Robert Sandall described Love as someone who sought out male musicians for her own gain, quoting an anonymous "friend": "She wouldn't take no for an answer." By going after "the hottest property in rock," Sandall concluded, grunge music had "a soap to rival the Lennons."

The idea that a female musician couldn't be successful on her own is nothing new. And Love was certainly aware that the public assumed Cobain was behind her music at her insistence—thanks to articles like Sandall's, as well as fan letters accusing her of scaring "poor Kurt into going out with her" (a line Love herself reads in *Montage of Heck*). Still, it bothered her more than other rumors. Buried in the Hirschberg hit job, Love is quoted as saying, "The worst thing is when people say Kurt's helping me to make it. If anything, Kurt has hurt me."

To be sure, the association, in some ways, was a burden burying her own musical aspirations. With the release of her album *Live through This*, her bassist Kristen M. Pfaff revealed, "We felt that pressure when we were recording. I think we all knew it had to be really good [to] get over the Courtney personality thing . . . the wife-of-the-rock-star thing and the girl-band thing." By all accounts, the album was good, with *Rolling Stone* calling it excellent and *Newsweek* insisting it "sounds like a young Chrissie Hynde, not Mrs. Kurt Cobain."[7] Nonetheless, public perception remained the same.

This particular attack differed somewhat from charges leveled at Ono or the Yoko tag itself. Instead, it was a play on the "gold digger" label, defined as a woman "who uses her sexuality and charm to seduce a man into a relationship where she can profit."[8] And it's been a strategy of disparagement at least since its early appearance in connection with performer Kay Laurell of the Ziegfeld Follies, when it was used against women seen as young, low class, highly sexual, and manipulative. As Brian Donovan chronicles in the book *American Gold Digger: Marriage, Money, and the Law from the Ziegfeld Follies to Anna Nicole Smith*, the term has been in this way a means to enforce traditional norms of womanhood as well as the family unit, which explains in part its redeployment against Love during a time of particular political concern around family values, with the "war against drugs" and a new focus on "moral renewal."[9]

The charge can also signify a referendum, to some extent, on manliness, those men who might be fooled, those who might be "led." Cobain's "fragile" appearance could have been provocation supporting this narrative, or perhaps it was his own upending of traditional gender roles, in particular the wearing of wigs and dresses. It probably didn't help, too, that he publicly called Love "the best f*ck in the world." As Love told journalist Gillian Gaar in an interview for *The Rocket*, "a woman, of course, can only use her pussy to get anywhere. Men can get by just playing good songs."

Love's look factored into the label, too—her blonde hair a callback to the quintessential "gold digger," Marilyn Monroe in *Gentlemen Prefer Blondes*, and soon linked with model Anna Nicole Smith, who married an eighty-nine-year-old billionaire in 1994. But Love's music did as well—with its firm place in a popular style, like Cobain's. Although the press could laugh at Ono's experimental music, dismissing her as "weird" and shrugging off the suggestion that Yoko helped Lennon musically, Love's sound warranted a different strategy. The press couldn't link Ono's sound with Lennon's at first, but they could link Love's with Cobain's. And so, for all of these reasons, a "gold-digging" star was born. She certainly wouldn't be the last (see chapter 5). And race, to be sure, would be a significant feature in similar labeling.

"IN MY LIFE"

As the couple's problems exploded into view, Love's Yoko tie—based in the gold-digger narrative as well as the couple's drug use—seemed a regular part of the negative press coverage. Two days after *The Times* swipe, Brian Rohan, writing for the *Irish Voice*, rehashed Love's *Vanity Fair* profile, describing "a sordid picture of the band, which was allegedly being torn apart by what was being built up to be the next Yoko Ono, Courtney Love." Five months later, Robert Hilburn of the *Los Angeles Times* profiled Cobain, calling the Beatles "Cobain's first musical heroes." To many, Cobain and Love were "the John and Yoko" of the '90s, not the Sean Penn and Madonna, a suggested parallel Love seemed to enjoy in the film *Montage of Heck*. The overlap, of course, wouldn't stop there.

Cobain was playing with fire, still actively caught up in drugs and spiraling. In July 1993, Cobain was arrested for domestic violence—his assault on Love. In the *Morning News Tribune* (Tacoma, Washington), Love defended Cobain: "It was a freak, insane, horrible thing." In Cobain's biography, Cross details the context of the dispute, including Cobain's increasing addiction, as well as Love's concern about Cobain's purchase of guns.

The following year, Cobain overdosed while on vacation with Love and his daughter in Italy. In "Kurt Cobain's OD Chills Nirvana Fans," Renee Graham of the *Boston Globe* reported March 5, 1994, that Cobain "showed signs" of recovering "from a drug-and-alcohol-induced coma." But just weeks after he woke up, he killed himself, dead of a self-inflicted gunshot. The headline in the *Chicago Tribune* announced, "Nirvana Star Kurt Cobain Dead: 'Lennon of His Generation' Likely a Suicide, Police Say." In the article, Cobain's mother, Wendy O'Connor, reflects, "Now he's gone and joined that stupid club," becoming part of a long list of other male musicians tragically dead young, at age twenty-seven: "I told him not to join that stupid club."

With Love "already cast in the role of Yoko Ono before she became a widow,"[10] it may come as no surprise that she quickly became the focus of the press's coverage of Cobain's suicide, just as Ono was for some after Lennon's death. And Love's anger did, too. She was "angry at her husband" but also at herself: "I listened to too many people. I'm only going to listen to my gut for the rest of my life. It's all my fault" (*Edmonton Journal*, April 12, 1994).

That anger was on full display at Cobain's memorial service in Seattle, with a recorded reading of Cobain's suicide note by Love along with her interjections, at times calling out his "bullshit." She clearly felt he could have done better, but she also seemed to question her own decisions. She helped stage an intervention for Cobain after his overdose in Italy, which she realized was a suicide attempt (as she revealed in *Dirty Blonde*), but shortly thereafter he checked himself out of a drug and alcohol treatment facility in Marina Del Rey, California. He then disappeared only to be discovered, five days later, dead.

At the Unity Church of Truth, during the funeral service, Goldberg spoke: "I believe he would have left the world years ago if he hadn't met Courtney." When the service was over, a song was played, at Love's request: John Lennon's "In My Life." The song is stripped and sparse as the singer considers those he's lost and yet still loves, a love still growing: "In my life I love you more."

TOXIC BLAME

The papers pushed Love's more natural "what ifs" toward a more toxic assignment of fault. On April 14, *USA Today* reported that Love was arrested for her own heroin use just a day before Cobain's suicide, supporting theories that Love's drug use was to blame. In truth, she was struggling, but part of her battle was her attempted protection and care of Cobain. Cross details Love's frantic attempts to help him, to find him, and to keep him alive. Her constant effort to save him was not part of the public narrative, nor was his history of suicidal thought pre-Love (tragically revealed in *Montage of Heck*). Her effort and her care didn't factor into the conversation because it hadn't been enough to keep him alive. Ariana Grande would find herself saddled with a comparable threshold of significance. Apparently, a woman has to succeed in fighting someone else's battle to avoid being blamed for the worst of that person's actions. Then, with the worst a reality, she alone is punished.

In Love's punishment, his death was her fault. Some of the related theories of Cobain's death spread online, in Usenet newsgroups, an internet-based discussion forum created in 1979 that expanded quickly, eventually reaching the masses when America Online allowed users to access the network in 1993. There, fans could interact with other fans, in a way they couldn't during the Beatles' breakup or in the direct aftermath of Lennon's death. The online forums fostered community among fans but also unchecked hate, the spread of misinformation without limits. Some of the early trolling maintained and supported claims that Cobain wrote Love's music; she was supposedly a groupie, nothing more. But, much worse, was the repeated line: "Courtney killed Kurt."[11]

The wild "evidence" circulated online was a strange mix of conspiracy theories and attacks on Love's general conduct: "The footage of her in the park the day after the discovery? She certainly didn't seem like a grieving widow to me."[12] Like other women seen as a general threat, including George Sand, Love was labeled a murderer. But, unlike the circulation of blame around Sand, new media supported and sped up the process.

This media attention recalled the press coverage of Nancy Spungen, who was murdered in 1978 at the age of twenty. Love was often compared to Spungen—with her addiction and a similar style. But, when Spungen died, the musical man, not the woman, remained behind. And this distinction was decisive in their respective coverage. Whereas Love was blamed for Cobain's death, credited with his suicide, Spungen's murder was never solved in the public imagination, even though her boyfriend, Sex Pistols bass player Sid Vicious, confessed to stabbing her to death. Love, in her grief, was reviled enough to inspire theories of murder with no basis in fact. Spungen's death, however, seemed to set off the opposite reaction—Vicious was exonerated with no basis in fact.

Vicious and Spungen had camped out at the Chelsea Hotel in New York, in a drug-fueled escape after the Sex Pistols' ill-fated tour of the United States. There were no other suspects and Vicious, who owned up to the crime, was arrested for the murder before overdosing in 1979. And yet, journalist Jessica Wakeman, writing for *Rolling Stone*, records the consistent doubt around Vicious's guilt—doubt that still existed in 2017. Photographer Eileen Polk, who knew Spungen, mused, "I think when Sid awoke stoned out of his mind and realized she was dead, he might have assumed he did it." Actor, screenwriter, and musician Victor Colicchio, who lived at the Chelsea at the time, also remains skeptical, even crediting Spungen with her own murder: "I don't think he would've killed her unless she told him to."[13]

A misplaced "himpathy," Kate Manne's term for the sympathy extended to men and only men, protected and still protects Vicious, even with his confession. If the roles had been reversed—Vicious dead instead of Spungen—I can only assume that the verdict would have been swift, Spungen guilty without a presumption of innocence. Like Love and like Ono. And like Grande, too (see chapter 9).

NO LOVE LOST

Despite the similarities between Love and Ono's romantic relationships as well as the treatment of Love after Cobain's death, Love would, at times, distance herself from Ono. In an interview for a profile for *The Guardian* (January 15, 1995), David Fricke asked Love directly, "Given the comparisons that have been made between Kurt and John Lennon, do you feel any affinity now with Lennon's widow, Yoko Ono?" Love realized then that she was "in the pantheon" of "rock couplehood," like Lennon and Ono. "I felt a lot of empathy for her," she said, "But I don't relate to her."

Almost two decades later, in a 2014 *Rolling Stone* interview, Love once again addressed the Ono label, explaining to Miriam Coleman that she had never "sat in on rehearsals" the way Yoko did. Rather than countering the Yoko myth in its entirety, Love again attempted to separate herself from it. In the interview, Love displays a certain hesitancy—revealing that her husband admired Ono but holding herself apart from that admiration. She explained that Cobain "thought Yoko was cool." "He was an early adopter," she said. But, when he gave her a Yoko Ono box set, she threw it "at his head." "I wasn't really a fan," she maintained. Even in her ode to Ono, "Twenty Years in the Dakota," she seems to support Yoko's guilt: "Well, you, you don't fuck with the Fabulous Four." Love didn't claim Ono's innocence. Yoko was "a virus" because she had violated the rules.

In short, Love stood up for Ono but only in part. She wasn't a fan, at least at first. She didn't sit in on rehearsals. She wasn't Ono and didn't want to be the "new Yoko" the Yoko the press was trying to make her out to be. The pull of self-preservation, given the litany of abuse Love experienced, must have been powerful. Love's reaction to Ono and her own Yoko tag also arguably reveals the true might of the Yoko myth, which Love unknowingly could have internalized. But her ambivalent response was, in some ways, a luxury. As a white woman, Love had the option to conform to the accepted standard—to downplay the Yoko parallel and maybe, just maybe, be accepted. That acceptance was part of the fame game, after all, and part of her reasoning when she dyed her hair blonde. In *Down Girl*, Manne makes it clear that misogyny "harms the most vulnerable women disproportionately." And it is often "white women, who tend to enable it, in ways that may be more or less connected with the aim of self-preservation."[14]

Still, Love was certainly aware of the contradictions of fame as well as its particular weight on women. In her journal, she wrote, "I am a Public figure unhappy with my share of the American dream. . . . If I wanted certain things, like respect and privacy I should have put out certain universal female symbols like chastity and ethereal mutedness." She recognized the price women had to pay to play in the business of fame. As she sings in the

Courtney Love. Photofest

catchy song "Celebrity Skin," from her 1998 album of the same name, "You better watch out / Oh, what you wish for." Toward the end of the song, she asks, "Have you ever felt so used up as this?"

In 2010, she praised Ono for staying true to herself within that suffocating system of celebrity. She told Robin Murray of *Clash Music*, "She sticks with her own thing." Ono, for her part, returned the compliment, when she told the BBC that "Celebrity Skin" was one of her favorite songs: "It's a brilliant, brilliant song by Courtney Love. The song represents all mothers of the world today: desperate, angry, totally sad, and also extremely intelligent. She's an incredibly complex woman and she has incredible vulnerability as well."[15]

At times, Love puts a positive twist on the worst of fame's cost. In an e-mail to Lindsay Lohan during Lohan's own harsh treatment in the press, Love offered the young actress some encouraging perspective. On January 7, 2006, she wrote of Hirschberg's 1992 article, "I thought the world had split open and was going to swallow me whole and all I wanted to do was kill that woman . . . I realize now that as hardcore as it was, it made me a lot more interesting and somehow employable."[16] Despite the spin and Love's admirable ability to acknowledge and, at times, counter an unfair standard, she shouldn't have had to do any of this. And she shouldn't have had to take any sort of stand in regard to Ono.

Cobain, who was remarkably progressive during his time, recognized the real problem. And it wasn't Love. In the liner notes for *Incesticide* (1992), Cobain wrote, "My wife challenges injustice and the reason her character has been so severely attacked is because she chooses not to function the way the white corporate man insists." She did not embrace "certain universal female symbols," as Love herself wrote. In the "logic of misogyny," a woman who does not conform, breaking with the accepted standard of feminine behavior, must be punished. And punished she was. But there's no excuse for that punishment, just as there's no excuse for Ono's. When Love dove into the celebrity world, like she did into that crowd in 1991, she should have been safe. The fact that she wasn't surely affected the women who admired her. Maybe it even stopped them. Despite Love's ambivalence, it never stopped her. And something in that courage is absolutely inspiring.

Reading a blog post of January 18, 2021, by Katelyn Campbell, I came across mention of another Love stage dive after the 1991 assault. She was performing on October 21, 1994, at The Metro in Chicago, during her *Live through This* tour following Cobain's suicide and the then recent death of Hole's bass player Kristen Pfaff, a heroin overdose. I clicked on the linked video of the show, even though Campbell warns her reader that Love is in danger. In the video, Love is on stage singing with rage in what could be a black mourning dress with a white Peter Pan collar. Then, she offers an encore rendition of the song "Olympia," which calls out the everyday sameness around her. With frustration, she pleads for change—"Make me real"—while wearing a new outfit: a black slip—a fashion fad, the slip dress, for which she later took credit. At one point, her eyes appear half open. Perhaps she's tired, perhaps she's unwell, or maybe she's simply done. But suddenly, she throws down her guitar, and I know what's coming. I want to stop her. I want to get her out of the building, away from all the people who want to tear at her or tear her apart. But it's too late.

They have her, and they're pulling at her clothes and her hair, ripping off her panty hose. Her security team has to fight off the crowd to get her back. They pick her up and help her back onto the stage. I think again of her name, Love, her stage name replacing her given name. She tried desperately to keep Cobain alive, fighting for her love, and it could have been her undoing, with the public punishing her over and over again with their hate. Still, once standing in front of the audience again, defiant in her black underwear, one bra strap broken, she yells into the mic, "Oh, do you do that to all of the guys?" It's an amazing line, in that moment. Just assaulted, again, she recognizes the double standard in her treatment and calls it out.

In some ways, it doesn't matter. She would still be Shannon's trashy whore and Hirschberg's unfit mother. But, then again, of course it matters. Love tried to conform to some extent—with her almost ironic but iconic look—and she didn't, with her musical messages and honest accounts of fame for women in music. She could not fully defend Ono, but she understood her plight. It was an incomplete protest but brave nonetheless. And many of Love's fans today admire her for that courage. Some embrace her as a "survivor," too. She survived assault, drug addiction, as well as her husband's tragic death. But she also survived the public's desire for her downfall. As Love herself said in 1995, "The American public really does have a death wish for me. They want me to die. I'm not going to die!"[17] If she had, she probably would have been celebrated. For the female celebrities the public has stalked and shamed, that's "the one happy ending." As

Sady Doyle writes in *Trainwreck*, "We love our dead girls. We love them pretty, and we love them young." Those who survive are rarely recognized for the tremendous strength of will behind that survival. Britney Spears is one of the few exceptions—the public is now generally embracing her after years of abusive attention. Of course, it took about thirteen years before that happened—time she spent in a prison of her father's making. And our making, too.

4

DRIVING BRITNEY SPEARS CRAZY

In her song "(You Drive Me) Crazy" (1999), Britney Spears describes losing sleep because she's so in love or infatuated with someone. It's a loss of control, this feeling of "crazy," "but it feels alright." In 2007, she was not calling herself crazy, but others were, and this use of the term had nothing to do with the sweet pain of late-night longing. On the cover of the *Daily News*, February 18, 2007, Spears looks calmly at the camera, her head partially shaved. "Britney Shears," the headline announced, along with the explanation: "superstar teeters on edge of a breakdown." And then Spears lost control for real, in a court of law, when she was placed under the infamous conservatorship at the insistence of her estranged father, Jamie Spears.

Throughout her career, the media would dehumanize Spears, boxing her into certain easy and pejorative categories reserved for women—"whore," "Yoko," "trainwreck," "white trash," and above all, "crazy." That abuse would peak alongside the popularity of gossip sites and magazines in the early 2000s, as digital platforms such as Twitter and Instagram began to climb in popularity—giving fans and celebrities themselves a more direct voice. But the damage, in Spears's case, was done and ruinous. The label "crazy"—a term with a history of female assault—would cage her in figuratively as it helped box her in legally when it was used as a tool in a 2008 court case that would ultimately lock her into an unprecedented conservatorship, one that only ended in November 2021. This particular toxic label, "crazy," then became action, action that had disastrous consequences for Spears as well as lessons for other women, watching from the sidelines, cheering Spears on or perhaps enjoying the spectacle of her downfall. In many ways, it is shocking that Spears was caged in a conservatorship for thirteen years, especially because she performed regularly during that period. But at the same time, given the historical connection between women and the term "crazy," it makes a terrible kind of sense.

MAD WOMAN

Women labeled crazy have been forced before to live under the control of men and then presented to the outside world for their consumption and viewing pleasure. In London in 1815, customers could pay a penny to view a lunatic in Bethlehem Hospital—but only on Sundays.[1] And that treatment relates to past understandings of "crazy," closely tied to women and, in particular, their anatomy.

In ancient Greece, the womb was seen as a sort of wandering animal, distrusted and out of control. Hippocrates then identified hysteria as "a catchall term for most female illnesses and emotional excesses, anything from a headache to an epileptic fit to using a swear word."[2] Again, that pesky wandering womb was the culprit, the source of women's "irrationality." During the Middle Ages, hysteria was further connected to demonic control and witchcraft, the gendered label "witch." Women as suspected witches were seen as uniquely powerful, a welcome change in some respects. But, of course, mortal men would respond, punishing women for the label men themselves had assigned them. Their ultimate fate would be fire.

The Victorian era took supposed remedy from flames to medical mutilation. At that time, confinement became increasingly common for the supposedly insane, and women, in particular, suffered as a result.[3] Hysteria was the go-to diagnosis, and any woman who didn't live up to the high expectations of female virtue could be diagnosed as such and committed to an asylum. In this system, men had all the control. Cheating husbands could blame suspicious wives, accusing them of hysteria. They could then force them into medical institutions, where men were once more in the lead. A doctor named R. Maurice Bucke worked at the London Asylum for the

Insane, which opened in Canada in 1870. He treated hysteria by removing the womb. He performed these "hysterectomies" until his death in 1902. Some male surgeons at the time were also removing women's clitorises for similar reasons.

Upon discovering the existence of this practice, author Eleanor Morgan was alarmed, to say the least. In her book *Hysterical*, she recounts how she thought her brain would combust, half-expecting to see her "gray matter" splattered across the "nice sweater" of a person nearby.[4] Reading her book, I could see only red. The reaction to women with reasonable emotions, displaying understandable anger or upset, was to strip them of the little autonomy they had and literally cut them apart for the perceived good of mankind. Do I sound hysterical? Can a book sound hysterical? And does my anger make me, its author, a woman, vulnerable to male judgment, dismissal, or control?

The removal of the clitoris, in particular, points to beliefs about the supposed root of female madness. It wasn't just being a woman that was a problem; it was a woman's sexuality or too much of it that was the real issue, as Elaine Showalter writes in her book *The Female Malady*. The sexual tie also suggestively frames the related historical display of women deemed insane. At least since the Middle Ages, the insane were used in this way as a means of education but also entertainment, and that spectacle had a certain erotic titillation.

In Romantic opera, music and "crazy woman" spectacle combined. A special convention—the "mad scene"—was defined by that mixture: the "mass popularity of madwoman representations, their frank appeals to sensationalism," and a tradition of "freak-show exploitation."[5] On the operatic stage, in the works of composers such as Gaetano Donizetti and Vincenzo Bellini, these scenes would climax with a woman going crazy. The popular device was partly a chance for the composer to write a virtuosic aria musically depicting madness, with wild leaps, repetition, unhinged chromatic play, and flashy runs. With these challenging and showy vocal lines, he could showcase his art through the prima donna's voice but at the expense of a central female character. *Classic FM* sums up the conceit, repeated in opera after opera: "woman is in love, something goes wrong, she loses her mind and dies," but not before delivering a showstopper.[6]

This history, as well as the tradition of male control in the realm of mental distress, cast Spears's conservatorship in a certain light. Although the surgeries have for the most part stopped, "crazy" is still a word wielded to enforce certain codes of female conduct. In a fascinating rumination on the term "crazy," in the book *Pretty Bitches* Mary Pols writes, "In our culture, the c-word is a warning . . . signaling acceptable parameters for behavior from female companions." Today, it's often a word used by men against women for their own reasons and possible gain. Pols offers the unsettling example of Martha Mitchell, married to Nixon's campaign manager, John Mitchell. Martha insisted that she had been taken from a hotel in Newport Beach in June 1972 and held against her will in an effort to squash the Watergate story. Evidently, she could have connected Nixon to one of the accused burglars, James McCord, whom she knew through her husband. And she was known to call reporters and voice her opinions. When she did eventually tell her story, she was dismissed. She became a punchline, even though the whole story was true.

I recently ran across a related story: the case of Christine Collins, whose nine-year-old son, Walter, disappeared in a Los Angeles suburb after he went to see a movie in March 1928. With national interest in the missing child, a boy in Illinois claimed to be Walter, and the LAPD happily called off the search and declared themselves victorious. Christine, however, insisted that the Illinois boy was not her Walter. With the police insisting that *she* was wrong, she produced dental records to back up her claim. He really wasn't Walter. Evidently the Illinois boy had thought becoming Walter would help him get to Hollywood. The LAPD, hoping to save face, then declared Christine crazy and had her committed to an asylum.

In these examples, the word "crazy" was flimsy justification for the heinous acts of men. And the women must have felt a bit mad in both examples. In the song "Mad Woman," Taylor Swift sings, "No one likes a mad woman / You made her like that." The lyrics potentially have multiple meanings, with mad defined as "crazy," "furious," or an understandable mixture of both. But, whatever the meaning, the man is most definitely responsible. In 2018 at *Variety*'s Power of Women Event, Natalie Portman similarly identified the root of a woman's madness in the actions of a man, instructing the audience, "If a man says to you that a woman is crazy or difficult ask him, 'What bad thing did you do to her?'" In Spears's case, so many different people participated in that "bad thing." So many participated in making her "crazy." And the men, once again, had their own personal reasons. They called her crazy, in turn driving her mad in its various translations. And they did so to further their own ends, as men have done for centuries.

"YOU MADE HER LIKE THAT"

In 1992, Spears found early success on *Star Search*. Standing next to the host, little Britney, born in McComb, Mississippi, in 1981, gracefully answered Ed McMahon's questions, foreshadowing so much of what was to come. He asked, "Do you have a boyfriend?" Spears, rightfully horrified, responded with an emphatic "No"; "They're mean," she explained. McMahon, more than double her size with gray hair and glasses, countered, "But what about me?"

Shortly thereafter, Spears appeared on *The Mickey Mouse Club*. And, at the age of only fifteen, she signed with Jive Records. A year later, in 1998, she was on television as a sexy Catholic-school girl, and the world couldn't get enough of her—her flesh, her body, and, oh yeah, that song. In 1998, Spears in an instant was everywhere, as was her single, ". . . Baby One More Time." As she herself said in *Framing Britney*, it was "overnight" celebrity—tick, tick, boom!

Britney Spears, ". . . Baby One More Time." Photofest

In 1999, Spears posed on the cover of *Rolling Stone* in an iconic image of sexy sweet, black bra and lots of pink. Alongside her popularity, however, backlash was already brewing. Sometimes, the love and hate existed together. In a study conducted during the summer of 1999, adolescent girls in a series of discussion sessions excitedly bashed Spears, often with real anger; at the same time, they celebrated her as a successful young woman. The girls' negative reaction had to do with a duality they perceived in Spears—competing messages of sexy and innocent, good girl and bad girl.[7]

It didn't help that Spears would soon be linked to Justin Timberlake of the boy band phenomenon 'N Sync. The group had formed in 1995, and with the release of their first single in the United States, "I Want You Back," in 1998, the band's audience increased with speed. In 2012, *Rolling Stone* cited 'N Sync in 1999 as one of the "top 25 teen idol breakout moments." Timberlake was easily a standout as the baby-faced heartthrob with angelic curls. With the arrival of Spears, it was a ready-made setup for audience upset, which a Fox News reporter, Roger Friedman, clearly exploited by linking Spears with Ono.

In 2002, during a pre-Grammy dinner, Friedman was able to speak with Spears, members of the boy band 'N Sync, which included Timberlake, as well as some of the musicians' parents. It was, in Friedman's estimation, "a congenial talk." When he asked the boys about their group's potential equivalent—the Rolling Stones or the Beatles—Timberlake was quick to choose the Beatles. Friedman then followed up, "Does this mean Britney is Yoko Ono?" Spears responded, "Who?" Preparing his description of this "happy exchange," Friedman wrote up front in his Fox News report, "You could guess that a girl without much of a formal education is no rocket scientist." But Friedman decided to "give her credit where credit is due": "Spears has a great little body and has done much to show it off in her videos and concerts." I honestly think I may have just thrown up a little in my mouth.

But Friedman wasn't done. Still speaking in that "congenial" way of his, Friedman then attempted to "save" Spears by offering her a chance to identify with Linda McCartney. Dripping with unchecked condescension, he asked her, "You know her name, don't you?" Sorry, Spears responded, "I'm very young."[8] Friedman explained the exchange by slamming Spears's intelligence, but he couldn't resist adding another dig, "She's not going to know much about the history of civilization, world economics, or how to split an atom," he wrote, but "you might expect" her to "know something in the category of pop music."

Really, though, what response would have satisfied Friedman? What could Spears say? In some ways, she was trapped, as Love was, too. She could have thrown Ono under the bus, insisting she was in no way a "Yoko." Or she could have righteously embraced the label—sure, I'm Yoko—which would have then made headlines absolutely everywhere, inviting in a toxic narrative and speculation, similar to the flurry of stories set off by the Hirschberg article in Love's case. I can see the litany of abusive articles that could have been, along with those that actually were. Love confronted these two sorry options and did her best with them, all things considered. But Spears, in her infinite wisdom (or convenient ignorance), found herself a third choice: playing dumb. And honestly, opting out in this way may have been Spears's best option under the circumstances.

Of course, Friedman's toxic take wasn't the only abusive response to Spears's relationship with Timberlake. On July 29, 1999, the *Boston Globe* reported, "Who knew we were breaking young hearts all over New England by reporting that the vivacious pop singing sensation Britney Spears had caught up with her new beau, Justin Timberlake." Who knew? Frankly, who didn't? In the article, Timberlake fans seemed incredulous, perhaps unable to accept the news: "Do you have any proof of this? A picture?" Of course, denial was kind compared to the blossoming hate, especially online. Already in 2000, a game at www.angelfire.com/ca3/antispears invited players to assassinate Spears. Another site collected harsh jokes about Spears:

What do you get when you give Britney Spears a penny for her thoughts?
Change.

And there were trolls, even then, hoping to take Spears's lyrics literally: "Hit me baby one more time." In an article in the *Wisconsin State Journal*, which chronicled this abuse (March 16, 2000), journalist Natasha Kassulke concluded, "We can assume it's all in good fun."

Obviously, Kassulke was wrong. In the *New York Daily News* (May 14, 2000), Spears herself tried to confront an overwhelming related focus on her body, in interviews and tabloid journalism, a focus all too common in the coverage of female musicians. With that media concentration, people also questioned her talent, insisting that any success depended on her appearance. With her good looks, they decided "that this [career] was just handed to me. That I didn't work for all this." On this topic, the media was relentless, with reporters asking her directly about her sexy look and even her breasts. In one televised interview, middle-aged Dutch host Ivo Niehe invited a then seventeen-year-old Spears to address the topic "everyone's talking about." Unaware of that topic, Spears gamely followed with a smile, asking, "What?" He creepily continued, "Well . . . your breasts." Spears kept that smile plastered to her face as she looked at the audience, confirming almost to herself Niehe's response: "my breasts." As rumors swirled about possible breast enlargement, Spears decided it was easier to choose to believe it was, indeed, "all in good fun," just a joke. "It was icky for me. But then I started saying it's a joke. That's totally how I look at it now. Whatever."[9]

After the birth of her children, the focus on Spears's body remained but in a different way. This time writers seemed to delight in her postpartum imperfections. The most notorious critique of this variety hit Spears after she performed at MTV's Video Music Awards in 2007 in a black bikini. The headline in the *New York Post*: "Lard and Clear." This attention—whether packaged as complimentary or not—could have been the basis of its own book. And much has already been written about the overwhelming pressure on women in music to conform to a standard look, including stories about Karen Carpenter and her related struggle with anorexia or Kelly Clarkson and the unrelenting media discussion of her weight, among many disturbing examples.

It's no wonder singer-songwriter Billie Eilish chooses to perform in baggy clothing, rather than displaying her body for public comment. In her song "Not My Responsibility," she asks, "Do my shoulders provoke you? Does my chest? Am I my stomach? My hips? The body I was born with, is it not what you wanted?" At the same time, she doesn't want the public to praise her decision to cover up and slut-shame those who don't. In a 2020 interview in *The Guardian*, she explained, "I don't like that there's this weird new world of supporting me by shaming people that [may not] want to [dress like me]." Either way, people are taking notice of her appearance, just as they always have in the coverage of women in music. "I feel you watching, always," she has said. And the relentless related commentary is a type of policing, whether it's celebration or criticism.

Men generally do not experience a similar policing. Men can take up space, any kind and amount of space. But women are only allowed certain kinds. As Sandra Bartky wrote in *Skin Deep*, "The properly feminine woman must never allow herself to spread into the available space." She must be contained and, of course, appropriately pleasing to the male gaze. Spears would be criticized for supposedly taking up too much space or the wrong type of space. But she was also subjected to creepy comments and disparaging scrutiny when she was judged superficially acceptable. As Eilish's example proves, apparently women in music have no way out of some sort of scrutiny and judgment around appearance—and it all can overshadow and even prevent real engagement with the work and true talent of these women.

In 2001, that malicious focus on Spears's body included what she did with it. At the MTV music awards, she danced with a yellow python. She was a snake charmer, a figure long seen as fascinating in Western culture.[10] Like that figure, she was sexy and exotic, but also sinister, directly aligned with Eve. And Timberlake was her Adam. Ostensibly waiting until marriage to have sex, Spears would soon field question after question about her activities with Timberlake: was she a virgin or not? Her 2001 song "I'm Not a Girl, Not Yet a Woman" was almost a public declaration. She was not quite the "femme fatale" of her 2011 Femme Fatale Tour, but she was on the cusp of maturity, and the world was watching.

The *Framing Britney* documentary ties this harassment to the times, including the Monica Lewinsky scandal in 1998. With the public discussion of then president Bill Clinton's affair with an intern, reporters were talking about sex in a way that they hadn't before. It was tawdry and direct, with ruthless blame heaped upon the women rather than the men, despite disparities in age and power, especially in Lewinsky's case.

Once the news was confirmed, Spears had had sex, the press was particularly shameless. Of course, the press was shameless in even reporting on the topic as news. But on December 20, 2001, *News of the World* blasted its headline: "Justin and I have great sex." She was not a charming Southern belle. She was supposedly "white trash," like that other famous Southern celebrity at the time, Anna Nicole Smith. The sexy Madonna was, to many, then officially a whore, or, in the words of the girls involved in the 1999 study, a combo of the words whore and slut, a "slore."[11]

All of these labels—white trash, slut, whore, even "Yoko"—worked to dehumanize Spears early, paving the way for her later treatment. But these labels also prepared the way for a specific label to come, "crazy." Given the historical link between a woman's sexuality and madness, this gendered focus on Spears's body and personal life played a role in making the term "crazy" stick, repercussions be damned. If Spears was slutty, or loose, she might be losing it. A "slore" would surely be crazy. The double standard is hard to ignore. Timberlake could brag about having sex with Spears, which he did. But Spears was condemned for her sexual activity. And that condemnation would feed into some of Spears's very worst moments of public abuse.

CENSOR-TAINMENT

In 2003, Madonna kissed Spears on stage at the MTV Video Music Awards—a passing of the torch that caught the attention of conservatives already concerned about sexuality in music and television. In a CNN interview after that kiss, conservative talking head Tucker Carlson awkwardly asked Spears about her experience with women—had she "ever kissed a woman before?" After Spears responded, "No," he continued, "What does your mom think?" The public was both titillated and repelled. Carlson, ever the hypocrite, was ostensibly criticizing Spears while playing the interview for its entertainment value. He no doubt knew that his viewers would enjoy the show, despite their moral platitudes. This was both censorship and spectacle, news as censor-tainment.

It's hard at this point not to hear the echo of Kassulke's conclusion: "We can assume it's all in good fun." And would the coming coverage still appear to be fun, the accelerated mania documenting and adding to Spears's real-life challenges: the end of her relationship with Timberlake, which he seemed to pin on her in his revenge song and video "Cry Me a River"? Reporters followed suit: "What did you do?" asked Diane Sawyer in an interview with Spears on November 23, 2003. Then there was her short marriage to friend Jason Alexander in 2004; her marriage to backup dancer Kevin Federline later that year; the birth of her two sons; and her bitter divorce from Federline in 2007.

Clearly, Spears was in turmoil—with life-changing events firing in rapid succession. She filed for divorce in November 2006, two months after the birth of her second child. Journalists Ronan Farrow and Jia Tolentino, writing for the *New Yorker*, tied the decision to Federline's partying in Las Vegas with his friends three weeks after that birth. When Spears texted him news of her divorce filing, Federline wrote on a bathroom wall at a night club, "Today I'm a free man—f**k a wife, give me my kids bitch!"

All of this happened alongside a growing public appetite for celebrity gossip, which tabloids responded to and supported. At the end of 2004, sales of magazines such as *Star, People, Us Weekly,* and *In Touch* were generally up 11.6 percent. Consumption would soon peak and start its decline in 2007. But celebrity blogs were there to capitalize, with gossip blogger Perez Hilton's traffic up 215 percent between July 2006 and July 2007.[12] Spears's every move was captured by this media market, and she was struggling. A picture of her walking in public barefoot earned her a nomination on "The American Trainwreck Awards," an *SNL* parody mocking women then in the news, including Courtney Love and Janet Jackson— or her breast—a reference to the 2004 Super Bowl wardrobe malfunction blamed on Jackson despite Timberlake's involvement. The label trainwreck signaled our then fascination—people couldn't stop gawking at the wreckage as female celebrities appeared "in some degree of high-gloss disarray," spiraling downward as we watched.[13]

In another *SNL* sketch from the period, Amy Poehler impersonated Spears with a heavy Southern accent, chewing gum, and holding a Big Gulp, all at a court hearing addressing her Federline divorce. This version of Britney, the "white trash" version, was apparently big fun.[14] Comedians capitalized. And Spears was quickly shamed for being shameless—for not trying, for not caring. It was another double standard. As William Cheng points out in "So You've Been Musically Shamed" (2014), society seems to believe that women should care in a way that men don't have to. Some men, such as Kid Rock, who have embraced the white-trash label, are even celebrated as outlaws. Kid Rock, to some, is wonderfully authentic, and he, as "white trash," is apparently a sort of treasure, whereas Spears was, well, just trash.

One of the only reasonable voices, especially in comedy, was talk-show host Craig Ferguson. In 2007, he reminded his audience that jokes have an "effect on real people." And "people are falling apart," including Anna Nicole Smith, who had died on February 8, 2007. "We shouldn't be attacking the vulnerable." And so, he said, he would no longer be telling any "Britney Spears jokes." The audience laughed, assuming the vow itself was some sort of joke. Or perhaps, at that point, the mere mention of Spears could elicit laughter. The audience, the public, was then so used to judging her from afar; they were so used to laughing at her as if she were less than human. On stage, Ferguson continued, insisting that Spears "clearly needs help." Again, the audience laughed. And the sound is chilling.

Spears herself seemed to give voice to her own frustrations in the song "Piece of Me," released on January 10, 2008, on her fifth studio album, *Blackout*. The song was cowritten and produced by Christian Karlsson and Pontus Winnberg, a Swedish team known by their professional handle Bloodshy & Avant. According to the blog *OhNoTheyDidn't*, Spears did not welcome songs about her personal life, but she made a big exception for this one. In the song, she asks, "You want a piece of me?" The answer is clearly "Yes," and she sings about herself from the paparazzi's perspective. She's not Britney; she's "Mrs. Lifestyles of the rich and famous," "Mrs. Extra! Extra!" She's "shameless." The tune is highly produced, with an electronic dance beat. It sounds playful and light, matching the song's video, which follows a group of girls, including Britney, wearing wigs and trying to evade the paparazzi. As the group descends a private staircase, the girls are smiling. But once outside, they have to run through the crowd to make their getaway. And one of the photographers is marked in the video with his own label: "paparazzo perv." It's a sanitized look at Spears's life that lightly hints at darker truths.

In the song, Spears acknowledges another reality: how the paparazzi pushed her, hoping to provoke her into making a newsworthy scene: "Who's flippin' me off / Hopin' I'll resort to startin' havoc." That menacing edge sounds in the repetition of the lyric, "You want a piece of me," which, after three background iterations, closes the chorus in a chromatic, almost jarringly off-balance descending line. The pitch play stands out against Spears's generally static melodic line, with rhythm and beat generating the song's real momentum.

In sentiment, "Piece of Me" echoes her earlier song "Lucky," released on her second album, *Oops! . . . I Did It Again* (2000). "Lucky," too, hints at the flip side of celebrity. But, in "Lucky," also written by a songwriting team, the tale is both much sweeter and more melodramatic, with Spears apparently isolated by fame. She's not in danger yet. She's alone, crying "in her lonely heart." And the music matches that mood, with the song in the style of a ballad, Spears showcasing her vocal range, from a kind of baby voice in a low register to a rounder tone on "why," the high note marking the question: "Then why do these tears come at night?"

In hindsight, some people have looked at these songs as cries for help. In 2019, in *Mashable*, Aisha Victoria Deeb published the article "Britney Spears' 'Lucky' Track Was the Cry for Help We All Ignored." And Courtney Love covered the song "Lucky" in a show of support for Spears in July 2021. In her version posted on Instagram, in which she accompanies herself on acoustic guitar, Love speeds up the tempo but pauses, still strumming, as she becomes visibly emotional. She eventually acknowledges that she herself is crying; the song had understandably struck a nerve, perhaps signaling a personal relationship to the song's subject matter. Love certainly had the experience to understand the song's depiction of fame.

In 2008, however, no one seemed to respond to these songs in these ways, at least not publicly, even though the signs that Spears needed help, as Ferguson recognized, were everywhere: images of her shaved head and images of her hitting a car with an umbrella, all related to her custody dispute with Federline. I have no way of knowing the specifics of Spears's condition then. Her mother, Lynn, in her book *Through the Storm*, cites the possibility of postpartum depression: "I believe Britney had postpartum depression, which, added to her brokenhearted spirit over the end of her marriage to Kevin and the enormous pressures of her career, brought her to the breaking point."

The picture of Spears with a shaved head, hitting that car, was taken on an especially difficult night in her dealings with her ex. In the *Framing Britney* documentary, paparazzo Daniel Ramos recalls following her back and forth as she attempted to see her kids and was refused by Federline. Eventually she parked at a Jiffy Lube, where Ramos approached her, hoping to ask a few questions. She then got out of her car and hit his. I remember seeing pictures of this incident in 2007. I remember the rage in Spears's eyes. But I don't remember the context—that this was the car of one of the many people relentlessly pursuing and harassing her, or that this incident immediately followed her desperate attempts to see her young sons, all of which failed. She clearly had reasons for her rage. Spears was in crisis, and the world around her was a source of ongoing trauma. As her mother wrote, noting her own experience dealing with the paparazzi, "When Britney beat that paparazzo's car with her umbrella, she was acting out my fantasy."

For Ramos, the context didn't matter either. It was a good night, he admits in the documentary; "it was a money shot." Blogger Perez Hilton said something similar then, thanking Spears for "being bad" because it's "good for my business." And he certainly capitalized, selling a T-shirt morbidly displaying a picture of actor Heath Ledger, who had overdosed and been found dead on January 22, 2008. He accompanied the picture with the words "Why couldn't it be Britney?" After years of treating Spears as an object and commodity, it's no surprise that the media or public at large had little sympathy for her. Instead, she was supposedly "crazy," an easy dismissal. It wasn't the world around her—apparently it was her. And, to people such as Hilton, her wrong was so great that her death would have been no loss. Worse still, Hilton may have been waiting for it, wanting it, much as witnesses wished for the deaths of Ono and Love—and much as witnesses sneered at troubled stars who would die tragically, such as Houston and singer Amy Winehouse. The world consumed their troubles until their troubles consumed them. For some, the fallen woman should fall. And rather than helping her up, she should keep falling, all the way down, while everyone else watches and laughs.

Spears had no recourse, especially when she lost custody of her children in October 2007, leading to a dramatic standoff on January 3, 2008, at her home. Spears was unwilling to part with her young sons, then both under three. Fighting back, appearing angry, only made her critics more convinced that she was indeed "crazy," hysterical. The tabloids ran with that "crazy" narrative, with cover stories such as "Inside Britney's Breakdown"; "Britney's Meltdown"; or "Mommy's Crying." After the standoff, with throngs of reporters on foot and overhead, circling in helicopters, Spears was rushed to the hospital for an involuntary psychiatric examination. According to *Us Weekly*, she went "completely psycho": "They had to strap her down like a mental patient and she was going between laughing and hysterics." In the words of an unnamed source, it was "a total psychotic breakdown. She just went crazy."

But it wasn't just the gossip sites. People close to Spears called her "crazy," too. Justin Timberlake had called her crazy much earlier, in 2004. Addressing the duo's breakup in front of a huge crowd at a show in Scotland at the Glasgow Barrowland, he said, "Have you ever had a girlfriend go completely crazy on you? She's crazy and I mean really crazy . . . out of this world crazy."[15] In 2008, apparently her record label thought she was crazy, too. Spears's former music video director, Joseph Kahn, made the issue public in 2019, explaining on Twitter that the record label had then refused to make the necessary funds available for Spears's music video, "Womanizer": "They gave me only two days to shoot Womanizer. When I asked for more budget the label said 'why would we give more money to a crazy person.'"[16]

Her family, however, to many in the #FreeBritney movement, was the worst offender. They used the "crazy" tag in an unusual move, the creation of a conservatorship normally reserved for the elderly, those unable to manage their own affairs in advanced age, or those otherwise incapacitated. This legal arrangement was established a month after that highly publicized standoff at her house and ordered by her father, Jamie Spears, on February 1, 2008. Jamie had been an absent figure in Britney's life, sometimes battling his own demons, including alcoholism. Lynn wrote in her book about his addiction as well as his verbal abuse. She also recalled a conversation in 2000 with Britney: "'Mama,' she said, 'do you want to live like this for the rest of your life?'" When her mother and father divorced in 2002, Spears was pleased. It was, she explained in *People*, "the best thing that's ever happened to my family."

But, with his reappearance, in the court documents readily available online, the court determined that "Spears does not have the capacity to retain counsel." This feature of the conservatorship, hardly unique in the conservator system, is a particular sticking point for those who urge legal reform. Even murderers have the right to choose their own counsel. But, on Spears's side, there was no official and trusted counsel or person she herself could appoint to plead her case as she was put in a legal prison. She was not even consulted as the paperwork was filed—the box checked to rationalize this treatment: "dementia."

The decision to make this move was supposedly about protecting Spears, given her erratic behavior, but there were also fears about certain influences in her life, including would-be manager Sam Lutfi and paparazzo-turned-boyfriend Adnan Ghalib. It was, in some ways, a power struggle for control over Spears, who wasn't close with her family at the time. Lynn explained the thinking, from her perspective, in her book, painting Lufti as a "predator": "Something drastic would have to happen for Sam to lose control and for Jamie to gain control of his daughter, who was, after all, an adult woman." The wording is striking—"an adult woman." Lynn emphasizes that point while ignoring the contradictions of her position. Lufti apparently shouldn't have control of this adult woman, but, according to Lynn, her father could and should. And with his court petition, he soon would.

As the supposedly temporary guardianship became permanent, Spears could not "make key decisions, personal or financial, without the approval of her conservators: her father, Jamie Spears, and a lawyer, Andrew M. Wallet" (as publicized by the *New York Times*, the *New Yorker*, and other outlets). The move effectively stripped Spears of the ability to make her own personal and professional choices. Her every purchase was recorded and, against her will, she herself was paying her father and Wallet, two men, to treat her in this way.

A documentary called *Controlling Britney*, the follow-up to *Framing Britney*, revealed that the conservatorship paid Jamie $16,000 a month. And he collected a percentage of her many professional deals. The documentary contends, in a convincing argument, that her right to see her children was used as leverage to force her compliance. A source from the security team, ostensibly used to protect her, alleges that all of her communications were secretly monitored. She was effectively silenced, and she remained so for more than a decade, subject to this conservatorship from 2008 through early November 2021. When Jamie Spears fought against his daughter for continuation of the conservatorship in 2021, he continued to reference mental health, claiming Spears was "mentally sick."

MAD SCENE

Spears's career did, however, continue, as she performed under the conservatorship. In fact, she pumped out new albums and toured immediately following the creation of the conservatorship and in the years to come, even establishing a lucrative residency in Las Vegas. She was apparently well enough, all along, to enrich those supposedly monitoring her "crazy." On the stage, she was allowed to express herself, while the team in charge handled her social media and choreographed the few interviews she was allowed to give. I can't get this blatant hypocrisy out of my mind as I look at photographs of her Circus tour, "The Circus Starring Britney Spears," which supported the release of her sixth album in 2009. That tour took place while Spears was supposedly not well enough to retain a lawyer or

Britney Spears on Good Morning America *(ABC), 2008.* ABC/Photofest

make any professional or personal choices, from March 3 through November 29, 2009, raking in millions of dollars for the conservatorship.

In it, she sang her song "Circus," from the new album: "There's only two types of people in the world: / The ones that entertain, and the ones that observe." The opening lines are deep and rough, related to a signature sound some categorize as vocal fry, a damaged and damaging sound.[17] With "all eyes on me in the center of the ring," it's clear what type of person Spears is. Next on the program, Spears sang "Piece of Me" from inside a cage. The image of her trapped behind bars as she recites her experience of celebrity is damning. With her fame and the conservatorship, she is caged twice over.

In a hearing on June 23, 2021, regarding her conservatorship, Spears told the judge, Brenda Penny, by phone, "My family is trying to make me feel like I'm crazy which I'm not." They had their reasons—they all had their own reasons—and those reasons had very little to do with Spears or what she needed. First, it was the paparazzi, pushing her, hoping to make her act crazy so they could get a story or a money shot. As she sang in "Piece of Me," they wanted her to start havoc. And flipping her off wasn't their only means of provocation. Paparazzi often worked in "triangle" formation, hoping to box her in, trap her. She would have no choice but to act out in order to get out. And then there was her family, her father controlling her life and her money, paying himself as he did so. He and his team enriched themselves by calling her crazy, setting up her performance on their terms. She was displayed, just as the insane used to be, both in real life and on the operatic stage. On the Circus tour, Spears was star and madwoman. A woman's undoing was and continues to be entertainment. A history of condemning and displaying women as crazy supported the labeling of Spears while her story became the modern version of both.

"YOU HAVE TO BE A GOOD GIRL"

Troubled male stars have not been subject to the same scrutiny and legal machinations. Everything about Spears's treatment, now, appears biased, gendered, and abusive. At a New Year's Eve show in 2008, at Madison Square Garden, comedian Chris Rock joked, "Britney Spears, boy. Even OJ [Simpson] kept his kids, and he even killed their mother." The crack, to me, works because it underscores the sympathy extended to men and only men. It underscores something that is ridiculous, awful, and absolutely true. Women must meet certain cultural expectations and, if they don't, the fallout outpaces anything a man might experience for doing the very same thing or things much worse.

Not only that, but insanity itself is treated in gendered ways in the arts. If Timberlake, the man, had been labeled crazy, the public may have praised him for it, the label another badge of honor for him. As Stephen Harper points out in *Madness, Power, and the Media*, mental instability is considered a part of creative genius for men—a sign of authenticity and greatness—whereas, for women, it's clearly not. Women, in contrast, are mocked and dismissed, though often sexualized at the same time.

Irish singer Sinéad O'Connor comes to mind in this context. With her own bald head, she did not follow the set pop script. When she boycotted the Grammy Awards in 1991, she was already being called "crazy." Many stars since have taken a similar stand, refusing to attend or perform at the Grammys in order to protest gendered or racial biases. But she was one of the first, writing a letter to the Recording Academy explaining that she didn't want to participate in the festivities because the awards "acknowledge mostly the commercial side of art." Then in October 1992, she tore up a picture of Pope John Paul II. During a performance on *Saturday Night Live*, she sang an a cappella version of Bob Marley's song "War," held up the photo, and then ripped it, yelling, "Fight the real enemy!" The controversial move was meant as protest, raising awareness about child sexual abuse in the Catholic Church. It also had a personal dimension.

Later aware of priests' abuse of children in Ireland, as a child she herself experienced horrific abuse at the hands of her mother. The picture she tore up on that stage was a photo that had hung on her mother's bedroom wall. In her memoir *Rememberings*, she wrote, "My intention had always been to destroy my mother's photo of the pope. It represented lies and liars and abuse. The type of people who kept these things were devils like my mother." The issue of the Catholic Church's predation is now public knowledge, especially since the release of the movie *Spotlight* (2015), which follows a group of mostly men as they track down evidence of the abuse—a movie widely praised and thoroughly celebrated. But, in 1992, when O'Connor, a woman, tackled the issue, it was in her own words "open season on treating me like a crazy bitch." In an interview with the *New York*

Times published May 18, 2021, she seemed to recognize that her treatment was partly gendered: "The media was making me out to be crazy because I wasn't acting like a pop star was supposed to act. It seems to me that being a pop star is almost like being in a type of prison. You have to be a good girl."

That prison was never for her. Even O'Connor's bald head was an act of defiance. When a music executive told her she should have longer hair in order to fulfill expectations of the pop princess, she decided it was time to act. That's when she shaved her hair off completely. And she has certainly made the connection between her experience and that of Spears. "Why were they saying she's crazy for shaving her head?" O'Connor asked, in the same 2021 interview. "I'm not." She added, "What they did to Britney Spears was disgusting."

Her own treatment was rather disgusting, too. Even before the *SNL* performance, people in the United States had been destroying piles of her CDs. They were upset by reports in 1990 that O'Connor hadn't wanted "The Star-Spangled Banner" performed before one of her appearances. In point of fact, O'Connor had been asked casually about adding the national anthem but had declined the offer. Her decision was not an anti-American rebellion, as the media would depict it. As she explained in her memoir, she just associated anthems with "squareness unless they're being played by Jimi Hendrix."

After the *SNL* performance, however, the harassment was far worse. She was banned from NBC, booed at a performance celebrating her hero, Bob Dylan, and her career never recovered. She was silenced on the world's stage while Spears was effectively silenced off of it. And the general consensus never considered an explanation or exoneration in genius, a positive spin reserved for men alone. Women can be stripped of everything whereas men, no matter their condition, remain in charge of their own artistic efforts, at times celebrated for signs of instability. Apparently, even with a history of addiction, men, like Spears's father, can remain in charge of a woman's artistic efforts, too.

FREEING BRITNEY

The label "crazy" allowed Spears's father and his team to control her. Like men before him, he used the term against a woman for his own benefit, without any of the positive connotations associated with the musical "genius" of men. The conservatorship was a modern way of committing a woman against her will and then displaying her as spectacle for the purposes of the men around her. There was also an education, or miseducation, in Spears's treatment. The gleeful reporting of her distress would surely broadcast certain messages to the public at large, especially to those similarly suffering. They, too, had to feel the negative portrayal—the dismissal and rebuke. And that reporting publicized a certain image of femininity—fragile, childlike, and about to break. That image fit the popular movie depiction of women as insane, beautiful but crazy—the "manic pixie dream girl," in Nathan Rabin's classic terminology. It's a femininity in need. Viewers see women not as strong but hysterical. And perhaps viewers understand women as such in real life as well.

Obviously, the ties between hysteria and women, in thought and medical practice, should not let anyone off the hook for what happened to Spears. So many people could have helped her but didn't. Ferguson saw the situation clearly. In 2009, so did Yoko Ono. In an interview, she said of Spears, "I think she's a survivor." In a way that other people perhaps couldn't, Ono recognized that "the world was not fair to her, and they're just using her and not dignifying her."

Less high-profile figures also sounded the alarm early. And with changes in online media and new digital platforms, their voices began to matter. Thanks to them, a new word started to become action—not crazy, but free. In fact, Spears might still be under the control of her father if it weren't for these fans and these changes in digital media, including the rise of Twitter and Instagram, which gave her fans a platform. Fans themselves have been called crazy—screaming and out of control. But that perception is misleading. Fans can be creative and productive. Fans can also be activists, as they were in the #FreeBritney movement.

An early voice among these fans was Chris Crocker. In 2007, Crocker became a punchline after they uploaded a video tearfully urging the world to "leave Britney alone": "Do we really want to see a 25-year-old woman to leave behind two children and die?" Early Spears activist Leanne Simmons, who runs the site freebritney.army, found herself mocked as well. But, as a fan of Spears, she felt ready for the dismissal. In 2021 she told NPR, "It was kind of a smooth transition from defending why I'm a Britney fan," dealing with the music snobs, "to defending her human rights."

In November 2017, Tess Barker and Barbara Gray became the central focus of the #FreeBritney movement after they began their podcast "Britney's Gram." The two women, both comedians, set out to unpack Spears's Instagram posts, which were delightfully "basic," Gray told *Rolling Stone*.[18] We know now that these posts were monitored by Spears's team, a company called CrowdSurf, which approved and uploaded her posts as long as they didn't mention the conservatorship. Barker and Gray initially found the posts charming but at times mysterious and even alarming.

In 2019, Spears stopped posting altogether, and the two took their speculation further: Was something else going on here? Was Spears OK? Spears would reappear with a cryptic post about needing "me time." But the post lacked Spears's typical use of multiple emojis. Gray and Barker doubted that Spears herself posted the message. Hours later, a report announced that Spears was in a mental health facility. Then, the next day, Gray and Barker received an anonymous phone call, which they replayed on the podcast's April 16, 2019, episode: "You guys are on to something."

The *Controlling Britney* documentary reveals that, at the time, Spears was not happy during rehearsals for her upcoming *Domination* performances, another Las Vegas run. And, as punishment for her pushback, she had been forced into the mental health facility. Initially #FreeBritney, for Barker and Gray, was a response to that forced stay. But it soon became a rallying cry against the conservatorship itself, as it had been for Jordan Miller, who started posting about the conservatorship on the fan site BreatheHeavy in early 2009. He would sign his posts "Free Britney." Miller, in an interview with Ronan Farrow and Jia Tolentino, recalls the backlash he received then, when other people doubted that Spears's family was abusing her. But Miller continued his campaign, galvanized in part by Jamie Spears, who, in a phone call, threatened to destroy him. After Gray and Barker's bombshell episode in 2019, the doubts were gone. The protests began, and even celebrities publicly addressed the #FreeBritney campaign, including Miley Cyrus, Olivia Rodrigo, and Paris Hilton.

In November 2020, Spears herself actively joined the movement, announcing through her lawyer that she would not perform as long as the conservatorship, with her father in charge, was still in place. She would no longer be on display, making money for those who sought to control her. The world was starting to see the truth—the full positioning of Spears as crazy and the exploitation of that narrative by those around her. Spears's call, during the court hearing on June 23, 2021, however, was the biggest reveal to date. It was a twenty-four-minute statement in which Spears outlined the abuse she had experienced, including the sick control over her that her father seemed to enjoy: "he loved the control to hurt his own daughter 100,000%. He loved it." And that control extended to everything she did—a grueling performance schedule, her love life, friendships, and, yes, her ability to have more children.

In that statement, Spears explained the repercussions for her: "I can't sleep. I'm so angry it's insane." She also made known her general distrust of the legal system as well as the public at large. After years as a joke, she was concerned that revealing her truth would prompt another round of mean-spirited digs: "I thought people would make fun of me or laugh at me and say, 'She's lying, she's got everything, she's Britney Spears.'" Spears was clearly empowered that day, finally able to detail all that she had experienced to a judge who was listening. And after thirteen years without being heard, she was worried about hanging up the phone, letting go of that connection. Toward the end of her statement, she told the judge, "I wish I could stay with you on the phone forever, because when I get off the phone with you, all of a sudden all I hear [are] all these no's—no, no, no."

After that call, however, it wasn't just "no." She started to hear a different answer—first the removal of her father from the conservatorship and then the end of the conservatorship as a whole. On November 17, 2021, with the conservatorship's end, she posted a message, speaking to her fans directly: "I honestly think you guys saved my life in a way 100 percent." And she also expressed hope that her story might help others suffering under conservatorships, those more vulnerable: "So, hopefully my story will make an impact and make some changes to the corrupt system." Fans, commenting on her post, were gleeful. On Twitter, skylar wrote, "This is beautiful. You're a warrior. Love hearing you speak about concern for others." Emily wrote, "We are here for you and so happy you can be human again."

There has already been more to come for Spears. We are learning new details of her life under the conservatorship and will no doubt continue to do so. Perhaps the legal framework that allows such abuse will experience real change. It should. There also may be more trouble for Spears. The media seems thoroughly chastened in this moment, blaming themselves, rightly, for the trauma Spears experienced. There are also those, like Kevin Fallon, writing for the *Daily Beast*, who have started to blame Timberlake, who seemingly benefited from his breakup with Spears, whereas she was condemned for it. He was able to rise, perhaps at her expense, much as he would in 2004 after the Super Bowl incident with Janet Jackson. But, if Spears makes a mistake post-conservatorship, people in the media could still be eager to pounce again. January 7, 2022, already brought a slew of negative responses to Spears's posting of nude selfies on Instagram, sparking defensive headlines such as "Britney Spears Isn't 'Crazy' for Posting Nudes on Instagram" (*Grazia*). On pause then, the scrutiny is certainly not finished *for good*.

For now, however, the labeling of Spears—the undoing of Spears— should be seen as a modern version of past treatments of women as crazy. Spears was called crazy and, in turn, driven crazy in many ways by the people around her. She was then forced under their control and displayed as spectacle. She could not communicate, openly explaining her situation, but she could perform. She was silenced, but she could still sing as entertainment. She lived in an operatic "mad scene," with the words used against her turned into action. And it took changes in social media and fan activism to end that particular performance at last.

The labels leveled at women clearly have enormous weight. Sometimes the message is subtle. In this case, it was not. And it had real-life consequences for Spears and for other women as well. Spears was the joke that other women, me included, did not want to become. She was the madwoman on display as entertainment—much as women are in the movies. But her display was also education and threat. In a popular internet meme, Spears appears bald and enraged, with the heading: "If Britney survived 2007, you can handle today." Is the message encouragement? Look on the bright side; it could be worse. People could take solace that their lot in life was not quite so bad. They could find comfort in the message, reassuring themselves that celebrities have their own troubles. But would the message have other effects? Was the meme a veiled warning? Keep it together; don't go to pieces. In some ways, both are messages of control: your life is not bad, so be content. Do not lose it. Do not strive for more. Do not demand more of yourself or those around you. The treatment of Spears was meant to control her. But it may have worked to control other women, too.

For some women, that message no doubt combined and reformulated based on other factors, such as race, gender identity, and sexual orientation. In the next chapter, we'll see how race impacted singer FKA twigs's particular experience dealing with media control and toxic labeling. Rather than a relationship with a musician, the foundation for that media blood-letting was her romance with the movie *Twilight*'s vampire prince, Robert Pattinson. And, to be sure, there would be blood.

5

FKA TWIGS AND THE TWI-TROLLS

Although FKA twigs belongs to the same story of misogyny in music as Love and Spears, she, like Ono, dealt with an interconnected racism. In twigs's case, this abuse was a complicated and aggressive experience of "misogynoir," a term that author Moya Bailey coined. In her book *Misogynoir Transformed: Black Women's Digital Resistance*, Bailey describes misogynoir as the "particular venom directed at Black women through negative representations in media." FKA twigs's encounters with misogynoir included comparisons to monkeys as well as references to her sexuality, which were built into the label "gold digger." The specific fandom around her onetime boyfriend, Robert Pattinson, conditioned the abuse. Though he wasn't in a band or a singer himself, like the other partners previously discussed, the fan frenzy around Pattinson was comparable to the hype around beloved boy bands. And his character and actions in the *Twilight* movie franchise only supported that fan investment, arguably in dangerous ways.

Twitter proved to be the platform of choice for this abuse. Although Twitter was part of Spears's solution, Twitter enabled the direct attack on twigs. Here, the immediacy of Twitter was truly a two-way street—a direct line for celebrities but also a means of harassing those same stars. And all were welcome to bully online, with very little oversight or regulation. In twigs's case, that activity on Twitter became part of her media coverage—in a vicious loop amplifying her initial toxic labeling.

RACIST LABELS

We have seen the gold-digger charge before with Love. Although it is often the blonde bombshell portrayed in this way, the label includes a racist imagining of the gold digger. As Sesali Bowen writes in the 2018 article "The Myth of the Gold Digger Endures," "We have a culture that does not trust Black women, especially those with money." That cultural truth appears in writing but also music, such as Kanye West's famous 2005 song "Gold Digger": "She take my money when I'm in need / Yeah, she's a triflin' friend indeed." The song's fierce popularity—ten weeks at the number one spot on the Billboard Hot 100—earned West entry into VH1's list of the greatest hip-hop songs ever created. Though Brian Donovan, in the book *American Gold Digger*, reveals the label's place in Black culture earlier, West's song in new ways ensured and propelled its varied place in contemporary popular thought. The gold digger was no longer just blonde. As Donovan writes, "While West's track 'Gold Digger' did not introduce the expression into African American vernacular, it certainly helped to solidify it."

This particular gold digger overlapped other notions of the Black woman in misogynoir, specifically the idea that Black women are hypersexual, regardless of age. In *Jezebel Unhinged*, author Tamura Lomax traces a rampant racist focus on assumed "black female sexual savagery and immorality."[1] Along these lines, the gold digger is supposed to be absolutely irresistible, deliciously sexed up, whether or not she wants to be. As West raps in "Gold Digger" after listing all his girlfriend's wrongs, "I don't care what none of y'all say, I still love her." Despite the warnings, he is powerless against her, unable to resist her superficial charm, though he's apparently powerful, too, at least in some respects. After all, he can still insult her publicly in song.

In the label, Black women are objectified. And a comparison is built in. She is less than an acceptable woman. As Donovan writes, "As a symbol, the gold digger operates through contrast." She's inferior. And she may even be less than human, like an animal—another thread in racist depictions and perceptions of Black women.[2] Overt analogy involving specific animals, such as the "monkey" charge in twigs's case, overlaps this history as well as a general racist strategy of casting groups of people as not quite human. Both Jewish people and Chinese people, for example, have been compared to rats and further connected to a rat's threat of disease. Even Ono was described by Albert Goldman, author of the Lennon biography *The Lives of John Lennon*, as "simian-looking." And popular Hollywood films have helped keep this history alive in the present, including movie versions of the story of King Kong. In this racist and sexist story, white women are under threat as a huge dark-brown ape invades respectable society.[3]

For nonwhite women, the hate is a tangled web in an ever-deepening pit. They are treated as hybrid subhuman and sub-men, entities with their own unique and hateful attributes.[4] The "monkey" insult has been unleashed in this way against Michelle Obama (she was called an "ape in heels" by a mayor in West Virginia and "monkey face" by a Colorado doctor, among other examples) and Meghan Markle, who was treated to her own Ono comparisons after she married Prince Harry.[5] BBC host Danny Baker was, in fact, fired after he posted a picture of Markle's baby depicted as a monkey.

The online attacks on twigs built on this history. But she saw the underlying issue clearly, calling out the racism involved in response. At the same time, she would internalize some of the hurtful messaging. After all, she was still processing prejudice she had experienced as a child. That early trauma was "a wound," she would later say—and she found it very much unhealed when the Twi-trolls attacked, ostensibly protecting Pattinson at her expense.

FOREVER KNOWN AS

FKA twigs, born Tahliah Barnett, recalled that childhood pain in an interview with Louis Theroux. On his BBC podcast *Grounded* in 2021, she explained that "nobody looked like me" (her mother is of English and Spanish descent; her father, who was not part of her early home life, is Jamaican). As an only child, she lived with her single mother in suburban Gloucestershire, rural and far less multicultural than other parts of England. Her mother struggled financially, but thanks to an academic scholarship, twigs attended a private Catholic school, St. Edward's, in Cheltenham.

In a 2014 interview with *Dazed*, she revealed that other kids at school "said horrible things about something I had no control of, which was tough." In another interview, with Ed Power of the *Irish Independent* (October 1, 2014), she tried to explain how it felt, sticking out in terms of appearance and race: "You're going to be self-conscious—your hair is a little 'wayward,' you have big eyes, big lips . . . everyone is staring at you. You're like a little creature everyone's gawping at. I remember in primary school someone not wanting to hold my hand in case the colour came off."

When she was seventeen, she and her mother moved to London so twigs could study dance at the BRIT School, a school that the British government funded; notable past attendees included Adele and Amy Winehouse. But she soon realized that she also wanted to study music. Rejected from the school's music program, she transferred to close-by Croydon College, where she studied fine art, literature, and philosophy. But she continued to pursue music as well as dance, performing as a backup dancer in the music videos of other musicians, including Jessie J. She also sang her own music at clubs and cabarets. She found support in the more experienced female performers around her, especially a group of Black women who hosted club parties internationally. They would send her to gigs, as needed, including one in New York, where she met visual artist Matthew Stone. In 2012, one of his shots would present her to the world on the cover of *i-D* magazine. Her first music release—mixtape, EP1—followed four months later.

Stone and twigs would work together later on her own projects, including the album artwork for her 2019 album *Magdalene*. The cover picture is a painterly rendering of twigs, biblical and all-knowing, with a medusa-like strand of hair curling down her neck. In a 2014 *Guardian* interview, Stone praised her talent and "star quality"—something he recognized when he first met her in 2012: "She has a strong idea of her own success that doesn't seem to revolve around compromising on her creativity. What's amazing is that she has found that magic recipe for being able to use her experimental work as a calling card that people connect to as something that is meaningful and progressive and pretty out there."

Writing her own music and directing her own videos, in 2014 she would be ready for her first U.S. tour. She had also released her mixtape follow-up, EP2, with her label Young (formerly Young Turks) the year before. It was then that she adopted the stage name FKA twigs. She had had the nickname "twigs" since she was a teenager—inspired by how her joints made noise, a popping sound, in dance class. And she wanted a stage name, rather than her given name, to front her musical work—a decision with certain benefits. After all, a stage name—one chosen by the musician—can be a way to control the narrative, to self-label before outside labeling. And that move brings potential protection. As Kevin EG Perry points out in "The Psychology of Stage Names—Why Musicians Create Personas for Themselves," when Bob Dylan chose his name, he managed to hide his Jewish background. A revelatory freedom and creativity also can come with a new name. As Lana Del Rey, real name Lizzy Grant, told Perry, "I just wanted a name for the music, that I could start shaping the music towards." The musician H.E.R. adopted her name and assumed a general air of mystery for similar reasons. But she saw it as a way to keep the focus on her music as well rather than who she was as a person. In 2016, she told NPR, "I really just wanted it to be about the music, and get away from, 'Who is she with?' and 'What is she wearing?'" For women, the stage name can, then, be a shield from the media scrutiny and toxic labeling we've seen over and over again—at least, in theory.

A pair of musical sisters, called the Twigs, forced twigs to rethink her stage name, and she eventually added "FKA." The specific letters are often explained in twigs's media coverage as an acronym for "formerly known as." But Emily Lordi, in a 2020 *New York Times* profile, also refers to FKA as "forever known as," suggesting that the confusion in meaning is somewhat beside the point. She chose the letters based on their sound above all. Actually, twigs had initially thought of the letters AFK, she told *Dazed*, until someone pointed out that "that stands for 'Away from Keyboard.'"

The rearrangement, in Lordi's telling, "amped up the name's androgyny and subverted" norms of celebrity culture, including a "one name," which female singers often adopt—a name that might loom larger than their work. In her interview with Lordi, twigs explained, "FKA Twigs felt like something to explore, rather than a female artist to become obsessed with." Clearly, twigs was keenly aware of the power of labels—including the potential effect of her own stage name on the ways people perceived her and her music. She chose a name true to her history but one meant to invite in listeners as an experience and potential challenge.

FKA twigs on The Tonight Show Starring Jimmy Fallon *(NBC),
February 24, 2016.* ABC/Photofest

LOVE BITES

In that same year, the artist now known as FKA twigs would see her new name plastered everywhere when she began dating "hunky actor" Robert Pattinson. London's *Daily Star* blasted its headline on September 4, 2014: "Sorry Twihards! Robert Pattinson Dating British Singer FKA Twigs." From the very start, the article made clear the direction of the relationship's coverage: readers would not like this news, and the media would support and respond to that expectation. *Sorry.* Clearly, trouble was ahead.

Immediately, writers introduced comparisons between twigs and Pattinson's former girlfriend, Kristen Stewart, who played his love interest, Bella Swan, in the *Twilight* movies. Pattinson and Stewart as an actual couple were a beloved real-life version of the romance in the films. Citing an anonymous source, the *Daily Star* article explained that twigs "is hoping that she avoids any drama with Rob's ex Kristen Stewart." In another headline, in London's *The Sun* (August 30, 2014), the related comparison was the whole story, and twigs was deemed completely different from Pattinson's popular ex: "R-Patz Secret Lover Twigged: Rising Star Is Opposite of K-Stew." This manufactured love triangle would continue to be a part of the media narrative during the entirety of twigs and Pattinson's relationship, quickly growing to include Stewart's supposed upset and Pattinson's continued devotion to Stewart. As Malene Arpe observed in the *Toronto Star* (September 14, 2014), "Kristen Stewart is 'bitter' that Robert Pattinson is dating English musician FKA Twigs." A month later, the headline in the *Brampton Guardian* announced: "Robert Pattinson Still 'Broken Up' Over Kristen Stewart."

Right away, twigs attempted to downplay the interest in her love life and keep the focus on her music. Asked about Pattinson, in an interview published on September 11, 2014, on mirror.co.uk, she said, "I think that I like to keep my personal life personal, but I'm really excited to be here today and to be talking about my music and my album." She seemed to know then that the focus on her romantic pursuits was also biased—coverage women confront in ways men generally do not. In the 2021 podcast interview with Theroux, she explained that she did not want to be defined by the relationship "because he doesn't have to be defined by it." But the fascination with twigs in light of Pattinson had already sparked into a fire. And nothing could assuage the fans invested in Pattinson and Stewart, fans who were irrationally incensed by Pattinson's relationship with twigs. Some of these fans expressed their upset in explicit manifestations of misogynoir, including the insult "monkey." And journalists covered these attacks, especially on Twitter, with anonymous trolls blown up as featured players in stories published about twigs worldwide.

The role of Twitter in twigs's story has some basis in what cofounders Noah Glass and Jack Dorsey envisioned for the platform. In 2006, they thought of Twitter as a music-specific tool. Friends could update friends about their activities and whereabouts. Twitter even had its unveiling at South by Southwest, the Texas music festival, in March 2007. Glass said, "This is why we built this thing! For concert and music shows!"[6]

Today, Twitter is deeply entwined with music, and many of the most popular Twitter accounts are those of big-name music celebrities. Their posts and responses to them have also become a primary starting point for journalists' coverage of music news. As Eric Harvey writes in "How Twitter Changed Music" (2019), "It doesn't even matter if you're not on Twitter; along with Instagram, it's now the origin point for most music stories that don't start with a press release." The popularity and attraction to social media make some sense. Twitter fosters the intimacy and immediacy many musicians seek to create in their music—dispensing with any go-betweens who might dilute their message or even prevent it in reporting. Tweets can also be raw rants or random stray thoughts—all a source of connection. But Twitter can amplify big problems, too, offering a safe haven for hateful trolls. And small problems can become bigger ones quickly while big attacks can snowball into an avalanche, with stars of all types occasionally shutting down their accounts to avoid the coming destruction. That avalanche, in twigs's case, fed the news cycle and continues to feature in stories about her, for better and definitely for worse.

Along the way, for twigs and many stars today, the music itself has become almost a secondary or coincidental consideration in their coverage and fame—despite their best efforts.[7] Their social media is the focus, with the music a means of promoting that primary interest. It's a strange reversal, to be sure, with their creative work an afterthought. And when torment takes over on social media, the music may not even be that—a vague idea overshadowed by online drama, all with real-world fallout.

TROLLING TWIGS

In September 2014, the ugliness confronting twigs took hold on Twitter—
with references to Stewart as a "queen" and twigs as a "monkey." These
trolls also put together side-by-side pictures, one of twigs and another of
a monkey in a similar pose. The onslaught was so intense that, for a time,
twigs began to think she might actually look like a monkey. On the Theroux
podcast, she admitted, "I remember it had this massive, dysmorphic effect
on me for about six months to a year, where every time I saw my pictures
and photographs I would think, 'Gosh, I look like a monkey, and people
are going to say I look like a monkey. So I need to really try and hide this
monkey-ness that I have, because otherwise, people are gonna come for me
about it.'" She added, "Obviously, I know now that's completely ridiculous.
But it is essentially bullying, and it does affect you psychologically."

Despite her struggles, on September 28, 2014, twigs did issue a response,
calling out the racist abuse, from similar "monkey" put-downs to use of the
N-word: "I am genuinely shocked and disgusted at the amount of racism
that has been infecting my account the past week." Ten minutes later, she
added, "Racism is unacceptable in the real world and it's unacceptable
online."

Many of the comments below these two tweets are now marked "unavail-
able" or have been removed entirely. But even the tamer responses reveal
the general bent of the hate directed at twigs. One account, "pattzstew"—
the name an obvious nod to the coupling of Pattinson and Stewart—wrote,
"You're so ugly, ridiculous, this is not racism." It was short, poorly argued,
and par for the course. Another, @Miliwait1D, wrote, "Also it's unacceptable that you are dating Rob!" To these bullies, twigs was in the wrong
simply because she was with Pattinson.

Stewart, in contrast, was the "right woman for Robert," as yet another
user wrote. And she was "right" to these trolls in part because she's white,
so white in fact that she had played Snow White in the 2012 movie *Snow
White and the Huntsmen*. Twitter trolls readily seized on this latter detail,
calling Stewart "beautiful snow white," the obvious choice. Pattinson, also
white, and Stewart were then part of the typical all-white fairy tale—prince
and princess. They supposedly fit. And it didn't matter that Stewart is
American whereas Pattinson and twigs are both English. The most important criterion of commonality was based on a racist standard, one alive and

well, even as recently as March 2022, when Indiana Senator Mike Brown suggested that the Supreme Court should not have legalized interracial marriage.

Not all the trolls made the issue obvious, but racial slurs, including the insult "monkey," as well as the basic put-down "ugly," signaled the perceived mismatch. And it wasn't just anonymous trolls who unleashed animalistic analogies as racist attack. Supposedly respectable journalists did, too, though the abuse was disguised to some extent. In an article about twigs in the *Sydney Morning Herald* (February 6, 2015), journalist Rachel Olding described twigs as a "beautiful, lithe creature"—"utterly unusual and painfully cool." The description is almost positive, but twigs is still reduced to the subhuman level of a "creature." Other writers stuck with standard adjectives that nonetheless made clear twigs's perceived difference from a supposed prevailing norm—she's called "edgy," "quirky," or "exotic." Some writers referenced her artistic decisions and output to amplify this portrayal of Otherness, much as they had with Ono.

Even her name became fodder in Arpe's coverage in the *Toronto Star*: "[T]he sentence 'Rob is happy with Twigs' brings about a lovely mental picture of him smiling goofily while caressing a large pile of sticks and assuring said sticks that his increasingly frequent trips to the gardener mean absolutely nothing." From animal to inanimate object, twigs was deemed lacking. And, in some ways, the *Twilight* movies themselves set up the harassment.

TWILIGHTMANIA

A journalist, identified as Aph, writing for wearyourvoicemag.com, first introduced the Yoko comparison in coverage of this abuse, drawing a connection between twigs's negative treatment and that of Ono: "One could argue that she's become the 'Yoko Ono' of our generation since the public spends more time engaging with her image as a destructive force that has broken up a sacred white union, rather than engaging with her actual work."

That "sacred white union" wasn't a band, though, like the Beatles. It was the group of megastars front and center in *Twilight*, including Pattinson playing vampire Edward Cullen and Stewart as momentarily mortal Bella. The extreme fandom around *Twilight*, similar to the frenzy around the

Beatles, was partly expressed in racist abuse. Indeed, the *Twilight* franchise had particularly devoted fans, most of them girls and women—80 percent in fact, according to Sara Klein in "Twilight: Changing the Business and Culture of Contemporary Cinema." The sheer scale of the fandom, too, was immense, with the films in total grossing $3.3 billion worldwide.[8] Those movies, which appeared between 2008 and 2012, were in the works even before the publication of the first book, on which the movies were based. And the success of the books ensured the success of the movies. As of 2011, the books had sold 116 million copies, printed in almost fifty languages. They were listed as a *New York Times* best seller for 302 weeks.[9]

The hype around *Twilight* actually attracted certain musicians to the franchise. Swedish musician Lyyke Li, part of the *Twilight: New Moon* soundtrack, told *The Guardian*, "when I thought about it, there are so few pop culture things today, where people are really crazy about something like Beatlemania, so I thought, how cool to be a part of something that so many young, open hearts listen to."

The movies also created fervent devotion to Pattinson as well as his romance with Stewart in a way that not even membership in a band could. Both the books and the movies unfold from the perspective of Stewart's character, Bella, as she falls in love with Pattinson as Edward. As Klein notes, this decision was deliberate and lucrative: "The movies and the books follow Bella closely by focusing the narrative through her perspective; the use of first-person narration creates a close identification with Bella on the part of her audience." Fans fell in love with Pattinson through Bella.

And Bella as a character invited that fan investment—as a clumsy, outsider every-girl who only becomes special once she captures Edward's obsessive attention. Fans, especially adolescent girls, identified with Bella and experienced their own sexual transformation under the watchful eyes of their beloved Edward, a vampire boy so beautiful he glitters in the sun. These fans, too, wanted to be special, like Bella when she is with Edward. And they wanted to be loved and protected by this especially beautiful and erotically dangerous character, which the *Twilight* marketing team supported with mega merchandising—posters, shirts, and buttons, all with his brooding stare. Older women, including the mothers of these fan girls, found their own reasons to fixate on Edward. For them, the movies were a "fountain of youth," a way to revisit the excitement of their past, before everyday chores or work overtook them.[10] Both groups could gaze at Edward while enjoying the charged tension between the lovers—as Edward initially tries to resist Bella. It was, in *Bitch* writer Christine Seifert's words, "abstinence porn."

The movies also made it clear that Pattinson/Edward belonged to Stewart/Bella. In fact, the movies supported this ownership in potentially unhealthy ways, modeling an arguably abusive tie. Bella in the movies is powerless against Edward's charm and in need of Edward. And Edward is, in turn, jealous and authoritarian in a dangerously patriarchal way.[11] In the first movie, he orders Bella to eat, though she isn't hungry, and she obeys. He also demands that she stay away from Jacob, a rival love interest. Even at the end of the first movie, Bella explains her decision to deal with another threatening vampire in secret as a way to get around Edward, who wouldn't have "let" her go if he had known. In the franchise as a whole, the relationship moves alarmingly fast, eventually isolating Bella as she cuts off friends and family, ending whatever dreams she might have had for herself as an individual.

Fans who felt the pull of this compelled coupling may have experienced Pattinson's relationship with twigs as a betrayal—not only of their investment in this storyline but also personally, as they vicariously fell under the controlling spell of Pattinson/Edward. The ugly response on Twitter had some connection, then, to a feeling of destined or meant-to-be romance. It was a winning formula at the box office, but the possessiveness linking fans and Pattinson was also potentially toxic. And it set twigs up for rejection and worse. This Twilightmania had no place for her. Her existence, like Ono's, was a disruption, no matter what she did or did not do.

GOLD DIGGER

The related racist harassment continued after twigs's initial response in 2014. Within that attack, she also dealt with ongoing questions regarding her sincerity or lack thereof—her imagined unsavory motives for dating Pattinson, both in online trolling and more mainstream media. Headlines included "Robert Pattinson Going Broke Because of 'Gold Digger' FKA Twigs"; "Is FKA Twigs Using Broke Robert Pattinson for His Money? His Pals Say So"; and "'Gold-Digger'—'She Knows How to Work Men.'" In the article "Robert Pattinson's Sisters Distrust Gold Digger FKA Twigs,"

Amanda Austin, writing for celebritydirtylaundry.com in 2015, voiced her suspicions along with the alleged concerns of Pattinson's sisters: "We can't ignore the fact that Twigs's music career and fan base have basically doubled since she and Rob began dating. So, in all actuality, Robert's sisters' suspicions might be valid." With rumors of their engagement circulating, Austin added, "the fact that Twigs and Rob still haven't signed a prenup is a serious cause for concern." Social media, of course, used the label in more personal digs. On Facebook, Georgie Henley wrote at the time, "I think FKA twigs is such as [sic] Gold digger, I mean no one knew who [she] was until she put her arm around My Robert Pattinson!!" The issue of ownership mixed with this invented tale of twigs's wicked and immoral quest for fame. Her very presence was both objectionable, with this labeling, and an act of selfish enrichment.

The same narrative of fame and money appeared again and again, sometimes combined with comparisons to Stewart. In the *Daily Star* (London), Emma Kelly (January 7, 2015) offered the headline: "What a Vamp! Robert Pattinson's Girlfriend FKA twigs Poses Topless." She then recounted how twigs was supposedly "stealing the spotlight from her superstar fella." In a write-up for HollywoodLife.com, Stewart allegedly saw this spotlight stealing for what it was. She was suspicious already, concerned about twigs's motives.

And then twigs did her thing, including talking to the press, which was apparently a sign of her treachery. An unnamed source shared, "It's so obvious to Kristen that this girl is just taking advantage of Rob . . . She's still very protective of Rob." Another headline made the contrast clear: "Kristen Stewart and Robert Pattinson Were a Private Classy Couple: FKA Twigs Is Using Rob for Career and Publicity." The gold-digger label and the Stewart references were, of course, complementary. The contrast implied in the label between the respectable woman and the "gold digger" had a ready-made visual, with white Stewart opposite twigs. Stewart was, then, part of twigs's labeling. She was both less than human and less than a particular human, Stewart—snow-white and therefore right.

In the gold-digger label, fans also had a way to exonerate Pattinson, *their* Pattinson. He was not to blame for choosing twigs because she chose him. Whereas Bella was powerless against Edward, here Pattinson was thought powerless against twigs, who supposedly was especially seductive but ethically deviant, using her sexuality for personal gain.

The fact that twigs, during her life, had to work extremely hard to create her career never mattered. She did not have wealth to support her musical aspirations, as many musicians do and must. And racism pushed her to work especially hard, partly based on the advice of her father. When she was only seven, he told her that she would have to radically outperform the white girls around her to make her ability incontestable. If it was close, the white girls would inevitably win. In her interview with Lordi, twigs revealed, "If I wanted to win a [dance] competition, I couldn't really afford to be good. I had to be excellent."

When twigs dated Pattinson, all of that fell away in the public imagination. Based in misogynoir and related myths of a Black woman's worth, she was nothing but a gold digger. That nothingness is key to the pernicious power of the gold-digger label. It presumes that a certain kind of woman has nothing to offer—not money, not talent, not worth. Leveling the gold-digger charge, then, strips a woman of her value until all that is left is her sexuality. She's an object, immoral and barely human, the "monkey" once more. And that charge, of them all, had to be especially painful for twigs. It was a direct attack on her hard-earned achievement. It was an attack on all that extra effort. And it was an assault on the words of her father. Referencing his advice, twigs told Lordi, "I really heard that."

MALFUNCTIONING AGAIN

The gold-digger label for twigs was leveled aggressively, with related racism in slurred language. That particular episode differs from the experience of other women similarly labeled. But certain contours of the stories match. In 2017, when Janet Jackson divorced her husband, Wissam Al Mana, she, too, was called a "gold digger." Much of the abuse, like twigs's, happened on Twitter and other social media sites, with trolls insisting the "marriage was a 5-year scam." The issue was one of timing, the fact that the two split after five years—generally a pay-off year in a prenup—and that Al Mana is a billionaire. Supposedly, Jackson stood to collect $500 million. On the Breakfast Club podcast, with DJ Envy and Charlamagne Tha God, the guys discussed whether Jackson should be labeled a gold digger. Maybe the move was even understandable, they said, because the number was "so big." And, really, her ex won, too: he got to have "sex with Janet Jackson," they crudely reasoned. But, still, they had to call "an ace an ace"—Jackson was, to them, a gold digger.

Unlike twigs, however, Jackson was not starting out in her career—far from it. She was already an icon, with plenty of money. Isabelle Khoo writing about Jackson's gold-digger controversy for *Huffington Post* meaningfully quoted a positive Twitter take (@shesalmostthat): "This Janet Jackson conversation just goes to show that no matter how much money a woman has, she can still be painted as a gold digger." Through the charge, Jackson was reduced to her sexuality, like twigs. The gold-digger label also negatively coded her sexuality while punishing her for it. Jackson had been so reduced and punished before—after the 2004 Super Bowl and her infamous reveal, termed then "Nipplegate." Despite her apologies after the fact, Jackson was blacklisted—both by CBS and Viacom—and she was no longer welcome to present at the Grammy Awards that year. Her album *Damita Jo*, which came out just a month after that Super Bowl, was not promoted as it should have been. And sales reflected the pushback. The level of punishment is all the more appalling when compared to the aftermath for Timberlake, who himself had made the mistake, pulling away more of Jackson's top than he should have.

Although Timberlake's career trajectory would remain on the ascent, as *Malfunction: The Dressing Down of Janet Jackson* makes clear, Jackson's would never fully recover. Author Treva Lindsey told Vanessa Willoughby, writing for *Bitch Media*, "When we look back at the moment, considering how much more explicit television is in 2020 than it was then, it was a very knee-jerk reaction to the problem of Black women's bodies that the nation has always had." The patriarchy has viewed Black women as alluring while also assuming a subversive depravity. That history clouded the Super Bowl narrative just as it clouded the response to Jackson's divorce.

The gold-digger label's presence in pop culture, supported by songs such as West's "Gold Digger," ensured widespread suspicion around Jackson's divorce. And her achievements didn't really factor into the coarse conversation. A comparable conversation would unfold around another Black woman in music, Ciara, in 2018. The rapper Slim Thug, speaking on Houston radio's Madd Hatta Morning Show, would suggest that the singer's marriage to NFL star Russell Wilson was all about "financial stability." He wasn't calling her a "gold digger," he said. Something was just "off." He insisted that he couldn't believe Ciara would honestly choose Wilson, someone he called "corny," especially because she had once dated the rapper Future, though he allegedly cheated on her. Of course, to clarify, Slim Thug was absolutely calling her a "gold digger." His backpedaling is a common strategy. When you want to say something that you know you shouldn't, just deny it up front while saying it all the same. It's a "get-out-of-jail-free" card, like "just kidding," when you know you're in the wrong.

Slim Thug would later apologize to Russell but not to Ciara. She was apparently fair game. Or perhaps the suspicion in that label is so common that it does not fully register as an insult, despite the inexcusable picture it paints of Black women in love—from Jackson to twigs, even as that love is falling apart.

"THEY WANT TO SEE US, WANT TO SEE US APART"

As a couple, Pattinson and twigs wouldn't last. The two parted ways in 2017. But, throughout her time with Pattinson, twigs dealt with this sadistic side of fame. The online abuse was not an isolated racist eruption, just as the negative articles were not. In a *New York Times* interview with Joe Corscarelli, published May 16, 2015, twigs would explain just how "awful" the cruelty was. She realized, "There's no amount of songs I can sing or dances I can dance that will prove to them I'm not a monkey." Though she felt powerless, on *Radio 1 Stories*, she explained her decision to respond directly to racist trolls: "I didn't want them [the fans] to see me being bullied and not stand up for myself."

Still, she later realized that she could have done more. In 2021, speaking with Theroux, twigs more fully addressed her experience dating Pattinson and explained why she didn't say more earlier, citing reasons of age as well as her ongoing attempts to be "twice as good": "If I was going through that now, I feel like I'd be able to talk about it, and do some good with it. But I don't know whether it was because of my age or whether it was because of the social climate or whether it was because being Black and from Cheltenham and from a low-income family and having to genuinely work twice as hard at everything I do to get a seat at the table." She was also processing the hate and, for a time, internalizing it by taking seriously what she believed for a time was "this monkey-ness." But, in 2021, she opened up, underlining just how "deeply horrific" that period had been. As the

Twi-trolls harassed and bullied her, she found that she was raw and vulnerable. Her experience with racism during childhood was right there, at the surface, the wound unhealed. She has since overcome the self-hate she felt then—when she felt "so self-conscious and so ugly"—but all is certainly not forgiven. She knows in full how "deeply unfair" her online treatment truly was.

That treatment left its mark on her 2019 album *Magdalene*. In the song "Cellophane," which she cowrote, it's twigs alone, with a sparse repeated motive in the piano accompaniment. She sings mournfully, "Why don't I do it for you?" She told *i-D* in an interview about the album, "It's funny that, as women, we're asking those questions without realizing how epic and iconic we are."[12] But her past haunts her, and the present stops, with only a light, beatboxed rhythm marking time. She quietly sings the next lines, "They want to see us, want to see us apart." She then asserts her own desires— "I don't want to have to share our love." And yet, the opening question remains, stretching on the word "I" as she scoops up an empty fifth, and even more so, when she repeats the same passage much, much higher. The pace picks up then, too, as the questioning builds into a frenzy. Then, it all drops away as she sings again in the song's initial register, before almost whispering, again alone, "They're waiting / And hoping / I'm not enough." With that line, the song ends in silence.

Critics have connected "Cellophane" in particular to twigs's relationship with Pattinson. But the album as a whole is not a "breakup" album. Instead, it's a reckoning with emotion, expectation, sexuality, and femininity. The album's title is also an indication of twigs's ongoing awareness of the labeling of women. Through it, she reclaims the biblical figure of Mary Magdalene, much as Sarah McLachlan had with Lilith, Adam's first wife, who refused to be subservient and was then cast as a villain. In Catholic school, twigs had learned only that Magdalene was a prostitute. She found out later that Magdalene was quite intelligent and worked in areas of healing and magic. As she told Theroux, she wondered, "Why is there not that much written about her in the Bible?" Only more recently, researchers have attempted to sift through fact and fiction. In doing so, some have concluded that Magdalene was never a prostitute. In fact, she may have been wealthy, supporting Jesus materially and emotionally as a central figure in his life.

For history.com, Robert Cargill, professor of classics and religious studies, shares the reason this truth has been twisted: "There are many scholars who argue that because Jesus empowered women to such an extent early in his ministry, it made some of the men who would lead the early church later on uncomfortable. And so, there were two responses to this. One was to turn her into a prostitute." The bending of her story resonated with twigs— "how the patriarchy can do that to women," their narratives changed, and then "the truth gets lost," or an invented "narrative becomes true." She underlined an example of this twisting in her own life, in media descriptions of her dancing as nothing more than writhing and sex. The beauty of the dance, her art, was lost in the telling.

Her album was meant to give back to women their many possibilities. In a 2019 interview with Jasmine Albertson, she pointed out the significance of Magdalene as "the Virgin Whore, the sacred prostitute": "As a woman, we can be both things, we can be innocent and pure and, you know, like a juicy little fruit, like a fresh flower. But we can also be sensual or knowing, healing, strong, powerful. We can be all of these things at the same time. And that's okay." In her interview with Theroux, the album's frame brought up twigs's early love of the pop duo Shakespeare's Sister, which similarly played on double standards and thwarted narratives of female power and genius. The duo's name, by way of the band the Smiths (and their song "Shakespeare's Sister"), references Virginia Woolf's essay about the fictional Shakespeare sister, who, if real, would never have been allowed to pursue her genius, at least not in the same way her brother could.

When the album came out, at the end of November 2019, twigs had plans to do festivals and videos, all showcasing her vision of *Magdalene*. But, when the pandemic hit, she had to cancel everything, as so many of us did. In this case, the disruption, as twigs told Theroux, was "quite poetic." Like Magdalene's actual story and the story of so many women, it was all "cut short."

In that creative vision, a powerful message persists. As twigs told Miranda Sawyer, writing in *The Guardian* in 2019, my work is "so much louder than my love life." And it needs to be. The negative labels affecting Black women, like those that grew up and around twigs and her relationship with Pattinson, resonate across "the populations depicted," impacting self-esteem and behavior. Young Black women may internalize societal expectations based on media depictions of other Black women. Those messages "direct interpersonal, community, and societal interactions within sexual contexts."[13] As Bailey maintains, they also affect material possibilities for these women "by justifying poor treatment throughout all areas of society."[14] To some, twigs is then something of a role model, as Jasmine Albertson pointed out in a 2019 interview on KEXP. In response, twigs said, "I don't know, really. I don't know, I'm very much still figuring out. So I don't know if I like, have the need or the want to be a role model, but I'm definitely okay with talking about things. For anyone who wants to join in the conversation." Like her name, twigs's music offers an immersive experience and a discussion about race, women, and the music industry. And it's definitely time that we all join or expand that conversation.

6

TAYLOR SWIFT AS A
MODERN MEDUSA

The public, in the case of Spears, was like a snake. They were waiting to strike. And her distress was the ultimate justification. For FKA twigs, it took just one actor playing a vampire for the public to bite with real anger and aggression. But, with Taylor Swift, the tide seemed to turn on its own.

In 2017, Brian O'Flynn in *The Guardian* wrote, "It's cool to hate Taylor Swift." And some people expressed relief that it was finally time for the pile on, as if that were her fate all along. In 2016, with #TaylorSwift IsOver trending worldwide, Shawn Cooke observed in the *Consequences of Sound*, "Longtime detractors had been waiting for public opinion to turn against the pop star, and now they seemingly can't wait to celebrate her demise." Comedian Katherine Ryan took full advantage in her 2017 comedy special *In Trouble*. In the performance, she describes Swift and her many famous friends in modeling. She at first conveys some desire to be part of the group but impersonates Swift and an imagined rebuff: I already have "one human woman" friend, the actress and writer Lena Dunham. Swift apparently was too perfect, with perfect friends to match. Otherwise, yeah, Swift and Ryan would have been friends, I guess. Got it, Ryan. Demonstrating what a good friend she would have been, Ryan then happily reports to her audience, "I knew that Taylor Swift would mess up if I watched her." "So," she says in a lower voice, "I did watch her . . . like a psycho." Ryan then gleefully describes a purported misstep, a post on Twitter addressed to musician Nicki Minaj that reeks, in Ryan's opinion, of "white privilege."

Those inclined to hate Swift, of course, had had a few opportunities to pounce earlier. First came Swift's involvement with boy-band members—Joe Jonas and then Harry Styles—a ready-made formula for abuse, as we have seen. But her ongoing clashes with Kanye West became the real backdrop for a more widespread revulsion. White privilege was a generic insult, one that could have applied to Ryan herself, especially given her entitled attitude toward Swift's friendship. But, in her feuds with West, Swift would, for many, then become a "snake." And that image and the related reputational fallout have endured, with little real analysis of the reasons why.

Some of the incomplete takes credit the animosity to her music. In *The Atlantic*, Spencer Kornhaber took on Swift in an article titled "Taylor Swift's 'Me!' Is Everything Wrong with Pop," writing in 2019, "One of the most impressive things about Taylor Swift is that she keeps finding a way to offend people simply with sound alone." But let's be clear: it was never about the "sound alone." The main offense was and continues to be gendered, reflected in the labels attached to Swift and her music.

To me, Swift's primary transgression was fighting back—not only in her music, but also in interviews, videos, tour imagery, and the recording studio. After she is insulted, she often calls out other people's abuse, including the wrongs of past lovers. Her songs are littered with these references. And, in the case of the "snake" label, she did so on a massive scale through her 2018 Reputation tour, which followed the release of her album by the same name. This response would have worked for a man, but for a woman, it couldn't. Her reception is, in some ways, Manne's catch-22 on loop. As Manne writes, any highlighting of misogyny "is liable to give rise to more of it."[1] Any attempt to decry the disparity, the inequality, or the unfairness potentially could make matters worse. And, in Swift's case, it did and does—memorably exploding into view in 2016 along with her second major confrontation with West and her subsequent labeling as a snake.

MANIPULATIVE SNAKE

Snake, as a label, is shorthand for the label liar but a particular type of liar. It's a person who lies in order to manipulate. A book by Ed Slack about dealing with manipulative people plays on that meaning in the title: *Two Legged Snakes: Understanding and Handling Manipulative People*. In the online "urban dictionary," those two-legged snakes are also "two faced." They're kind to your face while working deceptively toward their own ends. The snake as an animal supports the association with its slippery skin. It's hard to hold the snake, just as it's hard to grasp and understand a two-faced person. The label also builds on the appearance of a serpent in the Bible, an evil snake convincing enough in its lie to lead Eve and, ultimately, Adam astray. Negative expressions play on these associations: "snake in the grass," "snake oil," or "fake snake."

In cultural imaginings, that sneaky snake is often further connected to women—in the story of Eve, but also Medusa's magical hair and Cleopatra's asp. In some traditions, it's also related to women and performance. In the book *Belly Dancing: The Sensual Art of Energy and Spirit*, the authors insist, "Snakes symbolize the internal sexual energy represented by the goddess, and some dancers choose to dance with a snake to demonstrate the significance of the sexual energy to the flowing belly dance." The female connection is more explicit in some folktales, with the snake symbolizing the vagina and even responsible for menstrual blood. In that context, a snake bite is the cause of a magical wound that bleeds each month and never heals.[2]

The negative meaning behind the label is also routinely attached to women more generally—with and without the snake association. Women are culturally suspect. And they are saddled young with notions of their two-faced behavior and penchant for catty gossip. As adults, they are often considered manipulative or controlling, too, especially if they are particularly successful or in leadership positions. These powerful women, whether the boss or prom princess, are thought to be duplicitous, engaged in "indirect aggression"—slanderous gossip or some other version of behind-the-scenes machinations—all to get and keep the top spot. In "The Myth of the Mean Girl," Leslie Scrivener credits culture rather than observed fact as the basis for this gendered thinking: "Popular culture has been so consistent in depicting girls and women as treacherous, disloyal and devious that it has become a defining stereotype—even though there's a growing body of research suggesting that boys and men practice what is termed 'indirect aggression' as much and even more than females."

With this entrenched belief and attached cultural baggage, the snake charge was an obvious but lazy choice in the bullying of Swift, especially because she was at the height of her fame. She was so successful that people wanted to pull her down. With the snake tag, bullies had both a way to attack Swift and a way to discredit her achievement. Remarkably, Swift wasn't completely unfamiliar with the strategy or the bullying. Ever since she set her sights on stardom, as a young girl, the people around her had been doing something similar, though, of course, on a more localized scale disguised by the confusion of growing up. In fact, they had been taking cheap jabs all along, trying to keep her in her perceived place, below them and confined to the sidelines. As she would sing, "She's cheer captain, and I'm on the bleachers." But she wouldn't stay there for long.

THE GIRL ON THE BLEACHERS

Even before the full flowering of her celebrity, some people in Swift's life wanted to see her punished. As Ryan's Swift jokes make clear, early on Swift had certain basic points of potential backlash for those so inclined. In addition to being a woman, Swift is rich and white, "the Gwyneth Paltrow of Pop," according to Jennifer Gannon in *The Irish Times*. She's hardly the underdog we all want to celebrate. And her advantages apparently were instigation early on when she was just a girl. As author Chloe Govan chronicles in the book *Taylor Swift: The Rise of the Nashville Teen*, Swift was mercilessly shunned in school, in part out of jealousy. Her song "You Belong with Me" (2008)—which portrays Swift as an outsider, the girl on the bleachers rather than cheer captain—is based in that reality. When I first heard the song and saw the video, long before I knew Swift's biography, I thought it was somewhat inauthentic. It seemed like a stretch, imagining Swift as an outcast. I was guilty of making certain assumptions based on cultural standards of traditional beauty.

But, growing up in Pennsylvania, Swift, like her nerd character, didn't have a lot of friends. One local woman from Wyomissing recalled, "People used to call her stuck up, I guess because they were jealous. She wanted for nothing, when some of them couldn't scrape a few cents together . . . One girl I know would even fake retching when Taylor walked by." A former bully told Govan, "Because [Swift] liked the Dixie Chicks, our nickname for her behind her back was Dipsy Shit. . . . I admit that we made her life a misery, but she was so darned good at everything that it made me feel pretty good at the time to see her upset." Swift didn't seem to realize jealousy was a factor, telling *Teen Vogue*, "They didn't think I was cool or pretty enough, so they stopped talking to me." Like Ryan, however, they continued to talk *about* her, cutting her down to build themselves up.

During those days, Swift was already writing her own songs. Not only that, she had a clear vision of her future and was convinced she was meant for fame if she worked for it. Of course, many of the kids around her, who knew that she dreamed of a career as a singer, were not supportive. But Swift did move to Nashville, at fourteen, and after a few false starts, signed in 2005 with Scott Borchetta and his newly formed Big Machine Records. As interest in her music grew, with her first album in 2006 and second, *Fearless*, in 2008, so did interest in her love life. That focus brought with it a new type of bullying, with some still bent on containing and controlling her.

Swift's early high-profile boy-band beau, Joe Jonas of the Jonas Brothers, was kept secret for a while. Given the treatment of Ono, Swift might have had reason to avoid the press coverage. But it was Jonas's management that allegedly made that decision. Joe and his brothers had become a band in 2005 and were wildly popular thanks to their collaboration with the Disney Channel, including their own show and several movies. Much like the corporate interests behind K-pop, the brothers' management, in 2008, wanted Joe "to appear young, free and single." After the relationship ended, via a text from Jonas, Swift reflected, "When someone's not allowed to go out with me in public, then that's an issue."[3]

In 2012, Swift did, however, experience the ramifications of a public relationship with a boy-band member when she dated Harry Styles of One Direction, the popular English-Irish group that had shot to fame after their performance in 2010 on the British television series *The X Factor*. On December 10, 2012, newspapers widely reported that Styles flew on Swift's private jet, rather than with the rest of his band. An anonymous source told London's *The Sun*, "There was loads of room for the rest of the band in [Taylor Swift]'s luxury jet but he didn't even suggest they travelled together."

Despite the blame assigned to Styles—"he didn't even suggest"—*The Sun* announced, "Harry Styles' lover Taylor Swift has been branded the Yoko Ono of One Direction." The next day, the *Sydney Morning Herald* ran with the story, quoting that same anonymous source—"It's really not far off from the Yoko situation"—before reviewing the Beatles' split for anyone who might have missed the story of Ono's supposed blame. The paper also revealed that One Direction's female fans had been issuing Swift death threats as soon as the relationship was made public. On Twitter, one fan wrote, "I'll murder Taylor Swift. She will not date my Harry."[4]

The same thing would happen to another One Direction girlfriend when the group's Zayn Malik dated Perrie Edwards, singer with the group Little Mix. When the group parted ways in 2015, she was dubbed "the Yoko Ono of One Direction," or "Yoko Ono 2.0," according to the article "Ono! Has Perrie Done a Yoko and Split Up One Direction" (*Daily Mail*, March 27, 2015). But even with another so-called Yoko attached to One Direction, Swift would continue to be haunted by her relationship with Styles (a relationship dubbed online Haylor) and her related casting as "Yoko." Much of that hate is still readily accessible via Twitter—a hate with resilience. On March 18, 2014, well after the demise of Swift's brief relationship with Styles, @piscesrat posted, "Even though Haylor was in 2012 I still hate Taywhore cause she dated my Harry."

The hate is, in some ways, predictable, given the pattern we've seen play out over and over again in the press coverage of women in music. And yet, in Swift's case, it was not the ultimate impetus for the pervasive public turn against Swift in 2016. It may have helped prepare the way, but that turn involved another man, one she was not involved with romantically, despite his musical fantasies. Of course, I'm referring here to Kanye West, the rapper, Trump supporter, onetime husband of Kim Kardashian, and presidential candidate of sorts. I write here "of course" not only because the story is so well known but also because West often seems to get himself involved in the harassment of women, and well before his online attacks on Kim in 2022. More surprising, actually, is the fact that Kardashian participated and arguably led the ensuing bullying of Swift on social media. Even women and those subjected to their own online trolling—as Kim most certainly is—can bully other women. A pattern of learned behavior can turn victims into victimizers, as it may have in this "famous" case, though West was the central player and "jackass" of note.

"FAMOUS"

Swift had her first public issue with West after his interruption of her 2009 speech at the MTV Video Music Awards (VMA), an amazing moment that included both the direct silencing of Swift and a very public insult. At only seventeen, Swift at the time had successfully crossed over from country star to pop celebrity. During her cut-short acceptance speech, she said, "I always dreamed about what it would be like to maybe win one of these someday, but I never actually thought it would have happened. I sing country music so thank you so much for giving me a chance to win a VMA award." Before she could continue, West grabbed the microphone from her, "Yo Taylor, I'm really happy for you, Imma let you finish, but Beyoncé has one of the best videos of all time."

When West took the mic from Swift mid-speech, he challenged Swift's win—she didn't deserve the award, he believed. It should have been Beyoncé. He also made her speech all about him. In 2011, Lizzie Widdicombe writing for the *New Yorker* summed up the incident: "The moment, which had started out like a coronation, turned into something closer to a public shaming." The audience booed Kanye, but Swift revealed in the 2020 documentary *Miss Americana*, she thought the audience was booing her. Interviewed that night, right after the VMAs, Swift struggles to remain composed, as the documentary shows. Asked about Kanye—"any hard feelings?"—Swift responds, "I don't know him." She explained her thought process in the moment in an interview with *Wonderwall*: "I was really excited because I had just won the award and then I was really excited because Kanye West was on the stage—and then I wasn't so excited anymore after that."

West issued an apology and reportedly called Swift to apologize. To many, he was still clearly in the wrong, and even Barack Obama famously called him a "jackass." But the contrite West didn't last long, and he quickly seemed to switch gears in interviews the following year. On New York's Hot 97 radio station, he insisted that his timing was just off but the sentiment was justified. He also sought to set the record straight, addressing his then reputation by maintaining that he was not in fact "arrogant" but, instead, honorable. He was standing up for Beyoncé, he said: "That's completely selfless. That's like jumping in front of a bullet."

West's take seems less than honest, especially in light of other examples of his anger at awards shows. Even that night at the VMAs he was upset before Swift's win, but not for unselfish reasons. He was reportedly fuming backstage because he hadn't won anything himself.[5] In 2011, he tried to make the whole thing a joke while clearly acting again in his own self-interests. After Britney Spears's new song "Hold It against Me" outperformed his new single with Jay-Z, he wrote on Twitter, "Yo, Britney, I'm really happy for you and I'm 'a let you be number one but me and Jay-Z's single is one of the best songs of all time!" The post drips with condescension and self-entitlement—he'll "let" Spears be number one—while clearly implying that he deserved the win over Spears. But this time, he attempted to hide his true opinion and purpose behind humor.

Despite West's mixed messages, Swift tried to get past the events of 2009. In 2011, at the Met Costume Gala, the two "down low" high-fived, as widely reported by journalists still following the reported feud. Then, in 2016, she tried to cooperate with West when he contacted her about his 2016 song "Famous," which references Swift: "I made that bitch famous." In the "Famous" video, West appears in bed next to nude, look-alike wax figures of various stars, including Swift stripped of any cover. In the video, West, of course, is dressed and in control. Before the "bitch" charge, West raps, "I feel like me and Taylor might still have sex." The crude suggestion was that Swift owed him for her fame.

West evidently called to secure Swift's permission or at least run the concept by her before the song's release, a gesture Swift found respectful at the time. In a video recording of West on that call, made without Swift's knowledge, Swift responds gently to the lyrics, "It's like a compliment kind of." I am struck by Swift's generosity here, attempting to bury the hatchet and go along with West's rather gross use of her stripped image. After the fact, however, Swift was less than thrilled, unaware that West would not only rap about having sex with her but also call her a bitch in the song. Her fans, too, made known their disgust. Eventually, she also would object to West's claim that her success had anything to do with him.

In her 2016 Grammy Awards acceptance speech—for a win in the category of Album of the Year—she told the audience, seemingly referencing West, "As the first woman to win album of the year at the Grammys twice, I want to say to all the young women out there, there are going to be people along the way who will try to undercut your success or take credit for your accomplishments or your fame." Her representative, Tree Paine, was more explicit once "Famous" was released, making it known that Swift had not endorsed the song: "Kanye did not call for approval, but to ask Taylor to release his single 'Famous' on her Twitter account. She declined and cautioned him about releasing a song with such a strong misogynistic message. Taylor was never made aware of the actual lyric: 'I made that bitch famous.'"

Kim Kardashian then posted on Snapchat an edited version of the video recording of West on that call with Swift, insisting that Swift had given West her blessing. On Instagram, Swift wrote, "Where is the video of Kanye telling me he was going to call me, 'that bitch' in his song?" She answered her own question: "It doesn't exist because it didn't happen." But the mighty Kim and her many followers still labeled Swift a snake, a two-faced liar, topped off with a snake emoji. The online bullying was relentless after Kardashian posted, on Twitter, "Wait it's legit National Snake Day?!?!? They have holidays for everybody, I mean everything these days." The charge aligned with West's message. Just as the snake label implies manipulation and undeserved success, so did West's song and his not-so-subtle hint that he deserved credit, and then some, for Swift's fame.

Despite the fact that Kardashian's initial post made no mention of the line calling Swift a bitch, just as Swift and her publicist maintained, the snake label stuck. And it caught on in surprising circles beyond social media. In the *Daily Bruin*, the student newspaper at UCLA, Nina Crosby (October 23, 2016) insisted, under the headline "Taylor Swift Plays the Victim to Hide Manipulative Personality," Swift "is a snake," and she "has slithered among the music industry long before the iconic reveal by Kim Kardashian West." Swift was supposedly two-faced, playing "the American ideal" while under her polished facade it's just "scales and a forked tongue." Another 2016 story on *Page Six* chronicled a similar "cold manipulation behind Taylor Swift's sweet smile." A cited source and "Hollywood insider" shared with the publication, "There's this misconception that Taylor's a sweetheart, but she's quite calculated."

The incident and its drama made headlines again in 2020, when the unedited video recording of that call mysteriously appeared online. In it, currently available through a quick Google search, West begins, "So my next single, I wanted you to tweet it, so that's why I'm calling you. I wanted you to put the song out." He continues, mentioning a "very controversial line." When Swift asks to hear the line, he responds, smiling and obviously stalling: the song is "so so dope," he says. After asking her to "brace herself,"

Tweet

Kim Kardashian ✓
@KimKardashian

Wait it's legit National Snake Day?!?!?They have holidays for everybody, I mean everything these days! 🐍🐍🐍🐍🐍🐍🐍🐍🐍🐍🐍🐍🐍🐍🐍🐍🐍🐍🐍🐍🐍🐍🐍🐍🐍🐍🐍🐍🐍🐍🐍🐍

4:22 PM · 7/17/16 · Twitter for iPhone

183K Retweets **302K** Likes

Kim Kardashian, on Twitter, July 17, 2016

she warily assents, but he stalls again, noting the edge in her voice. As if it wasn't obvious, he asks, "Why do you sound sad?" Based on the guilty smile on his face, he knows perfectly well the reason. Swift responds, asking again about the line, which West still has not revealed: "Well, is it gonna be mean?" He insists it's not mean and then, after another attempt to convince Swift that the line is absolutely fabulous—his wife's favorite—he finally reveals the lyric in question, which would be slightly modified in the final cut. He tells her, "It says, 'To all my Southside n****** that know me best, I feel like Taylor Swift might owe me sex.'" Swift laughs but, in the end, asks if she can think it over. Again, he never mentions that he will call her a bitch, too.

The line he does share is gross enough—suggesting that Swift owes him and in a sexual way. But the bitch charge ups the insult. It would certainly not be the first time that Swift had been called a bitch, another label women in music—and women more generally—confront, one explicitly coded feminine (and the subject of the last chapter). In a particularly nasty published article, "The Hater's Guide to Taylor Swift," Drew Magary complained in 2010 of Swift's popularity: "I can't get away from this bitch." But just because she had been called a bitch before doesn't mean she was desensitized to its meaning, especially in the music of West—with his platform and their history. It makes no sense, in fact, that she would have approved her own labeling as a bitch if West had, in fact, revealed his song's complete lyrics in that call, which he absolutely did not. And yet, she remained the snake.

In 2020, after the full call appeared online, Kim tried to defend herself, claiming that Swift had lied about the call itself, citing an edited version of Paine's statement, that "Kanye never called to ask for permission." Kim also admitted that "the word 'bitch' was used without her permission" but attempted to argue that "nobody ever denied" that point. Paine then countered, making it clear that the original issue did, in fact, center around the label "bitch" by reposting her message in full.

Kardashian didn't acknowledge the resulting bullying or the snake label itself. Her attempted defense and this omission jarringly resound as I rewatch *Miss Americana*. In it, the camera pans the audience at a West show as he sings "Famous." The crowd chants, "F*ck Taylor Swift." At a concert in Arizona in May 2018, Swift addressed the cruel treatment: "A couple of years ago, someone called me a snake on social media and it caught on. And then a lot of people called me a lot of names on social media. I went through some really low times for a while because of it. I went through some times when I didn't know if I was going to get to do this anymore." And then she got mad. The history of the label and the sentiment behind it makes me ridiculously mad, too. Yes, "no one likes a mad woman." But, once again, they've clearly made her like that.

"BEAUTIFUL LIAR"

Although the labeling of Swift is somewhat unique in music, at least the specific tag "snake," the sentiment behind the attack is not. The manipulative charge is, in some ways, the ultimate default insult for a successful woman. She couldn't have achieved all that she has, apparently, without some sort of subterfuge. She can't be all that she is if it's threatening to a man. And, so, it's no surprise that some of the most powerful women in music have been blasted with rumors of their manipulation.

Madonna, a true legend, has been saddled with the charge. In the *Independent* (March 25, 2016), reporter Adam Sherwin ran down the findings of a study by brand expert Jeetendr Sehdev. The conclusion: millennials supposedly find Madonna "inauthentic" and a "media manipulator." Beyoncé was similarly tagged. In *The Atlantic*, "Beyoncé Is Expertly Manipulating Us All" (April 25, 2013), Esther Zuckerman asserted that Beyoncé is "an expert at manipulating her image and her audience." The alleged evidence: she has released songs attached to "lucrative sponsorship deals," and she's banned professional photographers from her tours, reportedly hoping to control the publication of "unflattering" shots.

Zuckerman's reasoning is egregiously double-sided. Men in music have certainly made use of advertisement and sponsorship deals without similar criticism. In 2014, West himself released a new song, "God Level," to accompany an Adidas ad campaign. Men have also banned photographers. In 2018, *The Guardian* reported on these bans as a trend, with Kendrick Lamar joining other stars in what was, in this context, described as a "stand." When fans take photos, the article's author Vanessa Thorpe insisted, it ruins the ambience. But Lamar, like Beyoncé, also banned professional photographers. The reason—not vanity in his case but an understandable desire to "protect his valuable 'brand.'" Just to help keep yet another double standard straight, let me sum up: A man can smartly ban professional photographers, but a woman doing the same thing is manipulative. OK; got it.

In 2016, as Swift was suffering her attack as a snake, the *Daily Beast* went after Queen Bey again, in the article "How Beyoncé Manipulates the Media." The writer, Amy Zimmerman, criticized Beyoncé's "OCD tendencies," her refusal to answer many direct interview questions, and her related maintenance of "total control over her story." She also questioned the sincerity of Beyoncé's then new album *Lemonade*, which came out in the wake of a cheating scandal involving Beyoncé's musical partner, Jay-Z. "It's important not to confuse this performance of intimacy with total honesty, or the surrender of any degree of control," Zimmerman wrote. "Beyoncé is pre-packaging the story of her husband's infidelity, manufacturing it as an art piece that then feeds directly into her pocket." Right, so a man can describe a romantic wrong, as men do in song after song. But, for Beyoncé, it's manipulation. Again, got it.

Honesty and authenticity are particularly valued in music. Attacking a woman for an apparent dishonesty or manipulative tendency easily clouds the weight of her music. And sometimes her only crime is her success. To some, she's too famous, too polished. And of course, she's a woman. Often, part of the problem is also her attempt to avoid the problem—like Beyoncé's reluctance to interview. Given Love's treatment after the Hirschberg interview, some hesitancy around journalists makes sense. But women who are successful and seek to maintain that level of achievement are in the wrong either way. They're trapped in a fame conditioned by gender. They can either take a hike or strike. In some ways, they'll lose regardless. But, I imagine, if a woman is strong enough, it could feel empowering to be that snake and bite. Watching Swift become a snake for her 2018 Reputation tour, I have to admit, I felt a little empowered myself. As she strutted across the stage in all black, I could live in that power for a while. It could be a short break from the double standards breaking us all.

"BE LIKE A SNAKE"

For a time, Swift would step away from the media spotlight, aware of the criticism as well as the press coverage supporting the bullying. But soon, she would find a way to respond, as she often does through her music. And she did so by harnessing the power of the snake. Initially, in Kim's use of the label and emoji, the snake was all negative. But the snake has explicitly positive ascriptions, too, in representations of the snake charmer and magic more generally. Snake symbolism also includes notions of power and renewal with the shedding of the snake's skin. That latter side supported Swift's appropriation of the snake, much as it had Spears's. Though Swift had been dubbed "the anti-Britney"—someone straitlaced, maybe even too straitlaced—Swift admired Spears's stage performance, including her use of a serpent: "What I love about Britney is that in every awards show perfor-mance, you're going to be surprised, whether she's doing a costume change on stage, kissing Madonna or walking out with a snake around her neck."[6]

During her Reputation tour, Swift would go further, reintroducing her-self with multiple snakes in tow—in song, in video, in costume, and even with a huge inflatable snake named Karyn. On that tour, she self-identified as a snake, reclaiming a label used against her while calling out past wrongs. As she told *Elle*, in a list of "lessons" learned, "Grow a backbone, trust your gut, and know when to strike back. Be like a snake—only bite if someone steps on you."

Swift advertised her new tour with snake imagery, and on the tour itself, she performed in stadiums in front of massive crowds of fans, some holding signs with snakes or snake stuffed animals. There, she would address the snake bullying directly and indirectly. In a 2018 Netflix recording of the final tour performance, the show begins with spliced sound and image—clips of negative press comments and frames of black snakeskin. The camera pans upward, along that seeming skin until we see that the skin is actually a dress Swift is wearing. Her transformation is complete.

In the concert's early song, "I Did Something Bad," Swift combines ref-erences to a man who wronged her and pictures, on a screen behind her, of flames and a snake as it strikes. With a bare and modern oompah-pah-pah accompaniment, the song begins quietly but with determination. With that same simple instrumental support, she sings, "'Cause for every lie I tell them / They tell me three / This is how the world works / Now all he thinks about is me." By the chorus, the music revs up like an engine, and Swift sings with power. The fire imagery on the screen behind her supports the song's reference to that other female-specific label, "witch," with Swift singing, almost as a meditation, "They're burning all the witches, even if you aren't one."

Her real display of force, however, comes in the next song, "Look What You Made Me Do," which introduces Karyn, the snake rising from nothing and eventually towering above her on stage. The song chronicles Swift's own rise after the West clash, when he lied but metaphorically "said the gun was mine." Rather than slithering away, "I got smarter, I got harder in the nick of time." And then she "rose up from the dead."

Toward the song's end, a ringing phone interrupts. On the screen behind her, Tiffany Haddish answers, saying "the old Taylor can't come to the phone right now." The reason: "'cause she's dead." In the song's official video, Swift emerges at the start of the song from her own grave. She's a zombie version of herself but soon assumes her throne, dressed in red, with snakes providing her tea. The song itself opens with ethereal instrumental play, string sounds, and otherworldly percussion. But the sound eerily slides up and away, as the fantasy turns into a nightmare, and Swift begins her rhythmic recitation: "I don't like your little games." The song, like "I Did Something Bad," is nothing like Swift's early ballads. Instead, these songs are raw and rhythmically intense, with a pulsing energy meant to support a stage strut or the assembling of an army.

In a stage address, Swift explains the meaning of the tour's title, creating an intimate moment between her and the fans, despite the massive size of the setting and crowd. She mentions the light-up bracelets audience members received up front, revealing that the accessory is a way for her to "see every single one of you." With that connection, she outlines their commonality, which, in her opinion, is the quest for "something real," a real friend, a real relationship. But, she says, "a bad reputation"—set off by a rumor or name calling—can get in the way of that. Reputation, in this way, matters. It's not always fair or deserved, but it has real consequences for everyone.

DISORIENTING OR DOUBLE STANDARD

This was not, of course, the first time Swift had fought back in her music or on stage. As she explained during the Reputation tour, her songwriting is often a way for her to "get past or understand something." And that necessitates personal revelation, including mention of those who have hurt her. In the song "Dear John" (2010), for example, about her relationship with singer John Mayer, she records his wrongs: "Don't you think I was too young to be messed with?" In "Cold as You" (2006), she sings, "And now that I'm sitting here, thinking it through / I've never been anywhere as cold as you." In "Tell Me Why" (2008), she croons, "You could write a book on how to ruin someone's day." Her references to her real life in song, including those who've wronged her, can create a sense of intimacy between her and her fans. The fans piece together details of Swift's failed romances or other life events, and they feel as if they really know her. That candor shows a seeming authenticity or honesty, at least for some. But for others, this was part of Swift's snake problem and reason for backlash.

In fact, Swift's response, including callouts of past wrongs, for some was rather gross. She wasn't a powerful snake but, to them, a complainer who enjoyed playing the victim. In 2018, in the article "Taylor Swift: Why Is It So Difficult to Support Her?," Jennifer Gannon identified this "victim" role as the reason for Swift's lack of support. To be clear, Gannon was blaming the victim, with no mention of those who victimized Swift. In Gannon's words, she was "fueled by the notion of being treated unfairly." Hurting her supposedly gives her power. And so, she can be hurt; in Gannon's thinking, maybe she should be hurt. In "Ten Years of Taylor Swift: How the Pop Star Went from Sweetheart to Snake (and Back Again?)" (*The Ringer*, 2019), Kate Knibbs wrote something similar, admitting that she's sick of what she describes as Swift's "innocent victim" act.

To some, the West feud included an ugly racial element as well—with Swift "a little too comfortable painting herself as the victim of an angry black man."[7] The whole thing was, then, a sort of "racial melodrama."[8] But to Gannon, Swift's supposed victim complex was more "mean girl" than racist. As she wrote, Swift's feuds have a "distinct, inescapable adolescent stench." And she allegedly plays it all up for the press. Her general insult and diss in song are, then, evidence of "a transparent opportunist that will reignite a dormant feud to insert herself back into the headlines and hashtags."

Even more thoughtful articles took issue with Swift's defiant response to abuse but for different reasons. Leah Donnella, writing for NPR, called Swift the twenty-first century's "most disorienting pop star," crediting the label to Swift's use of insult in her songs, a tool Donnella called a rap strategy. According to Donnella, Swift is too privileged, too white, to make diss work for her: "To take on the stylistic elements of that narrative without being situated in the same reality is both brilliant and, at times, deeply unsettling." Although the "disorienting" charge makes some sense to me, given rap's history, Donnella's reasoning doesn't cover the issue entirely.

Plenty of insults are included in the music of plenty of other non-rap artists, such as Bob Dylan and Frank Zappa. Both are considered musical geniuses, powerful and clever. They certainly haven't been saddled with the same "disorienting" charge. Even the Beatles went after each other. In a song aimed at Paul McCartney post-Beatles break-up, "How Do You

Sleep?" John Lennon sang, "The only thing you done was yesterday / And since you've gone you're just another day." Male artists have also addressed failed romances without pushback—even high-profile romances. On *Medium* in 2018, Kelsey Knoploh singled out the Weeknd's album *My Dear Melancholy*, a response to his breakup with Selena Gomez. She rightly noted that "even when people found alleged references to Gomez, they did not call him desperate or clingy." He was actually praised for his "depth of emotion." Meanwhile, Swift is just "boy crazy," catty, opportunistic, and "disorienting." And that reaction begs the question: Why? Men can insult in song or call out the misdeeds of others. Why can't Swift? Was she just supposed to accept her toxic labeling and mistreatment without voicing objection or fighting back?

Women in music risk censor by standing out and standing up. And if they don't always take the high road, instead calling out their abusers in song, apparently the toxic labels will just keep coming, even multiply. To be sure, it's a public and musical realization of Manne's "catch-22," cycling without end. Swift's public stands, in online posts and diss songs, incite the counterattack. She asserts her power through insult, playing against traditional gender norms, and so she's punished, her power stripped. Swift displays strength, in her career and music, and is censored, shamed as a snake in order to enforce behavior customarily accepted and expected of women. It doesn't matter that other people attacked her. Apparently, she still has no right to break with supposed rules assigned women. And when she does, often calling out the bad behavior and misogyny in song—with reference to snakes and witches—she is further punished in gendered ways. She can try to avoid the public shaming, but as she explained in *Miss Americana*, she'll then just get criticized for that attempt, shamed for strategizing.

NO SCOOTERS

Swift continues to be a target with her rerecording of her early music, the creation of a second set of masters. In her original contract, which she signed with Borchetta when she was just fifteen, she gave up the copyright to her initial recordings. But she writes her own songs, which gives her ownership of the music itself. And the period of time in her contract that forbids rerecording has ended. Though she is legally allowed to rerecord, her decision to do so is still exceptional. In truth, she is not the first to make that move. In the article "Why Swift's Rerecording Her Old Songs," the *Washington Post* identifies Joanna "JoJo" Levesque as an artist who made the same decision earlier, after her past label, Blackground Records, removed her music from streaming services, ostensibly holding her music "hostage." But the move is not the norm. And, with Swift's superstar status, the plan was sure to attract attention, especially given the connection once again to West.

With their original deal, Borchetta and his label had thrived alongside Swift's success. In 2017, her six-album contract with Borchetta ended, and she left the label. In the summer of 2019, Borchetta sold his label and, along with it, the masters of Swift's catalog, for $300 million to Scooter Braun, someone Swift hates and someone she purports Borchetta knows she hates. Shortly thereafter, on Tumblr, Swift called Braun a bully: "Any time Scott Borchetta has heard the words 'Scooter Braun' escape my lips, it was when I was either crying or trying not to. He knew what he was doing; they both did. Controlling a woman who didn't want to be associated with them." Of Braun, she wrote, "All I could think about was the incessant, manipulative bullying I've received at his hand for years." "Essentially, my musical legacy is about to lie in the hands of someone who tried to dismantle it," she explained.

Braun is one of the most powerful music executives, with a team of high-profile stars including Justin Bieber, Sheryl Crow, and Ariana Grande (though Grande has left). He has also managed Kanye West. Braun's "manipulative bullying," Swift made clear, had to do with his work with West, in particular the rapper's 2016 song "Famous."

In a blog post on his label's website, Borchetta responded to Swift's upset, beginning, "So, it's time for some truth . . ." He continued, "Taylor had every chance in the world to own not just her master recordings, but every video, photograph, everything associated to her career." "As to her comments about 'being in tears or close to it' anytime my new partner Scooter Braun's name was brought up," he added, "I certainly never experienced that."

This questioning of Swift's honesty—a sentiment built into the snake tag—as well as the divided response to her own insults in her music are both reactions related to gender. Swift herself seems well aware of gender inequality more generally. Not only does she address the misdeeds of specific people in her music, she also at times highlights this gender imbalance in her work. In a 2019 song, "You Need to Calm Down" from her album *Lover*, Swift responds to her haters. Confronting the line "You need to calm down," a phrase often used to silence or dismiss women, she sings, "And snakes and stones never broke my bones." On the same album, she gets at the issue more directly, imagining how she would be treated if she were a man. In the song "The Man," she sings, "And I'm so sick of them / Coming at me again / 'Cause if I was a man / Then I'd be the man." Despite the subject matter, the music doesn't have the same dark energy as "Look What You Made Me Do" or "I Did Something Bad." Instead, it's an upbeat fantasy with bounce: "When everyone believes you / What's that like?" In the video, released in early 2020, Swift appears as a man, voiced by the muscular actor Dwayne "The Rock" Johnson. In one scene, a "No Scooters" sign is visible; in another, Swift's man manspreads on the subway.

I would guess, then, that she recognizes the ways this gendered system has impacted her own reception. As she explained in a 2019 *Rolling Stone* interview, she's in a "mockery echo chamber," a public opinion trap. "People had so much fun hating me," she continued, "And I couldn't figure out how to learn from it. Because I wasn't sure exactly what I did that was so wrong." In *Miss Americana*, she remembers her beginnings as a star, when all she had wanted was approval, to be the "good girl." But in no way could she be both the good girl and stand up for herself. And there seems to be no solution still. Even Swift's rerecording has been viewed in a negative light. In the *New Yorker* on November 29, 2021, Carrie Battan described this effort as "the kind of emotional gesture that Swift lives for: a counterpunch designed to punish her transgressors while fortifying her legacy." She's that "mean girl" once more.

THE MAKING OF MEDUSA

Men generally can insult and feud in music without the pushback women experience. The diss songs written or performed by men and their own public beefs can seem celebratory and fun, "boys will be boys." But for women, insults make matters worse, stones hurled that bolster walls women must already confront in music. And those stones are gender specific— bitch, witch, snake. It becomes clear that some groups of people have greater authority already, permission to insult without consequence. And through that insult, they can further maintain their authority, their social ranking above other people. Women simply don't have that level of authority, not even privileged white women such as Swift. That right, apparently, still is reserved for men—some men more than others, because race, sexual orientation, and gender identity remain significant factors for them as well.

So, what's Swift to do? What are women in music to do? To some, the answer is clear: take the high road. How many times have I heard this phrase or Michelle Obama's powerful version, "when they go low, we go high"? Certainly, the high road is the noble choice. But, still, I have to write: Why should women *have* to take the high road? Sometimes, I, for one, would like to wallow in the unfairness of it all. Then I would like at least the option of getting away with the low road, the way some men do. That choice seems all the more important when women are taken to task for saying or doing anything at all, no specific words or deeds necessary. It's one more double standard in the path before women in music—a double standard in the very authority to take action or level toxic labels in the first place.

In that double standard is yet another warning. Don't fight back, even if the world around you has forced you to consider fighting. Hide yourself. Do nothing. The story of Medusa, with her snakelike hair, seems particularly apt in the telling of Swift's story and this lesson. I wasn't fully aware of the specifics of this Greek myth until my eight-year-old son, reading a children's book about mythology, told me that Medusa wasn't always a monster. In his version of the story, Athena was jealous of Medusa's beauty and, for that reason, turned her into a monster.

In other versions, including the Roman poet Ovid's description in the *Metamorphoses*, the sea god Poseidon raped Medusa in the temple of Athena when she was just a young maiden. Athena, angry about Poseidon's desecration of her temple, then punished Medusa by turning her into the dangerous femme fatale of monster lore. That's right, Athena punished Medusa for Poseidon's violence. Once again, the world around the woman made her into a problem—a mad woman, or, in this case, a monster. And it was the world around Swift that turned her into a snake. Like Medusa, she was depicted as the one in the wrong. His role in the story never mattered.

Medusa, for being the monster that Poseidon and Athena had turned her into, would be killed, decapitated by another male character, the demigod Perseus. Then, in popular tellings, Perseus would use her severed head for his own gain, transforming his enemies into stone through her corpse gaze. That image, of the victorious man holding Medusa's head, has been used, too, by artists such as Caravaggio and Cellini, and in pictures of powerful men in political power, such as Trump, with female adversaries portrayed as the Medusa figure, including Angela Merkel, Theresa May, and Hillary Clinton.[9] As Jess Zimmerman makes clear in *Women and Other Monsters*, women are demonized over and over again as monsters when they deviate from a standard and accepted model. Women are killed over and over again in order to demonstrate the power of men. And so, Swift, a modern Medusa, probably will keep encountering her punishment, though the crime itself was never hers.

7

KESHA SEBERT VERSUS DR. LUKE

Romantic connection is obviously used in the toxic labeling of women in music. Women involved with male musicians can be muses, or unwelcome interruptions, or something much worse. Whatever she is, it's all about the man and his creative genius. The male partner may even be credited with the success of his partner, as was the case with Love. Some of the women who have avoided similar labeling, at least in connection with their romantic pursuits, have shrewdly hidden that part of their lives. Hip-hop icon Missy Elliott, for example, has remained relatively beloved for well over two decades. In 2019, she earned an MTV Video Vanguard Award, marking her longevity and influence. I suspect that it's no coincidence that she also refuses to discuss her personal life. True, twigs tried this strategy, but Pattinson's star status was simply no match for her silence. In Elliott's contrasting case, journalist Rachel Kadzi Ghanash writes in *Elle*, "Her refusal to discuss her personal life has allowed her to deftly deflect any inquiries about her real life toward her surreal life," the one she inhabits in her music and videos.[1]

Another example is the country icon Dolly Parton. She, too, has remained beloved, even while straddling competing identities and perspectives. As Emily Lordi writes in the *New York Times* (November 30, 2020), Parton is "country without being retrograde"; "feminine but not fragile"; "God-fearing and gay-loving"; and both "authentic and artificial." She, like Missy Elliott, also does not spotlight her romantic pursuits, and her partner has not attracted the spotlight with his own pursuits. She has been married practically her whole life to a man named Carl Dean, who rarely appears publicly, let alone by her side. And again, I imagine her long-standing positive reception and the limited attention paid her husband are in part related.

But it isn't just romantic relationships with men that factor into the labeling of women in music. Non-romantic relationships can, too. Kanye West, for example, took credit for Swift's fame. And Swift's word was discounted by both West and Borchetta—she was then supposedly a "snake." In the case of Kesha Rose Sebert, known professionally as Kesha, it was her producer, Dr. Luke, real name Lukasz Gottwald, who was credited with her success. And that narrative exists even though he's still actively trying to destroy her.

THE MAN BEHIND THE WOMAN

Musician Lily Allen recognized the pattern—the regular mention of a man as the reason for a woman's success, whether or not the man claims credit. In 2014, she told *NME* that "of those big successful female artists, there is always a 'man behind the woman' piece." Whitney Houston, for example, was famously tied to producer and A&R executive Clive Davis. By some, she was thought of as "a mere vessel" for his genius.[2] For Allen? In her own words, "It was [songwriter and producer] Mark Ronson and the same with Amy Winehouse." In the article "The Disturbing Trend in How We Talk about Female Musicians," Natalie Morin concludes, "Our culture considers female musicians only as strong as the men who support them, and that's a huge problem."

The desired message is potentially veiled: a woman can't possibly succeed on her own. She couldn't be a genius. And it's horribly insulting, as Houston herself made clear: "I don't like it when they see me as this little person who doesn't know what to do with herself—like I have no idea what I want, like I'm just a puppet and Clive's got the strings. That's bullshit. That's demeaning to me, because that ain't how it is, and it never was."[3]

But there is another lesson: a woman *shouldn't* be allowed to succeed on her own. The standard narrative reflects a societal problem with women standing alone on stage, independent and powerful. Media sources respond, stepping in to remedy the issue by boxing up these women in more palatable packages of two. And women themselves may seek out and rely on a partnership they do not need. Along these lines is an additional concern. What if that man, connected to that woman, does *not* support her? What if that man receives the credit while undermining her, manipulating her, or even abusing her?

In the book *Can Music Make You Sick?*, authors Sally Anne Gross and George Musgrave identify a potential danger in the manager-musician relationship. They interviewed a female singer-songwriter, identified only as "M," who told them, "Having a manager who I'm employing in a way but is technically sort of in charge of me; basically, calling the shots to some degree . . . the dynamic is that he knows more about the industry and he is the one liaising with all the other people and I'm just hearing it filtered back through him, so he's got this sort of overarching control and I'm just sort of subservient to that to some extent." Another musician, "F," suspects that those managers interested in taking advantage of this power structure might specifically target younger women in music: "I think this is why they love young artists, because there's a level of manipulation and control that they love. And that's why most female artists over 25, no one's bothered. Like 'Oh no, no, you're just a bit too old.' What? No: that's because you can't tell me what you want . . . me to do. You don't have that power and control."[4]

A similar dynamic can exist in the producer-musician relationship, especially when musicians sign deals with producers and labels potentially spanning decades. In the case of Kesha, that's precisely what happened. Though Gottwald supposedly made Sebert famous, he's also the reason she was branded by some a "liar." And no cute snake emojis were involved in that labeling. The "liar" charge was explicit, and at court, it was legally binding. Sebert has remained bound to Gottwald, with no way out of her contract with him, despite her attempts at court. And in her case, he was more than controlling; he's also her alleged rapist. The legal system has not only failed to help Kesha; it has actively participated in labeling her, blaming her, and justifying Gottwald's continued power over her and her music. With a history of cultural suspicion around women, Sebert's experience with the legal system is sadly somewhat standard in cases of sexual abuse and rape. Her fame and relative privilege, in this case, could not protect her. If anything, her spotlight fueled his aggressive defense as well as his ongoing offense.

LIAR

Long-held beliefs position the woman as suspect and the man as something more. Even when confronted with evidence to the contrary, men and some women tend to avoid the reality of women's accusations to protect a certain positive picture either of themselves or men in general. It's a sympathy extended only to men—in Manne's wording, a "himpathy." In "Why Don't 'Good Men' Believe Women?" Soraya Chemaly confirms, "Denying that sexual harassment and assault are part and parcel of so many women's daily lives is a form of identity protective cognition—a documented phenomenon in which individuals who encounter new information that is inconsistent with their beliefs and cultural identity tend to dismiss or diminish that information."

For those willing, able, or forced to accept the realities of rape—with studies showing, according to Sweeny, that roughly 14.8 percent of women in the United States have survived rape or attempted rape, though only about 30 percent of cases are reported—societal pressure to stay silent can still be tremendous. Even renowned psychologist Sigmund Freud, for this reason, found himself unable to fully embrace the reality of sexual abuse. He almost did, with the publication of his *Studien über Hysterie*, which blamed men and their widespread sexual abuse of women for victims' bouts of hysteria. But, after its publication, his peers and colleagues mocked him. "I am as isolated as you could wish me to be," he wrote to a friend. In response, he changed course, insisting the abuse never happened—the women were liars. Their testimony, he reasoned, must have been "only fantasies that my patients had made up."[5] Even an expert on human psychology, then, gave in to the bias and his own desire for self-preservation.

With the case already stacked against women, the burden of proof at court falls heavily on the shoulders of victims. Evidence is often dissected in ways that both retraumatize the victim and skew unfairly in the man's favor. What was she wearing? What was she drinking? His clothes and his beverage consumption are immaterial. Author Julia Serano notes this unequal distribution of trust, writing in "He's Unmarked, She's Marked," "people will tend to trust his side of the story because (by virtue of his being a man) his account will seem unquestionable to them."[6] It doesn't matter that the rates of false reports about sexual violence are so small, roughly 2 percent.[7]

It also doesn't matter that in the era of #MeToo, women who outed an abuser were often trashed as liars when they, in fact, had much to lose in even asserting their truth. The testimony of Christine Blasey Ford and its aftermath, including the confirmation of her victimizer, then Supreme Court nominee Brett M. Kavanaugh, is a case in point. Related public ridicule only supports victims' self-silencing.[8]

In Sebert's case, she would be presumed guilty, dubbed a liar, as the abuser was assumed innocent. The court system protected a presumption of innocence at the expense of the victim. For Sebert, even a simple exit from her contract with Gottwald was impossible legally. Gottwald deserved his control, the court seemed to suggest. After all, as his lawyer made clear, she was "no one" before him—the values around partnerships in music here justifying that dismissive thinking. She needed him. She owed him. It was the sentiment in West's song "Famous" backed up by the law. But it did more than negate Sebert's value. It also helped hide Gottwald's abuse. The toxic bias in the coverage of women in music, in this case, had legal ramifications, adding to the burden of proof already heaped upon victims of rape, even when they're the lucky ones—stars seemingly on top of the world but, instead, living an American nightmare.

"THE PARTY DON'T STOP"

At age eighteen, in September 2005, Kesha signed with Gottwald. And Gottwald convinced her to move from Nashville to Los Angeles to begin their work together. The contract terms covered six albums, to be recorded and published with Kasz Money and Prescription Songs, though, in 2011, Gottwald would cofound Kemosabe, a Sony imprint, and Kesha's contract would transfer to that label. Just a month after she signed with Gottwald, the two went together to a party at Nicky and Paris Hilton's Hollywood home (Kesha had appeared briefly on Paris's show *The Simple Life*).

At the party, as Sebert would reveal in her lawsuit, Gottwald gave her something he called "sober pills." According to the *Vulture* article "The Complete History of Kesha's Legal Fight against Dr. Luke," which relies

on both Sebert's lawsuit and the account of her mother, Gottwald then took
Kesha back to his hotel room, where he "raped her while she was uncon-
scious." When she woke up the next morning, naked in the hotel room and
feeling strange, Sebert called her mother, Pebe Sebert, a songwriter herself: "Mom, I don't know where I am. I think we had sex. I'm sore and sick.
I don't know where my clothes are. I think I need to go to the hospital."
Sebert did not then file a report, though she suspected that the "sober pills"
were the date-rape drug GHB. She had explained to her mom, "I don't
want to be a rape-case victim. I just want to get my music out."

The following year, Sebert tried to work with another manager—with
DAS Communications—who attempted to find her work independent
of Gottwald. But she had no easy way out of her contract with Gottwald,
though the two had yet to produce anything of substance at that point.
During the first four years of her contract with Gottwald, she would instead
write songs for other singers. But then she had her first hit as a singer in
2009, when she made an appearance in the studio during Flo Rida's recording session. He was working on the song "Right Round," a song cowritten
and produced by Gottwald, and the rapper realized he needed a female
voice in the song. Her participation was something of an accident, and
Kesha is still uncredited on the track in most versions.

After that song, Sebert quickly found herself center stage with her debut
single, "Tik Tok," a song that was absolutely everywhere in 2009. The song
defined her as fun—the "party don't stop"—and, in pop culture, she was
suddenly the ultimate party girl who brushed "her teeth with a bottle of
Jack." Kesha has since revealed that the song was supposed to be somewhat
ironic, like the Beastie Boys' "(You Gotta) Fight for Your Right (to Party),"
but she was encouraged (maybe even pressured) to lean into the image
of the reckless, good-time goddess. In a 2016 interview in the *New York
Times*, she explained to writer Taffy Brodesser-Akner that Gottwald told
her at the time, "Make it more dumb. Make it more stupid."

She readily admitted that she does enjoy a night out but insisted that
that aspect of her personality is not all she is or all she wants to be. At
the same time, she was surprised by reactions to that song—by those who
condemned her for her party-girl image. Though it wasn't the image she
necessarily wanted, she still felt that she should be allowed to inhabit that
character without censure. After all, many men have sung about partying
and drinking without similar repercussions. She told Brodesser-Akner, "I

am allowed to do, and say, and participate in all the activities that men can do, and they get celebrated for it. And women get chastised for it."

Even with criticism, Kesha had arrived. Her first album, *Animal*, took the No. 1 spot in January 2010. She had finally achieved a version of the success she had been chasing. Behind the scenes, however, Sebert was struggling. In 2013, after the release of *Animal* as well as her second album *Warrior*, the press started to report on some sort of tension between Sebert and Gottwald. But the extent of the issue remained secret publicly. In a glowing profile of Dr. Luke in the *New Yorker*, journalist John Seabrook clearly sided with Gottwald when he broached the subject of his relationship with Sebert, noting that "now that her pop-star dreams had come true she was proving hard to control."

Frankly, that sentiment is stomach turning, with or without knowledge of the assault. The assumption built into Seabrook's statement is that Dr. Luke was supposed to control Sebert. And, if he couldn't, that was a problem, with Sebert the one to blame. Seabrook finished his discussion of Kesha by explaining, "When I asked Gottwald what was up with Kesha . . . he shrugged and said, 'I haven't heard from her in a while.'" Seabrook didn't follow up by asking, Why not? What had Gottwald done? Instead, the relationship was strained because something "was up with Kesha." Enough said.

Part of the public narrative around Gottwald and Sebert's relationship at the time centered on Kesha's song "Die Young," which had been released as the first single from *Warrior* in the fall of 2012. On December 14, 2012, a shooter would kill twenty-six people, including twenty young children, at Sandy Hook Elementary School. Kesha's song, with lyrics about partying hard "like we're gonna die young," was pulled from radio stations shortly thereafter. Sebert responded on Twitter, voicing her own earlier concerns about the song's message: "I understand. I had my very own issue with 'die young' for this reason. I did NOT want to sing those lyrics and I was FORCED TO." She also apologized, "I'm so so sorry for anyone who has been effected by this tragedy and I understand why my song is now inappropriate. Words cannot express." Reviewing the "Die Young" controversy, Seabrook added in his profile, "Kesha had previously claimed to have written the lyrics by herself." She was already cast as a liar, and that was before the full extent of her issues with Gottwald would come to light. The night of the Hiltons' party was resurfacing; the party really hadn't stopped.

"WARRIOR"

In January 2014, Sebert checked into rehab, hoping to treat an eating disorder. Her mother publicly blamed Gottwald, explaining in an interview that he berated Kesha for her weight. At the rehab facility, Sebert also told doctors about the 2005 assault as well as subsequent sexual and physical abuse she suffered in her dealings with Gottwald. She then filed a California lawsuit against Gottwald on October 14, 2014. Although she detailed the abuse and assault, she did not file criminal charges. She simply wanted to be released from her contract. The following year, at Gottwald's request, that lawsuit was blocked on a technicality. According to the terms of Kesha's contract, all legal disputes were to be settled in New York, not California. Also on October 14, 2014, Gottwald filed a countersuit in New York, denying Sebert's allegations and claiming defamation. His suit was dismissed, again based on jurisdiction.

In September 2015, Sebert tried once more, filing an emergency preliminary injunction in New York. Again, her only goal was release from her contract. The injunction, readily available in its entirety on scribd.com, would be a heartbreaking loss for Sebert. But the case gained national attention and became the basis for the #FreeKesha movement, another rallying cry meant to uplift a female singer shackled by the forces around her, including the legal system. In Spears's case, those forces were tied to her father. The legal system in that case seemed apathetic at best and broken at worst. But reading the court transcript of Sebert's injunction, just under one hundred pages long, I was struck by the court's language—the court's participation in the caging of Sebert.

During the hearing regarding Sebert's injunction, Judge Shirley Werner Kornreich spoke directly with the legal teams representing both sides, Sebert and Gottwald. Attorney Tina Glandian, representing Sebert, outlined for the court Gottwald's abusive "course of conduct," which in addition to sexual assault involved dominance and control, often through name calling. After the judge asked for specifics, Glandian stated, "He would tell her, 'You're not going to—it doesn't matter what lyrics you want, I'm going to say what goes in . . . you're not that pretty, you're not that special, there's a million girls out there.'"

Other artists have since confirmed similar behavior. Singer Kelly Clarkson, who had worked with him on the song "Since U Been Gone," one of her early successes, has made it clear that Gottwald is "not a good guy." She would also say, for the court record (in a deposition related to later litigation between Sebert and Gottwald), "People have said he is belittling, the same kind of things that I say. He is very, I mean, just to be blunt, he can be kind of a bully and demeaning. I don't like him as a person."

Pink, responding to Sebert's allegations against Gottwald, echoed the sentiment: "I know that regardless of whether or not Dr. Luke did that, this is his karma and he earned it because he's not a good person." Even the positive *New Yorker* profile hints at Gottwald's problematic personality. Of course, that ugliness is described as a positive, in a sort of manly framing of creative genius. The article cites a friend from Gottwald's student days at the Manhattan School of Music: "The thing that made Luke hilarious back then, apart from the pot smoking, was that he was completely arrogant." Related hilarity ensued when Luke tried out for the *SNL* band. He walked in and said, "You can stop the auditions right now"—totally "hilarious," said musician Lenny Pickett, overseeing tryouts that day. That sort of brash overconfidence, which some embraced, might not have endeared him to everyone in the band once he was, in fact, given the job. "I think I was fired five times," bragged Gottwald. And let's not forget that he would give himself the honorary title "Dr.," a move I can't quite picture a woman getting away with in the same way. In these ways, Gottwald fits a certain image of masculinity in the arts—arrogant and self-important—one that has excused aggression and sexual entitlement while helping others spin both as "valued expressions" of manliness.[9]

During the hearing, the judge found her own way to counter any indictment of Gottwald's behavior: "If you're saying he told her she was heavy or he called her fat, I'm not sure what your allegation is, because it's not clear from the record or when it happened, but they have a business relationship. I don't know what the standards are, I don't know why it was said, I don't know how it was said." She then added, "What I'm trying to say is that this was a business relationship and, in fact, he did have control of her—her career because of the contracts in place." The court's understanding of a business relationship is unsettling. Apparently, a business contract could entitle Gottwald to control and manipulate Sebert, sometimes through abusive language. In this relationship, the court seemed to accept Sebert as less valuable than Gottwald. He could do as he wished; she could not. And she had no recourse because they had a contract.

When it was the opposing side's turn, attorney Christine Lepera, representing Gottwald, found it necessary to state, for the record, that "when Kesha was discovered by my client she was no one." The implication was that Gottwald was responsible for Kesha's fame—the false narrative of so many men connected to talented women—but also that she should be grateful, despite his purported bad behavior. In a way, she was still no one or, at least, could be treated as such. Although the judge would call out attorneys when their discussion seemed to wander off topic, this observation, which Lepera offered, was accepted without objection. The conventional thinking about women in partnerships justified the unnecessary dig. And a site of supposed justice sanctioned the double standard without comment.

Attorney Mark Geragos, also representing Sebert, tried to cut through the bias around Gottwald's importance to make a basic argument: that Sebert would suffer "irreparable harm" if she remained in her current contract with Gottwald because she could not work with him, given the abuse. Something had to be done, and fast, because "she has, as most pop recording artists do, a very slim window within which to perform." Ageism was here a recognized music industry truth, highlighted to encourage a quick contract end. But the judge countered, highlighting Sony's offer to have her record without Gottwald's involvement. Geragos insisted that that was "an illusory promise" and voiced skepticism that Sony, with its allegiance to Gottwald, would promote Sebert. Again, the judge's understanding of routine business standards would not allow her to follow Geragos's logic. She insisted that "a business like Sony will do what is in its best interest." These are "business people," she maintained.

The court also voiced some doubt about the veracity of Sebert's abuse claims. The judge noted, "There is not one piece of paper from a doctor saying this." The onus was clearly on Sebert and her legal team to prove that she was not lying, whereas Gottwald was assumed credible.

With the judge's understanding of a business relationship and skepticism around Sebert's abuse claims, the court on February 19, 2016, ultimately ruled that "there has been no showing of irreparable harm." Pictures of Sebert in the courtroom that day show her crying. She had no hope with this injunction of convicting Gottwald. All she wanted was the end of her legal tie to him, her contract. As Stacy Malone, executive director of the Victim Rights Law Center, writes, "each sexual assault victim defines justice differently."[10] With a 2.8 percent national conviction and incarceration rate

for rapists, victims in some ways have to find and pursue their own definitions of justice. But Sebert's limited version of justice was still denied. She
would have to push forward tied to Gottwald, as her song's titular "warrior":
"Love us or hate us, nothin' can break us."

"PRAYING"

Sebert, with her notoriety and privilege, had some advantage over other victims. But wider issues of societal misogyny still clearly affected her case. She
was inevitably treated as a liar. In the days following the injunction, Gottwald
would accuse Sebert on Twitter of lying because she was "motivated by
money." His supporters would also point to video footage that surfaced
shortly after the injunction—footage that shows Sebert in 2011 denying the
rape. The video was part of a lawsuit involving DAS Communications. The
company had sued both Sebert and Gottwald, accusing Gottwald of pressur-
ing Sebert to cut ties with them. Geragos explained the video, insisting that
Gottwald had "threatened to destroy Kesha's life and the lives of her family
if she didn't cover up her sexual assaults in a 2011 deposition."

Meanwhile, Sebert would remain committed to her primary aim—to get
out of her business relationship with Gottwald. Right after the injunction
loss, in a letter to her fans, she would respond to Gottwald's claim that she
was just trying to renegotiate that contract by reasserting her aim: "This
case has never been about a renegotiation of my record contract—it was
never about getting a bigger, or a better deal. This is about being free from
my abuser." But the legal system couldn't even give her that. In the *Rutgers
University Law Review*, Erin Hodgson noted in 2018 that Sebert's case
highlights a problem in the legal system—no contractual remedy is available when "the breach is a traumatizing act of sexual violence." And Sebert
wouldn't accept an out if it meant accepting the label "liar." On Instagram
in April 2016, Sebert revealed that Gottwald offered to release her from her
contract if she renounced her accusations against him (a spokesperson for
Gottwald called her post a "publicity stunt"). His terms didn't match her
understanding of justice either, so she remained trapped in her contract.
She remains so as of this writing.

Amid mounting court losses—including a counterclaim of abuse that was
thrown out, with a judge stating that Sebert was acting "unreasonably"—Sebert

was able to focus in 2016 on performing and delivering new music. Just as Geragos warned, however, attempts were made to block these efforts. When Sebert wanted to perform at the Billboard Music Awards, Gottwald tried to keep her from appearing on stage. She was able to perform, in the end, but she was prohibited from mentioning Gottwald or the lawsuit. Still, Sebert found some support among other musical women.

In the week following the injunction loss in February 2016, musicians and celebrities spoke out on behalf of Sebert, including Adele and Lady Gaga. Swift also donated money—$250,000—to help pay Sebert's legal bills. Lady Gaga and Swift both had had their own experiences with abuse. In 2017, the world began to hear about the many, many other women who did, too, when actress Alyssa Milano asked women on Twitter to write "Me too" (a phrase that had originated with activist Tarana Burke a decade earlier). In 2018, Sebert was the face of music's "Me too" when she performed her new song, "Praying," at the Grammy's along with stars such as Cyndi Lauper, Bebe Rexha, Camila Cabello, and Andra Day—all supported by the Resistance Revival Chorus. Radically contrasting her party hit "Tik Tok," "Praying" is a plaintive ballad with piano accompaniment and sentimental string sound. In it, Kesha quietly sings, "Well, you almost had me fooled / Told me that I was nothing without you." She sings directly to her tormentor, holding him accountable for putting her "through hell." But then, in an ascending line, her voice grows in strength as she insists "now the best is yet to come." The song is hopeful, brimming with renewed power and a desire for rebirth in repeated emphasis on the words "praying" and "changing." Introducing Kesha, Janelle Monáe said, "We . . . have the power to undo the culture that does not serve us well." And that culture, still today, protects the music industry's musical monsters.

MUSICAL MONSTERS

In the context of abuse and trauma, the music industry, like everyone else, tends to protect its men while viewing its women with mistrust. The proof is everywhere. In 2009, even singer Rihanna would be seen by some as suspicious, though R&B singer Chris Brown would openly admit he assaulted her. To be fair, he couldn't really deny it when photos appeared of Rihanna with bruises on her face and a swollen lip. But, after the abuse,

Brown found a different reason to call Rihanna a liar. He had made an apology song, "Changed Man," insisting he had played it for Rihanna. She, however, denied hearing the track. He told ABC News's Robin Roberts, "I played the song for her . . . the day I did it . . . a month after the situation. She called when she first heard the song. And I mean, I'm not trying to say—call her any liar or anything like that. But I played the song for her when I first wrote it. And she cried." He wasn't calling her a liar, but she had lied, he insisted.

It was the same trick construction that Slim Thug had used. *I'm not saying what I am, in fact, saying.* Most egregiously, on ABC Brown was given a platform to play the victim while he was, in fact, the victimizer, casually referencing his abuse as "the situation." And the media aided and abetted him. The musical world also stood by him, with Brown still performing, even as new assaults made headlines. After his light sentence for assaulting Rihanna, he was accused of attacking fans as well as other girlfriends, including his ex, Karrueche Tran. In 2019, he was also accused of rape in Paris. And he's not the only high-profile musical man who performs while criminally monstrous.

R. Kelly, of course, continued in the music industry for decades despite the many disturbing charges against him, including rape and kidnapping. He was finally found guilty in a court of law in 2021. But even then, he was depicted as a victim in a headline in the *Chicago Tribune*: "R. Kelly Was on Suicide Watch after Conviction in New York" (October 20, 2021).

Metal's Marilyn Manson performed in music for decades, too, operating as a "monster hiding in plain sight," according to a *Rolling Stone* article documenting his many sick sexual assaults (November 14, 2021). Earlier, producer Phil Spector similarly worked, producing songs for the Beatles among other high-profile acts. And he did so while abusing the women around him, including his onetime wife, Ronnie, of the girl group the Ronnettes. In 2003, he would be convicted of murdering actress Lana Clarkson. When he died in 2021, the BBC initially tweeted, "Talented but flawed Producer Phil Spector dies aged 81."

Notions of male creative genius clearly contribute to the problem. How many movies have depicted a difficult, obnoxious man as a winning creative force? The trope is so prevalent that audiences get the distinct impression that a man must be terrible in order to create real art. It's a winning cover. He is not a sadistic monster; he's awful because he's a creative genius. A woman in music would never benefit from a similar conclusion. And when the woman has to face one of these so-called musical geniuses, the associated cultural capital is one more obstacle in her way. She must be the liar because he cannot be in the wrong. And if he was aggressive, it's all due to his genius. Men are almost encouraged and rewarded for their bad behavior whereas women can't make a false move or expect a basic level of protection when they are, in fact, the victims of these men. As Robyn Autry wrote in 2018, the music industry has "arguably lagged behind Hollywood and other entertainment industries in terms of #MeToo accountability."[11] The lag is due, in part, to societal thinking around music and women, supported and propelled by the labels we use—liar for women and genius for men.

"HIGH ROAD"

After Sebert's court loss, Gottwald was not content with his win and began his own legal campaign against her. Based on his personality, the offensive move makes some sense. He needed to both control Sebert and punish her. Really, the counter-maneuver supports characterizations of Gottwald as bullying and manipulative. But cultural values around genius surely encouraged him, too. He was entitled to abusive behavior and full vindication for that behavior, even though, like Brown, he was able to continue to work in the music industry despite Sebert's claims (in the immediate aftermath of the high-profile injunction in 2016, Gottwald would work under other names, such as Made in China, Tyson Trax, and Loctor Duke).

In that litigation, he would continue to insist that Sebert was a liar, relying on evidence that did not account for a trauma response—all of which may have played a part in that 2011 video for the DAS Communications lawsuit as well as a birthday card from Sebert that Gottwald would try to introduce as exonerating evidence. The thrust of his case was an argument that both Sebert and her mom defamed him. The basis for this claim included a private text exchange between Sebert and Lady Gaga, real name Stefani Germanotta, in which the women discuss their belief that Gottwald had also raped singer Katy Perry. According to the women, a music executive had told both Germanotta and Sebert about the alleged assault.

The court transcript, especially Germanotta's deposition in September 2017, again reveals the tremendous burden on the victim in cases like these.

In one of the many ugly exchanges with Gottwald's lawyer Lepera, Germanotta described what she knew about Sebert's 2005 rape claim. Lepera asked her if Sebert "was drinking" that night. Germanotta made it clear that her opinion of Sebert's claim "was formed based on the fact that I had seen Kesha in Luke's studio in her underwear when she was young, and I was there." Lepera wondered why Germanotta would believe a rape claim if she had not seen the rape itself, asking her, "You think there has never been a false accusation of rape?" Germanotta countered: "How about all of the women that are accused of being liars and how she was slut shamed in front of the world, how about this?" In another tense exchange, Germanotta asked Lepera, "Why on earth would this girl tell the entire world that this happened? Why on earth?" She continued, "Do you know what it's like for survivors? Do you know what it's like to tell people?" The transcript does not describe Lepera's facial expression, but Lepera clearly reacted dismissively. Admonishing Lepera, Germanotta responded: "Don't you role [sic] your eyes at me. You should be ashamed of yourself."

Despite Germanotta's impassioned testimony, in February 2020 Sebert was found guilty of defaming Gottwald. Perry denied the rape; and that music executive, named in the deposition "Mr. Janick," denied telling Sebert and Germanotta about a rape. Again, Sebert was the liar, and this time Germanotta was, too. And it didn't matter that the conversation about the alleged rape was only made public after Gottwald subpoenaed Sebert and Germanotta's private text messages. Once again, the legal system supported Gottwald and his claim. Though New York Supreme Court Judge Jennifer G. Schechter decided the texts were a "publication of a false statement," her decision, made at Gottwald's insistence, had created that publication by making a private rape accusation public. In short, the court system punished Sebert for its own actions.

Sebert and Gottwald would soon gear up for another courtroom showdown regarding the text exchange with Lady Gaga. Frankly, the legal back-and-forth is dizzying. Whatever the ultimate outcome, it's clear that Sebert's relationship with Gottwald has defined her in so many ways—as a liar, a party girl, a nobody—and it will continue to do so. For the most part, the legal system has participated in and sanctioned the name calling. Sebert challenges these labels with her music—music she continues to release under the contract she signed with Gottwald, though without his input as producer.

Her fourth album is aptly named *High Road*, though that title has a double meaning, with Kesha overcoming her past but also "high as hell." It's a return to some of the lightness of her first album but also an attempt to celebrate her independence. In the upbeat song "My Own Dance," Kesha sings with punctuated male "yeahs": "You're the party girl, you're the tragedy / But the funny thing is I'm fucking everything." Music critic Megan Buerger, writing for *Pitchfork*, finds the album "loaded with tension, like someone trying to portray freedom and free-spiritedness—even a recovered sense of identity—who isn't quite there yet." To me, that tension makes perfect sense. Sebert is wading through the complications of being herself in music when she isn't completely free. Under these circumstances, I don't know how she'd ever get "there"—unburdened and at peace.

It's also hard to imagine a scenario in which Sebert emerges in the public mind independent of Gottwald. Perhaps, for those that believe her, she will be a victim or survivor. But, whatever the position or label, she is still connected to Gottwald—if not an abuser (a big if), then clearly a jerk. I don't know what he was drinking or what he was wearing that night in 2005, but based on the testimony of other women who worked with him as well as the "hilarious" recollections of his boasting, Gottwald is not a nice person. I don't understand why he would keep Sebert locked into a contract she does not want for so long—after all of this—if he is in any way a decent individual.

In *The Atlantic* article "The Pop Music You Listen to Really Does Matter" (July 6, 2021), Spencer Kornhaber quotes an influential industry figure, "Luke's an asshole—everybody knows it." And the fact that he still has power—that he still works with other stars and young up-and-comers—is confirmation that the musical world has not yet confronted the realities of its power inequalities, its history of abuse, or the ways in which it supports its monsters. Meanwhile, Sebert has had to fight to get her music out. She has had to fight to be herself. She has had to fight to be seen as herself. And the difference in the effects of this "he said, she said" is yet another double standard confronting women in music.

The way Sebert has been treated is tragic but also a signal that the road ahead (within the law and not) for those without her privilege is even worse. The abuse can be as well. In 2013, Swift made that point when she accused radio DJ David Mueller of groping her during a photo op. The DJ was fired. He then sued Swift for millions in a civil case, claiming she falsely accused

him of assault and thus destroyed his career. Swift was forced to counter-
sue, maintaining that the assault did happen; she was not a liar. The very
public trial took place in August 2017. In a *Time* article, Swift explained
why she originally reported the incident to the DJ's then employer: "I
figured that if he would be brazen enough to assault me under these risky
circumstances and high stakes, imagine what he might do to a vulnerable,
young artist if given the chance." Swift won the case and was awarded a
symbolic one dollar, a dollar she has yet to collect.

Music is, indeed, about relationships—between the musician and the
music, between the musician and those who support the musician, and
between the musician and the other musicians involved. Those relationships can be transcendent or toxic. And, for women in music, those toxic
relationships can mark them with a label for life. The systems and structures
around these women may support that labeling. In the case of Sebert, the
court system helped create the label "liar." In the press and public opinion,
she's been marked by that label as well as others. As she sings in the song
"High Road," she's "that bitch you love to hate." Other women in music
similarly have been marked by abusive relationships, such as Rihanna. In an
interview in *Vanity Fair*, she recalled a 2014 incident when the NFL and
CBS chose not to use her song "Run This Town," with Jay-Z and West, in
light of the abuse she suffered and an abuse scandal involving NFL player
Ray Rice. She was, in Jay-Z's words, punished "for what happened with Ray
Rice." Rihanna realizes it's another label she cannot shake—victim—and
"the victim gets punished over and over."

Remarkably, Gottwald, working within the legal system, is still not satisfied. Apparently, he wants to punish Sebert completely. And the law affords
him the right to do so. Clearly, he can weather the continued association
with Sebert. He'll continue to work regardless, just as he has, unless big
changes are made in the music industry and supporting systems. And that
change, if it happens, must reckon with the language and thinking in and
around music—words such as "genius" and "liar"—but also the word "diva."
The music-specific label "diva" might seem less controversial than the other
insults or condemnations reviewed so far, but it, too, supports a gender bias,
one disguised this time by the fun of a larger-than-life singer with a voice
and personality to match.

8

IT'S MARIAH CAREY, DAHHHLING!

Although Gottwald has dealt with very little reputational fallout despite a rape charge, women can be harassed for absolutely anything, even rumors. Based on gossip that she requested sorted M&Ms and a supply of puppies backstage, Mariah Carey has long been labeled the ultimate "diva." In *Glamour* magazine (2006), television presenter Jamie Theakston took credit for starting the latter rumor: "When she performed on Top of the Pops we started a rumor she'd demanded puppies in her dressing room and it became instant Mariah folklore." Plenty of other moments are, of course, cited as evidence of Carey's diva-ness, including additional backstage demands, lateness, her glamorous self-care rituals and appearance, and, most especially, her MTV *Cribs'* episode in 2002. While watching the show more recently, I found Carey absolutely delightful—charming and funny. But some people didn't, or didn't in the same way. *Vibe* magazine (February 2003) described the episode as "painfully self-indulgent."

Sometimes the diva tag is assigned with less condemnation. It can be outwardly neutral or comically flippant—for example, in the various lists of the top divas (such as the 2009 list compiled by music-news.com, with Carey at number one). But to me, whether it's lobbed as serious criticism or a casual joke, the label has bite. And that bite once again is related to gender. In fact, it's hard not to notice that women dominate these diva listings. Surely, musical men make their own demands.[1] Surely, men in the spotlight have elaborate grooming routines, too. They're also definitely late—with Guns N' Roses and Kanye West both notoriously tardy. Why are men allowed these luxuries, or at least extended some benefit of the doubt, whereas women are labeled and penalized as divas?

As this chapter makes clear, in the "diva" label, the underlying thinking betrays yet another double standard in the treatment of women in music. Men, apparently, have legitimate reasons for specific requests whereas women are being "difficult" or "high-maintenance." Men can take care of themselves and act in their own self-interests; women can't, or shouldn't. Throughout her career, Carey has been subject to these double standards. And her labeling is a warning. Certain people—women, and especially Black women—simply can't reach beyond an accepted behavioral standard without public censure.

A SINGING GODDESS

The term "diva" is the most musical of the toxic labels covered in this book. Early use of the word diva during the nineteenth century was reserved for female singers alone, a gendered and music-specific put-down. But it ascribed to the operatic lead soprano a celebrity status beyond mere "prima donna." That's not to say the term prima donna was wholly neutral. Though it was initially rather impersonal in the seventeenth century, the label evolved in meaning, marking a female singer as "a self-important or temperamental person."[2]

That change coincided with the public appearance of female singers, who weren't allowed on the opera stage before the seventeenth century. During Italian opera's spread in popularity, the complete prohibition ended as the leading lady became a necessity. Still, various popes imposed various bans on women, limiting their access to the stage. Men could perform publicly, but most women then confined their singing to smaller chamber settings. Somehow a modest stage was more appropriate. In 1798, the last official limits were lifted.[3] But unofficial censoring took their place in the ways people talked about female singers. In Victorian England, the condemnation was linked to a violated expectation of womanly virtue. Women were expected to be modest, private, and subservient. A woman who pursued

a public singing career, whatever her general character, could not do so
without undermining her supposed ideal femininity. As a singer, she had to
watch out for herself and her career interests, and yet she was condemned
for that necessary self-protection. These singers were seen as rebellious,
seductive, and "marginally 'feminine.'"[4]

The sexualized view of female singers related to the display of the female
body on stage as well as the mysteries of vocal sound, something invisible
and sensual. The siren from Greek mythology supported the sexualization,
as did a link between the singer and the courtesan in preceding centuries, something played up recently on the Netflix show *Bridgerton*. In the
series's first episode, the unwed opera singer is seen having sex, despite the
rules constraining the other women in the series. And she does so outside,
in the open air. She's a loose woman of ill-repute but wholly unprotected.

The diva label overlaps these notions of the prima donna and amplifies
them, with many characteristics exaggerated. Generally, the association
was positive—her singing as a diva, for example, was divine. She was an
opera singer of "otherworldly vocal power and beauty."[5] But other associations were even more negative; her behavior was especially scandalous. By
the 1880s, the term also condemned female stars outside of opera—any
celebrity perceived as dramatic, assertive, or high-maintenance. As Tracy
C. Davis writes in "From Diva to Drama Queen," "These women are incon-
siderate as they claim dominion over others, no matter how great or inconsequential the realm." According to Oxford Languages Online, the diva is,
then, "a famous female singer" as well as any "self-important person who is
temperamental and difficult to please."

Reading between the lines, the diva was and is criticized for a certain
confidence—for knowing what she wants and going after it. Her sense of
self-worth may also translate into an investment in herself and her appearance, with carefully curated hair, nails, and clothes—all further fodder.[6] But
the condemnation is clearly a trap, especially in music. To be successful, a
female singer needs that confidence and related investment. It's another
no-win. Basically, by being a celebrity, the diva is violating lingering perceptions of women as caretakers and humble providers. The same sort of Victorian values work subtly through the label, damning a woman for simply
taking up space in music and on the stage.

Not all women in music attract this misogynistic labeling. But all women
performing in the spotlight are vulnerable to it. And then, with a perceived

misstep, one can be labeled as difficult when she is most likely doing what she has to do to be successful, often capitalizing on a remarkable talent. As Laura Miller and Rebecca Copeland write in *Diva Nation*, "divas are not born"; they are created from "the friction produced when female genius meets social stricture." For women, the initial bans on making music publicly may have ended, but similar social codes persist. With that, female singers are subject to lingering limitations and double standards around musical performance. Women, such as Carey, still aren't truly free to sing, caring for themselves and their careers as themselves. And the ongoing labeling of women as divas is their constant reminder and punishment.

SING SING

At times, Carey has uniquely played with her diva reputation, expertly turning it into a laugh. In the comedy *Popstar: Never Stop Never Stopping* (2016), she declares mock seriously, "I'm probably the most humble person that I know." But not everyone's in on the joke or what she's had to fight through to deliver that punchline.

Her career began when the CEO of Sony Music, Tommy Mottola, discovered her after hearing her tape in 1988. In quick succession, he signed and married her, despite a more than twenty-year age difference (the two divorced in 1998). Though Carey was then aware of ideas of her as "some sophisticated gold digger," as she writes in her memoir, *The Meaning of Mariah Carey*, she was really far from savvy. She was under Mottola's control and, for her, the marriage was a prison, with Mottola obsessively watching her and monitoring her activities. In her memoir, she refers to her home with Mottola as Sing Sing, which works on several levels. She had music but was "lonely and trapped." And she was trapped just north of New York City, not far from the actual Sing Sing prison.

Like other abusive men in music, Mottola still found a way to take credit for her success. In his 2013 memoir, he wrote, "Was I obsessive? Yes, but that was also a part of the reason for her success." Really? The biggest reason, let's be clear, was Carey's voice—with its five-octave range and her ability to hit staggeringly high notes while pulling off big runs and dazzling melismas. When her mother, a classically trained opera singer, first heard Carey sing in her highest register, she said, "You're going to hurt yourself."[7]

Mariah Carey and Whitney Houston, in The Prince of Egypt *(1998), directed by Brenda Chapman, Steve Hickner, Simon Wells Shown.* DreamWorks SKG/Photofest

With that "divine" voice, Carey would be included in performances involving other big-voiced legends, such as VH1's *Divas Live* show, a 1998 tribute to Aretha Franklin.

Thanks to her operatic mother and this early experience with legendary divas such as Franklin, Carey had some positive early association with the label diva. In her memoir, she includes a chapter by that title, "Divas," with discussion of Franklin—for whom she has "an ocean of gratitude"—and Diana Ross, who was honored in the 1999 *Divas Live* performance. She also includes Whitney Houston, with whom she presented at the 1998 MTV VMAs. At the show, the two had a staged "Clash of the Divas" skit, with dueling dresses. Early on, Carey was often compared with Houston, and headlines played up a supposed real-life clash. In the *Chicago Tribune*, the article "Houston Recaptures Diva Status" (1992) explained, "For the last year or so, pop diva Whitney Houston has seen her star eclipsed by hot new comer Mariah Carey." In her memoir, Carey observed, "Everybody wanted to pit us against each other in some 'battle of the divas'—a tired but pervasive pathology in music and Hollywood that makes women compete for sales like emotional UFC fighters." At the 2022 Grammys, musicians

Dua Lipa and Megan Thee Stallion riffed on their own rumored rivalry as well as the original Carey/Houston skit. In this way, the cycle of pathology continues.

But the connection to other supposed divas with dazzling voices wasn't the only source of Carey's labeling. She was also rumored to have extravagant tastes and demands. Carey herself has revealed a penchant for the finer things in life as well as a few unusually decadent habits, including bathing in milk. She didn't grow up in a world of luxury, and her mother struggled financially. With her own success, Carey could indulge in extravagances she couldn't as a child. And she found that she enjoyed the pampering and excess. Honestly, it makes sense.

In a beloved but infamous 2002 episode of MTV's *Cribs*, Carey offers viewers a glimpse of her newfound luxury, inviting them inside her very first independent apartment, a penthouse in New York City. She had purchased it after leaving Mottola, and it was "the kind of home I dreamed of as a child." During the episode, Carey shares that fantasy but also leans into her reputation as a diva in truly hilarious ways. She shows off her "shoe room," with her favorite type of shoe—the high stiletto heel. Favored brand? "Whoever's gonna stick to that motif," she says, smooth as butter. She describes her wall color, neutral, not jarring, because "life's jarring enough." And then she takes us to the bathroom, with affected emphasis on the first syllable, the British open "a," BAHthroom. With chandelier overhead, Carey settles in for a bath, candles lit and bubbles ready, while still wearing her towel.

Other highlights include her many wardrobe changes, her use of her exercise equipment while wearing heels, her dog pulling down her cat by the tail, her in-house salon with hair stylists at the ready, and Carey explaining how she fixed her beautiful fish tank by convincing her fish to be nocturnal—so they'd be on her schedule.

After 2002, discussions of Carey's "diva antics" rarely failed to mention some aspect of this episode. In 2021 in the *Daily Star*, "Mariah Carey's Biggest Diva Moments," it was that bath. But, really, it's hard to ignore Carey's clear comedic chops. She's playing a character—a character she can't shake. In an MTV special, years after the *Cribs* episode, Carey addressed the episode more directly: "I didn't really take a bath. Like, hello?? I had on a bodysuit, what do people actually think?" After an off-camera laugh, Carey added, "Like, I'm really gonna be stripping and taking a bath—I guess they do think so, 'cause that's gotten me in trouble before. Whatever."

The "trouble" she mentioned had to do with another MTV appearance in 2001, on the show *TRL*. In it, she arrives in an oversized T-shirt, pushing an ice-cream cart. It was a poorly conceived publicity stunt that involved her stripping off the shirt to reveal a skimpy "eighties *Glitter* look," as she put it in her memoir. In a 2007 interview in the *Chicago Tribune*, she recalled her desire then to change the critical narrative around her recently released movie *Glitter*. She was dealing with a tremendous amount of stress at the time, but she had thought the segment would be funny and had hoped that the show's host, Carson Daly, would riff alongside her, adding to the fun. Instead, eyeing her as if she had gone "crazy," he said, "What are you doing?" As Carey told the *Chicago Tribune*, it "was so blown out of proportion. . . . It was meant to be funny! And now I realize I can't do that on TV." The *Tribune* journalist smartly responded, "Only boys get to do really stupid things on TV in the name of comedy."

That gendered response to humor has only supported Carey's diva punishment. Studies have shown that women value humor—they often like a man who can tell a good joke. But men would prefer women who can laugh at a joke rather than tell one. Although a woman might find a funny man more alluring, men tend to find women who use humor "slightly *less* alluring." Even worse, as *Atlantic* writer Olga Khazan writes in "Plight of the Funny Female," "The way men and women laugh and joke has been so different for so long that it's hardened into a stark, oppressive social norm. Norm violators get punished, and often, that means funny women are punished, too." Carey has looked to humor throughout her life. Early in her career, she had even found some release by creating an entire album as an alter ego, a "brooding Goth girl," all while she recorded her hit album *Daydream*. But Carey's humor has not only been misunderstood; it may have fueled the haters. With Carey's failed *TRL* bit, she had unwillingly lit a match, and the press was ready to see her burn.

The post-*TRL* response was Carey's earliest experience with media abuse. In her memoir, Carey reflected, "The press devoured my silly *TRL* stunt and me right along with it. It was the first time I had experienced the phenomenon of a public fail that woke the monster in the media, that vicious vampire that gains its strength by feeding on the weaknesses of the vulnerable." Carey felt as if the media were just waiting for a complete fall: "The monster in the media is only satisfied when you are destroyed." And they almost got it. Soon after, Carey found herself exhausted and overworked. She tried to hide away at her mother's house, but her mother didn't understand. Her brother Morgan—a frightening and destructive presence in her life—convinced her soon after to check into a rehabilitation center. But, she writes, "I did not 'have a breakdown.' I was *broken* down—by the very people who were supposed to keep me whole." In the *Daily News*, the headline announced, "Mariah's Crack Up! Mother's Desperate 9-1-1 Call as Diva Unraveled." For a time, she was treated as a trainwreck spectacle, like Spears and others. But, as the media made clear, she was a diva, too—*diva unraveled.*

During the summer of 2001, rumors about her mental health were everywhere—Was she "crazy"? Was she suicidal? She attempted to diffuse the situation in interview. She also performed, picture perfect, for the troops after 9/11, offering as tribute her song "Hero" (1993). At the end of 2001, she joked about her troubles again with David Letterman, explaining that she had been "sleep-deprived" and, "No," she had not had a "breakdown." As the scrutiny continued, so did her explaining.

At the end of 2002, Carey sat down with Matt Lauer for a longer interview on NBC. In that interview, he asked her directly about her diva reputation. She defined the term as "a singer who maybe is a little bit dramatic and also, you know, sometimes has a reputation of being bitchy or difficult." Was she one? She admitted then, "I don't know." But she insisted that she's not hard to work with or demanding: "I didn't even demand sleep for years. How demanding could I be?" Her reply uniquely connected her exhaustion during the summer of 2001 to her diva reception. Perhaps part of her exhaustion had been related to a reluctance to feed the diva narrative. To get sleep, she would have had to say "No." She would have had to demand time for herself, which she wouldn't or couldn't without criticism.

As for her glamorous world and the staff supporting her, she insisted that that life was part of her celebrity and not something she necessarily wanted. The entourage—with people doing her hair and makeup—is "part of the whole swirl of, you know, show biz as a female artist." To be successful, she had to maintain a certain image. But she was criticized for that effort. If she appeared otherwise, however, the media would blast her, too. Carey was caught in an abusive cycle, as a lot of female celebrities are. And so, she was unfairly punished, as she would be either way. But the problem was once again society's understanding of what a woman can have and do for herself, with race a particular factor, as it often is for those labeled diva.

DIVAS IN CONCERT

The limitations set for female singers play out, of course, in the reception of other icons in music. Houston was the diva to which Carey initially was compared. She had that big voice, with her signature song "I Will Always Love You." At the start of her career, she also maintained a carefully curated facade, glamorous and perfect. In the 1980s, her management felt that she had to appear especially polished in order to earn mainstream respectability. As Gerrick Kennedy writes in *Didn't We Almost Have It All*, "Before Whitney, the country hadn't collectively christened a Black girl as America's Sweetheart." Black musicians were not then featured on MTV as the fledgling music station began to make its mark. And radio operated similarly. To break through that racial divide, Clive Davis, the powerhouse record label exec working with Houston, actively sought to market her as "universal," rather than "ethnic."

Once Houston was a success, she would be criticized by some in the Black community for not being Black enough. She would be criticized for being a diva, too. In 1999, Houston performed at Ohio's Blossom Music Center, dressed to the nines, resplendent, and referring to herself in the third person. She said from the stage, "Whitney must take her time." A few days previously, journalist John Soeder had interviewed her, asking her directly if she considered herself a diva: "Um . . . yeah," she said. "I suppose. Sometimes."[8] In headlines later in her career, she would be called the "tragic pop diva" or "troubled diva," as she battled with addiction.[9] As with Carey, criticism of her diva-ness could exist alongside criticism of everything else.

Women in music have reacted in different ways to their treatment as divas. Beyoncé worked to reclaim the label, twisting and reframing it as a means of self-empowerment. In the fast-paced song "Diva" (2008), Beyoncé sings "diva is a female version of a hustla," a stereotypically Black male figure who is similar to an entrepreneur but without the "bourgeois respectability."[10] In a looped sample, she powerfully announces: "I'm a a Diva."

In contrast, Jennifer Lopez, who was treated as a diva in the early 2000s, couldn't get past the label's gendered duality, though at first she tried. Just as journalists worked to pit Carey and Houston against each other, the media had fun speculating about Carey's relationship with the new diva on the block, Lopez. Asked about J. Lo, Carey famously said, "I don't know her." That statement has been additional reason for Carey's diva tag; it was supposedly the ultimate burn. But, as Carey told *Pitchfork* in 2018, "I really was trying to say something nice or say nothing at all. I really was."

When Lopez hosted *SNL* in 2001, she used her monologue to address her reputation and possibly flip the narrative. Appearing in a robe, she wonders aloud why she's considered a diva. Staff members appear perfectly synced, pampering her as she talks, and she eventually strips off the robe to reveal her iconic low-cut green Grammy dress. More than a decade later, however, Lopez was no longer laughing when she addressed the label. In a 2017 roundtable interview with other famous women, she said, "I've always been fascinated by how much more well-behaved we have to be than men." She revealed that her diva reputation made her feel as if she couldn't speak up for herself. But men could say whatever they wanted without the same punishment: "I was always fascinated by how I could see [a man] being late or being belligerent to a crew and it being totally acceptable; meanwhile, I'd show up 15 minutes late and be berated."[11] In another interview two years later, she connected the label to issues of race, explaining, "Because I was Latin, and I was a woman, and I was Puerto Rican, . . . they were not giving me the same pass that they gave everybody else."[12]

Carey's treatment as a diva takes on new meaning in this context. Carey's father is Black, though music industry officials did much to disguise her background, as Davis did with Houston. For Carey, this issue of race was at the center of several painful moments during her childhood—including one in school when she used a brown crayon to draw her father. The other kids laughed; the teacher did, too. They all insisted she had "used the wrong crayon." She was left feeling "humiliated and confused."

The most notorious diva in the opera world, Kathleen Battle, is also Black, a detail that makes her achievement all the more remarkable in the whitewashed world of classical music. And yet, her success is almost eclipsed by her colleagues' negative assessments of her as a person. At one point, past collaborators at the San Francisco Opera even created and wore T-shirts emblazoned with the declaration "I Survived the Battle." Though Lopez highlights the issue of race more generally, author Jaap Kooijman ties the condemnation in the term "diva" to the specific treatment of Black singers. Reading his "Fierce, Fabulous, and In/Famous: Beyoncé as Black Diva," I couldn't help but think of Battle. He writes, "Although diva has been applied to female stars of various ethnicities, there is a specific connection between the diva and black female performers, based both on the positive connotations of strength and survival within a white-dominated entertainment industry as well as on the negative connotations of excessive and unruly behavior, often based on racial stereotypes."

As we've seen, diva is another way to contain and restrain a woman. The label says that she is demanding too much, or more specifically, more than society generally feels she's allowed or worth. That proscription easily overlaps racial stereotypes, both in its positive and negative application. As a diva, a woman singing on the stage is stepping beyond society's standards based on gendered proscriptions as well as racial ones. She may be celebrated or condemned for that defiance. Sometimes, it's a little bit of both. In either case, the label communicates a notion of what is expected of women and, more specifically, Black women.

As a student of classical music, I have long believed the stories regarding Battle's poor attitude and outrageous demands. But, in light of this biased treatment, I'm starting to wonder if perfectly appropriate explanations don't exist. In the 2016 article "A Defence of the Diva as Kathleen Battle Visits Toronto," Pater Goddard writes, "Divas are monumentally self-centered, opinionated and demanding, we're told. They're not easy to work with. (Check out Diana Ross or Nina Simone.) But maybe that's what it takes." Given all that Battle had to push through to become successful, it makes perfect sense—according to the patriarchy's twisted logic—that she would be called out as a diva. In fact, it may be more surprising that more women aren't when simply stepping on stage or saying "No" is enough to earn the label—at least for some women.

WONDER WOMAN

In 2017, several male actors described Carey as a diva for doing just that—simply telling them "No." She was hired to appear in the comedy *The House*, with Will Ferrell and Amy Poehler. But, first, she was late. The exact lateness seems to vary in the telling—three or four hours. And there was a song she didn't want to sing, though she proposed a different one as substitute. On *Watch What Happens*, Will Ferrell told host Andy Cohen that the main issue centered on a scene. In the script, Carey wrote,

"I don't want to do this scene." Ferrell explained that the scene "was totally approved at the time." By who? He doesn't say. I would venture to guess, though, that it wasn't approved by Carey.

Ferrell conveniently left out the details of the scene. But another actor involved, Rob Huebel, clarified in an interview on SiriusXM's Entertainment Weekly Radio that Carey didn't want to be murdered, which was the scene's end. She was supposed to be shot and killed but objected to her on-screen killing. She made some suggestions, still hoping to make her appearance work. Huebel shared, "She was like, 'I don't think my character would get killed by bullets. What if I deflected them like Wonder Woman?'" The production team was not interested: "We have you for one day. We don't have time to argue with you. Just do it." But she didn't. That's the story. I could easily imagine Paul McCartney refusing to be murdered on film without pushback. I would guess Paul Simon could get away with a script note without a public airing of grievances. But Carey? A woman? She must be a diva.

For this failed cameo, she earned headlines everywhere: *In Business Insider*, "Mariah Carey Caused a 'S—t Storm' on the Latest Will Ferrell Movie"; on Hollywood.com, "Will Ferrell Hints at Mariah Carey's Diva Antics on *The House* Set"; and, on movieweb.com, "Mariah Carey's Diva Behavior Got Her Booted from Will Ferrell's *The House*." In all of the many write-ups about this incident, I couldn't find a single response from Carey. It was just these men frustrated that she didn't do what they wanted her to do. The lone sane voice, that of journalist Sesali Bowen, saved me from completely exploding with frustration: "While Huebel was wondering 'fucking what is going on with her?' he should be considering what is going on with him—and anyone else who thinks that working with a legend like Mariah Carey doesn't come with some conditions."[13]

And why didn't Carey respond? After the difficulties of 2002 and with therapy, Carey found a new sense of freedom, celebrated in her album *The Emancipation of Mimi* (2005). The last track is both declaration and prayer: "Don't let the world break me tonight." And she has since realized that the media's monstrous appetite for her failure doesn't really matter in the same way, not with all the changes in online reporting and social media. She found her own voice, as she writes in her memoir: "*We* are the media."

Still, the diva label wasn't going anywhere. And so, she had a choice: fight it or embrace it. Given her positive association with the term—the connection to the traditional operatic diva, her mother—she's been able to own her reputation in a way that other stars haven't. With her sense of humor, it was fun in a way to play that character, with the big sunglasses and heavy use of the word "darling."[14] In a 2020 interview with *Guardian* writer Hadley Freeman, Carey commented on her diva rep: "Who the fuck cares? Honestly! 'Oh my God, they're calling me a diva—I think I'm going to cry!'" To be clear, she does not own "diva" in terms of the rumored backstage demands, which she denies, or any cruel treatment. But she enjoys luxury, sequins, and insanely high heels. And she makes a useful point: "I fucking am high-maintenance because I deserve to be at this point."

In some ways, Carey and other female singers are in violation of perceived feminine virtue just by taking center stage. As a singer and one with a big voice and personality, Carey has found herself mistreated according to a long history of associated baggage. Like early female singers, she's been seen as too independent and too demanding—labeled a diva in the media and punished for that labeling. But, to be there, she has had to demand certain conditions, as men do without pushback. Even men dubbed divas (and there are some), such as Prince, are arguably called the term with reverence (though that application comes with complicated additional implications around gender and sexuality). Generally speaking, the term's negative connotations are reserved for women alone. In the 2006 interview, Theakston said, "I think some women disagree with [Carey's] diva-like behavior, but without her, the world of entertainment would be a much duller place." As I laugh at her insistence that she swims "in evening gowns and heels," I couldn't agree more.[15]

But I wonder about the damage the label has done. How many women haven't spoken up, afraid they might be labeled a diva? And for Carey, though she has embraced her reputation, it has surely held her back at times. In 2018, she shared her struggle with bipolar disorder. She was diagnosed with the disorder during that summer of 2001. But in *People*, she explained why she didn't reveal the issue then: "I was so terrified of losing everything. I didn't want to carry around the stigma of a lifelong disease that would define me and potentially end my career." Given the ways the media defined her as a diva, her fear seems well-founded. If she had felt free to reveal her truth, she would have inspired others, no doubt, to do so as well—others who needed help. The label diva is meant to contain and silence women. In some ways, Carey pushed past the label. But in other ways she didn't, or couldn't. But really, she shouldn't have had to contend with a reputation so thoroughly based in gender bias—and one so uniquely attached to women in music. Their only crime: appearing on that stage, in the spotlight, on their own, and being absolutely fabulous.

9

ARIANA GRANDE AND THE "DANGEROUS WOMAN"

Like Carey, Ariana Grande has been called a diva. Carey was one of Grande's inspirations, along with the other female singers she and her family loved to play at home, often on their at-home karaoke machine. "The soundtrack was Whitney, Madonna, Mariah, Celine, Barbra," Grande told Rob Haskell writing for *Vogue*, "All the divas." Grande gained early attention for her singing when she took her private passion public by posting online a version of Carey's song "Emotion" in 2012. But she gained toxic attention in 2015 when she was captured on security footage licking a doughnut. Even more criticism was to come—most of it focused on her performance style, dress, and romantic relationships. This attention would implicitly and explicitly rely on one of the ugliest female-specific labels— "slut"—an indictment of her expressed and unexpressed sexuality as well as her perceived mishandling of men.

The term "slut" has hovered around many of the women featured in this book. The focus on romantic partnerships and appearance in the media coverage of women in music slides all too easily into gross name calling. In our fascination with both, there is always judgment, often harsh and sometimes hidden with moral platitudes about decency and morality loaded like a weapon. In the case of Grande, similar judgment was part of a deadly attack. In 2017, a terrorist group targeted her and her concert in

Manchester. We can distance ourselves from such extremism or the role
that the policing of gender played in that bloodshed. But we all participate in a system that puts men first—their needs and wants—with women
severely judged by association. And sometimes, that judgment can become
violence.

SLUT

Like many of the labels in this book, "slut" has a long history. In the early
1400s, according to the *Oxford English Dictionary*, it was "a woman of
dirty, slovenly, or untidy habits or appearance." It could also be "a woman
of a low or loose character" in an alternative meaning dating back to the
late fifteenth century. That second definition became more common in
the nineteenth century and crystallized in today's definition: from Oxford
Languages Online, "a woman who has many casual sexual partners." In so
doing, the term falls in line with a long-standing trend in insults—words
that define women as sex objects—as well as the consistent punishment of
women for their sexuality. Either way, there's no way out.

As Amanda Montell writes in *Wordslut*, "Even a brief scan of our language's slang for women will reveal that female desire is worthy of shame
no matter what a woman chooses to do with it, which can only be one of
two things per our culture's rules: having a lot of sex, which earns her the
reputation of a whore, or opting to withhold it, which gets her labeled a
prude." As is often the case, women have no safe course of action—damned
if they do or do not do it.

Men, of course, live according to a different set of rules. They can have
all the sex they want. They'll be celebrated as studs. Their actions and
desires define them. In contrast, women are defined and labeled based on
what men want. If he wants sex and she doesn't, she's an "ice princess." If
he thinks she's had too much sex, she can be called a "slut."[1] Those double
standards have real repercussions in our rape culture—a culture that con-
gratulates men for their sexual dominance and penalizes women if they are
forcibly dominated. Within that culture, a woman can also be punished,
of course, based on what she's wearing, as we've seen. She can appear to
be a slut and treated as such, whether or not she wants to have sex. Men
are supposedly "naturally more sexual" whereas women aren't.[2] And so the

responsibility falls on women to make sure that everyone behaves appropriately, even if they are not willing participants in the first place. The shame and judgment embedded in the word slut support this system as well as the bias in rape's prosecution and coverage by the media. That judgment also supports thinking that saddles women with the wrongs of men. In Ariana Grande's case, it played out in response to both her music or, more specifically, how she presented her music, as well as her romantic partnerships. She could not be herself without reference to a man and what he wanted. Her needs and desires were inconsequential.

DOUGHNUTGATE

For a time, however, she couldn't be herself without reference to a doughnut. In July 2015, a video appeared online of security footage taken at a doughnut shop. In the video, still available on YouTube, Grande is seen with an apparent boyfriend and some friends in front of a display of doughnuts. At one point, she seems to lean toward one of the doughnuts on top of the display case, perhaps stealthily sticking out her tongue for a lick. When another tray of doughnuts appears, she says, "That's disgusting." More controversially, she comments, "I hate Americans"—which she has explained since as a reaction to the unhealthy diet of many children in the United States.

The offhand statements, never meant for public dissemination, landed her in the hot seat, and she quickly posted an apology video: "Seeing a video of yourself behaving poorly, that you have no idea was taken, is such a rude awakening, that you don't know what to do—I was so disgusted with myself." This moment, dubbed "doughnutgate," caused much backlash. And Grande even lost a performance spot at the White House gala later that year. The incident is still brought up in any write-up about Grande and her supposed "diva" behavior. And there are many.

Immediately following the incident at the doughnut shop, *Cosmopolitan* set out to chronicle a time line of Grande's bad behavior, answering the headline's question, "How Did Ariana Grande Get Such an Awful Reputation?" *Buzzfeed* already had "A Full History of Ariana Grande's Alleged Diva Behavior," so it merely had to update its write-up, adding the doughnut incident. Both of these histories start with Grande's work on the

Nickelodeon show *Victorious*, which features Grande playing the character Cat Valentine as she attends a performing arts high school. The show
was canceled in 2012 after a two-year run, but Grande found herself in a
spin-off show, *Sam & Cat*, with another actress, Jennette McCurdy. The
two apparently didn't always get along, at least that was the rumor. When
the show ended, McCurdy made a Web series with an obnoxious pop-star
character she called Glorianna, the rhyme obviously suggestive. Grande
also seemed to have an issue with another actress, Victoria Justice, whom
she blamed for the initial cancellation of *Victorious*.

Both write-ups also highlight fan controversy, with reports of Grande
cutting one signing short and a photoshoot gone wrong in Sydney, Aus-
tralia. The photographer, Chris Pavlich, told the world that Grande
wouldn't allow shots of her right side and left the session before it was
finished. Grande countered, insisting that she was just changing her
shirt. In an interview at the time on an Australian radio station, she
maintained, "It was just a photographer or something who got mad at
me because I left to change my outfit mid-photo shoot because I didn't
like my top."

By the end of the year, the stories grew increasingly strange; a *Life &
Style* report announced that Grande insisted other people carry her places
when she didn't want to walk. Her boyfriend at the time, rapper Big Sean,
responded in an interview on *The Breakfast Club*: "That don't even sound
logical. No, man, she don't get carried. I remember I was with her one time
and she got carried but it was 'cause her foot was bleeding. She busted her
foot, you know, dancing and stuff."

In each of these stories, Grande was demanding too much. Just as the
media criticized Carey, writers found reasons to limit Grande and call out
her choices. From there, it wouldn't take much for them to get specific,
focusing on how she chose to present her sexuality. In some ways, the early
criticism set up the attacks to come. She would be asking for too much
again. But this time, she was too much in a particular way. And that violation demanded a specific type of scorn. In this treatment, the men around
Grande were significant, even a decisive factor. At the same time, they
were merely a reference point in her condemnation. Like Ken dolls with
no backstory, they became props in Barbie's story and the telling of all she
supposedly had done wrong. This opposition suggests that women can hold
the spotlight entirely when the name of the game is shame.

GETTING DANGEROUS

Sadly, some early criticism around Grande's performance style came from a seeming ally, singer and actress Bette Midler. In 2014, Midler told *The Telegraph*, "It's always surprising to see someone like Ariana Grande with that silly high voice, a very wholesome voice, slithering around on a couch looking so ridiculous . . . But it's not my business, I'm not her mother. Or her manager. Maybe they tell them that's what you've got to do. Sex sells." In Midler's opinion, "You don't have to make a whore out of yourself to get ahead." Grande responded, posting on Twitter on November 25, 2014, "Bette was always a feminist who stood for women being able to do whatever the F they wanted without judgement!" Referencing Midler's mermaid character, Delores De Lago, Grande added, "Not sure where that Bette went but I want that sexy mermaid back!!!"

Though Grande spoke up quickly, addressing the criticism directly, the issue was far from dead. When she released her "Dangerous Woman" video in 2016, she would be condemned on Facebook; and the post, which labeled her a "whore," compounded Midler's scorn. In the "Dangerous Woman" video, Grande sings in black lingerie, sometimes standing, sometimes in a bed. She's aroused and "open," but as she makes clear in the very first line of the song, she doesn't "need permission." She would, however, continue to defend herself in light of the public criticism, as was fast becoming a necessary habit: "[W]hen will people stop being offended by women showing skin / expressing sexuality? [M]en take their shirts off / express their sexuality on stage, in videos, on Instagram, anywhere they want to . . . [T]he double standard is so boring and exhausting."

Honestly, it really is.

The history of this sort of condemnation is immense and immensely hypocritical. As Jarune Uwujaren points out, women are rewarded for "performing sexy" and then routinely punished for it. Is the performance empowering, or is it playing into the male gaze? Even feminists such as Midler can fall into this trap, focusing on the actions of individuals rather than the underlying issue and contradiction. As Uwujaren concludes, "Understanding and judging the actions of women in a patriarchal context shouldn't be focused on labeling their actions feminist or disempowering, moral or immoral. It should be focused on constantly challenging the notion that a woman's value should be judged by her sexiness to begin with."[3]

In some of the related criticism, Grande's appearance and romantic interests would blur. Her presentation of her sexuality in her music became part
of the story around her relationships. The men involved were mentioned in
passing whereas she would be dissected and defined by her association with
them. A month before the doughnut event, for example, during the summer of 2015, she confronted in interviews question after question about her
recent breakup with Big Sean. The attention surrounding that split struck
Grande as yet another double standard. She was sick of the questions or
the label "Big Sean's ex." Again on Twitter, she wrote, "I am tired of living
in a world where women are mostly referred to as a man's past, present
or future." And then she went further, addressing the way her love life is
treated in comparison to a man's: "If a woman has a lot of sex (or any sex
for that matter), she's a 'slut.' If a man has sex, he's a STUD, a BOSSSSSS,
a KING." The man is celebrated, and she's labeled in connection to him
when, as she wrote, women "are more than enough on their own."

The following year, Grande started dating musician Mac Miller, which
prompted the same speculation and storyline—she was Miller's present.
That focus reduced her. She was an object, *his* object. And perfect strangers felt fine treating her as such. On December 27, 2016, she described an
encounter with one of those strangers and how it made her feel. While she
was out with Miller, this person (a man, obviously) said to Miller, "Ariana is
sexy as hell man I see you, I see you hitting that!!!" "This may not seem like
a big deal to some of you but I felt sick and objectified," she wrote. When
someone on Twitter blamed her for the encounter—she was apparently
asking for the attention with her "sexual" music videos—she took to Twitter
again: "Expressing sexuality in art is not an invitation for disrespect!!! Just
like wearing a short skirt is not asking for assault."

In 2015 and 2016, Grande clearly dealt with a lot of animosity. And she
fought back admirably, thanks in part to social media. When she hosted *SNL*
in March 2016, she was ready to try a different line of counter-messaging:
comedy. During her monologue, she addressed her early work as an actress
as well as doughnutgate: "It can be tough growing up in show business,
you know? A lot of kid stars end up doing drugs, or in jail, or pregnant, or
get caught looking at a doughnut they didn't pay for." After insisting she's
ready to move beyond doughnuts and into "a real adult scandal," she sang
a tune called "What will my scandal be?" Frankly, she had already been
dealing with weighty issues of misogyny, including age-old Madonna-whore

condemnation repackaged and refined by the music industry's hypocrisy around female sexuality. She didn't need another scandal, let alone an "adult" one. And yet, just a year later, she found herself confronting something far worse.

REAL ADULT SCANDAL

On May 22, 2017, a suicide bomber arrived at Grande's concert at Manchester Arena. The tour was organized to promote her album *Dangerous Woman*. Grande sang at one point with video behind her emblazoned with words of empowerment: "wild," "free," "not asking for it." In her song "Dangerous Woman," she was "skin to skin," and it's her decision. Her voice is big and resonant, and the song showcases her range, which has earned her comparisons to Carey. In another song, "Side to Side," she also focused on sex, decorating her melodic lines with runs and embellishments, again similar to Carey. She's "been here all night," and it's got her "walkin' side to side."

The explosion, which occurred right after her final song, killed 22 people and injured 116. One of those who died was an eight-year-old girl. In the immediate aftermath of the bombing, parents and loved ones searched for their kids in the ruins of a fun night out turned nightmare. ISIS immediately took credit for the bombing. The former chief crown prosecutor for northwest England has since categorized the attack as one directed specifically at women and girls, or "gender terrorism." He said, "It was obvious to me. I looked at the death toll and how many girls there were."[4] ISIS has a history of victimizing women—through forced marriage, kidnapping, and the rape of women within perceived enemy groups. But the attack was also a means of value enforcement, and those values have a long, sordid history. As Sophie Gilbert wrote in *The Atlantic*, "The impulse to hate and fear women who are celebrating their freedom—their freedom to love, their freedom to show off their bodies, their freedom to feel joy, together—is older than ISIS, older than pop concerts, older than music itself."

Grande herself was not hurt in the explosion, but she was reportedly seen in hysterics leaving the venue. She would tweet: "broken. From the bottom of my heart, i am so so sorry. i don't have words." She flew home right after the concert, and certain on-air personalities criticized her for doing so. On

May 25, broadcaster Piers Morgan posted on Twitter, "She should have stayed to visit her injured fans." His criticism was not a one-off. In another post, he wrote, "I can 100 per cent guarantee you I would stay and visit those who had been killed or wounded watching me perform." It was an easy pronouncement for someone who wasn't there and does not perform. People such as Morgan ignored the fact that Grande herself was no doubt grieving and processing the trauma of that night. She was, like many of her fans, quite young, too, only twenty-three at the time.

Just eleven days later, Grande did return. She organized the benefit concert One Love Manchester, which took place on June 4. She performed the raunchiest of her songs there by request. A victim's mother thought the sexed-up songs were only appropriate, after a *Daily Mail* article maintained that the bomber targeted the concert in part because of Grande's sexy image. But what about those who had targeted her before? The attack in Manchester was a real-life manifestation of the dangerous power behind words such as "slut." Grande's sexy image was, of course, not the problem. She was not inviting the attack, as the *Daily Mail* suggested in some ways. The problem was the way we consistently have thought about a sexy image. More specifically, the problem was—and is—the way society polices a woman's performance of her sexuality through language.

THE MARS BAR

Regulating female sexuality, without discussion of societal standards and values, is everywhere in music. We've seen it in the media frenzy around Spears and in the abusive attacks on Love. We've seen it in interview after interview by hosts who emote their put-on concern while asking about the sexual activities and dress of women in music. Disapproval is implied even as they ask for more and more detail, entertaining their audiences while affecting a pose of moral authority. And the women under the microscope are often very young, sometimes publicly transitioning from childhood to adulthood, as was the case with Spears and Grande.

That was also the case with singer Miley Cyrus, who grew up on screen as Hannah Montana and later was denounced for performing nearly nude while swinging from a wrecking ball at the 2013 VMAs. Social media sites have ramped up the spread of that sort of treatment even as they have given stars a platform for response. On October 4, 2019, Cyrus called out the particular fervor around her image and sexual choices, writing on Twitter, "Men (especially successful ones) are RARELY slut shamed. They move on from one beautiful young woman to the next MOST times without consequence." Women are called "sluts," she wrote, whereas men are "legends."

Like Grande, one of those judging Cyrus was another female celebrity, not Midler but Marianne Faithfull. In 2014, she had told ITV that pop stars "like Miley Cyrus and Rihanna" are "completely rubbishy sluts actually." The issue, for Faithfull, was the way they dress. But Faithfull, of all people, had to recognize the hypocrisy: how she was trashing women in the press just as she herself had been trashed, and for similar reasons. She had to know the damage, too, because her treatment is understandably a sore point for her. She was the focus of one of the more depressing media witch hunts, and one that occurred quite early, in 1967, before the full flowering of media harassment or even the birth of cyberbullying. The setting of her downfall was a party at Keith Richards's home, in West Wittering, Sussex, with Mick Jagger and other Rolling Stones members in attendance. As Jagger's then girlfriend, she was there, but the party must have been rather sedate, because, at one point, she decided to go for a walk. She then came back, took a bath, and wrapped herself in a rug, still naked. She didn't know the police were on their way, hoping to bust the band for drugs.

News of the bust spread quickly, even then. And Faithfull was collateral damage. Soon, she wasn't just nude at a Rolling Stones party; according to the reports, at the time of the bust, Jagger supposedly was eating a Mars bar out of her vagina. (Honestly, I can't believe I just wrote that sentence.) The story is so ridiculous and ugly. In her autobiography (2000), she reflected: "The Mars Bar was a very effective piece of demonizing. Way out there. It was so overdone, with such a malicious twisting of facts. Mick retrieving a Mars Bar from my vagina, indeed! It was far too jaded for any of us even to have conceived of. It's a dirty old man's fantasy."

In a 2001 interview in *Salon*, Faithfull told David Bowman that the story bothered her a lot, even some thirty-three years later: "I never will find it funny. I went into complete insanity trying to figure out who started the rumor." She recognized in the story the role of society's double standards. The men were glamorized, despite the drugs, whereas, as she put it in an interview with AN Holmes in *Details Magazine* (1994), "A woman in that situation becomes a slut and a bad mother." The criticism is concentrated on the woman, despite the men involved. The story became legend as the men were celebrated as legends. And it doesn't matter what the men did or didn't do. It was all about the woman, as long as she could be mocked and disparaged.

In Cyrus's case, Robin Thicke was also on that VMA stage just as Timberlake was with Jackson. But the men never matter when a woman is there to blame or shame. And that's true even when the man should very much matter—as in the case of Monica Lewinsky. In that coverage, an intern ranked as more significant than the president of the United States. And all because there was a woman to both fetishize and censure—never mind Bill Clinton's power, age, or marital status. With that blame, the women are defined and labeled forever. They are reduced to their sexual appeal—they are a tasty treat themselves, like a doughnut or a Mars bar. But, in that reduction, they are both everything and nothing more.

THE "YOKO EFFECT"

A year after the Manchester bombing, the media's focus returned to Grande's romantic relationships. This time the criticism related to Miller, then her ex-boyfriend. The condemnation would combine much of the criticism she had dealt with before as a referendum on her sexuality as an independent woman as well as her right to care for herself. But in that verdict, critics took a stand on behalf of Miller as well while at the same time actively diminishing him. That treatment is not unique in the patriarchy's handling of musical women in love. The same argument could be made about the coverage of Cobain and Lennon. And it's an interesting twist. Women are treated as subservient by nature, yet they hold all the power when things go terribly wrong.

During Grande's two-year relationship with Miller, he had struggled with substance abuse. In a *Vogue* profile of Grande, journalist Rob Haskell described Grande's desperate attempts to help him. He wrote, "Friends with her during the *Dangerous Woman* tour recall a woman up at all hours, desperately tracking his whereabouts to ensure he wasn't on a bender." In her song "Everytime" from the album *Sweetener* (2018), she seemed to allude to that struggle: "I get tired of your no-shows / You get tired of my control." And yet, as she sings in the chorus, she always went "back to you," despite the toxicity.

But in May 2018, she didn't go back. Soon after she broke up with Miller, she was reportedly involved with comedian-heartthrob Pete Davidson, and the two were engaged quite quickly (by June 11). On May 17, Miller was arrested for a DUI. He was also charged with a hit-and-run. The Twitter abuse was immediate, with Elijah Flint posting, "Mac Miller totalling his G wagon and getting a DUI after Ariana Grande dumped him for another dude after he poured his heart out on a ten-song album to her called the divine feminine is just the most heartbreaking thing happening in Hollywood." (Grande has said only the song "Cinderella," on Miller's 2016 album *The Divine Feminine*, was inspired by their relationship.)

Many other comments of a similar nature blamed Grande for Miller's behavior. But Grande responded to Flint: "How absurd that you minimize female self-respect and self-worth by saying someone should stay in a toxic relationship because he wrote an album about them. I am not a babysitter or a mother and no woman should feel that they need to be. I have cared for him and tried to support his sobriety and prayed for his balance for years (and always will of course) but shaming / blaming women for a man's inability to keep his shit together is a very major problem."

Apparently, Grande was supposed to stay with Miller because he needed her. Never mind what she needed. With her supposed betrayal, thinking about herself as men do, she was in the wrong for his wrongs. As Toni Van Pelt, president of the National Organization for Women, put it, "[M]en in particular are taught to think of themselves first. Women are always extolled to take care of others first, to put themselves second. If they think of themselves first, then they're considered selfish." Grande was clearly judged from a similar perspective, despite the obvious bias.

When Miller died of a drug overdose on September 7, 2018, a crueler blame was immediate, with gendered slurs and general declarations of her guilt. The pile on was so intense—both on Twitter and Instagram—that Grande disabled the comments on her Instagram account and did not respond for several days on Twitter, which was noteworthy given her normal rate of activity on the platform. *Rolling Stone* writer Brittany Spanos, in "'You Did This to Him': Ariana Grande, Mac Miller and the Demonization of Women in Toxic Relationships," connected this incident to a "Yoko effect." She defined the effect as fans' "desire to connect female partners to actions they may not comprehend," something also at work in the toxic blame Love experienced. The assumption was that Grande should have put other people's needs before her own. She should have done more to help Miller, despite what it might have cost her. As in Love's case, the actions of the man were not his own but, instead, her responsibility and her fault.

On September 9, Grande posted a message of mourning and tribute: "i'm so mad, i'm so sad I don't know what to do. you were my dearest friend." She added, "i'm so sorry i couldn't fix or take your pain away." Culturally, many people still expect women to take care of men; when they can't, or can't prevent the worst, society reacts with anger. Grande was grieving while trolls blamed her for Miller's death. That expectation was part of her mourning—"*i couldn't fix or take your pain away.*" But fixing Miller was never really Grande's responsibility. The idea that women should be there in this way for men is, of course, unfair. She is the giver. He's the taker. As she sings in "Dangerous Woman, "'Cause I'm a giver, it's only nature."

In 2019, she told Haskell, reflecting on her relationship with Miller, "By no means was what we had perfect, but, like, fuck. He was the best person ever, and he didn't deserve the demons he had. I was the glue for such a long time, and I found myself becoming . . . less and less sticky. The pieces just started to float away." She didn't deserve those demons either. She tried to fight them with him and for him, as was expected, but she definitely didn't deserve the blame for those demons and their ultimate course in the end.

In some ways, it was easy to blame Grande. The skeptics were already there. From the start she was in violation of perceived feminine virtue. As a singer and one with a big voice, she was mistreated according to a long history of associated baggage. She had also been consistently defined in relation to men. Her treatment, when Miller died, followed suit. Some could not see her as an individual; they could not separate her from him.

And the words we use back up that treatment. They continually define and punish women based on their proximity and relationship to men and what men want or need. The men are generally treated as individuals with power. The only time they're not, apparently, is when they're in the wrong or in distress. But that only happens, of course, when a woman is nearby to blame and shame. Then she has all the power, *his* power. But it's a negative, inauthentic power. It's a power that was never hers and never should have been assigned to her. Through that reassignment, her real power is limited and lessened until she's nothing of value, and he's nothing, too.

"THANK U, NEXT"

Grande has worked in her music to move past the spectacle. In her song "Thank U, Next," released in November 2018, she confronts interest in her love life directly, listing the relationships of media fascination, including her romances with Davidson and Miller. She insists that each man "taught" her something and so she's thankful, singing in the chorus: "Thank you, next / I'm so grateful for my ex." The song is heavy in sentiment at times, with reference to Miller being "an angel." But the delivery is light, as is the supporting video, a parody of four different movies, each with romance and a brutal breakup as part of the plot line: *Mean Girls*, *Legally Blonde*, *Bring It On*, and *13 Going on 30*. She is able to proclaim her growth—"I've learned from the pain"—while playing with her reputation. The video begins with rumors, much like the movie *Mean Girls*, and Grande's clearly at the center. Like the villain Regina George, she pores over her burn book, but she also heroically leads the girls at the beauty salon, much like heroine Elle Woods in *Legally Blonde*. She's good and bad, but all of it's fun, with cameos sprinkled throughout the video, including an appearance by Kris Jenner as her too-enthusiastic mom.

In another song, "7 Rings," from the album *Thank U, Next*, she similarly makes use of parody, this time riffing on the infectious melody "Favorite Things" from *The Sound of Music*. The song is catchy and once again light, with Grande rapping about a fun time out with the girls. "Been through some bad shit, I should be a sad bitch." But that's not the course she chooses. In fact, she often chooses to fight back, confronting and calling out bias in the music industry and, society more generally. In 2018, that righteous fight was directed at Piers Morgan, who was once more picking on women in music. He had accused the girl group Little Mix of "using nudity to sell records." Grande responded, "Women can be sexual AND talented. Naked and dignified. It's OUR choice. & we will keep fighting til people understand. I say this w all due respect but thank u, next."

She had, at one point, hesitated before responding to people such as Morgan. In a 2020 interview with Apple Music's Zane Lowe, she explained, "I stopped doing interviews for a really long time because I felt like whenever I would get into a position where somebody would try to say something for clickbait or twist my words . . . I would defend myself. And then, people would be like, 'Oh, she's a diva.' I was like, 'This doesn't make any sense.'"

But ultimately, she decided she needed to speak up. With the bias she has faced, she has had a lot to say and a lot that society needs to hear. To Lowe, she explained the turnaround, "And I do want to do interviews and share with people, and not be afraid to be myself." By speaking up, other women might not be afraid to speak up, too. With her example, they might be able to embrace their sexuality and define themselves as individuals despite any romantic involvement. If we can change the thinking behind the words in these statements, maybe they can be respected as legends, too.

10

TAKING BACK BITCH

"Bitch" is a more common way to disparage a woman than "diva." It's less fancy, with none of diva's grand operatic lineage and less musical in its origins. But there's plenty of overlap. Both are gender-specific put-downs. In episode 3 of Netflix's *History of Swear Words*, which is devoted to the word bitch, Nic Cage calls it "the most frequent" slur with gendered connotations. And many women in music have experienced the insult. In 2002, Dave Grohl publicly called Courtney Love "an ugly fucking bitch."[1] West, of course, called Swift a bitch in his song "Famous." And, in the world of country music in 2003, the right-wing website the Free Republic dubbed Natalie Maines "the Dixie Bitch" after she commented on the Iraq War: "We do not want this war, this violence, and we're ashamed that the president of the United States is from Texas."

"Bitch," unlike the other words chronicled in this book, features prominently in music itself, in lyrics and performance, often with men referring to women as such, especially in rap. Sure, we've seen "gold digger" pop up similarly. But bitch appears over and over. And I'm not talking about long, long ago. As Kyle Eustice asked in his *Hiphopdx* headline, "Why Is Male Rappers Calling Women 'Bitches' Still a Thing in 2020?" But bitch has also been reclaimed in songs by women. The most popular early example is the 1997 song "Bitch," cowritten by Shelly Peiken and singer Meredith Brooks.

Peiken got the idea for the song while driving in her car. She told me, "I was thinking to myself, 'Well, that would be a really great idea for a song,' because I never heard a woman do it."

Reclamation of words can be powerful in changing the way we talk and think about women. And we've seen other women flip words and ideas in this way—such as FKA twigs's embrace of Magdalene, or Beyoncé's version of "diva." Bebe Rexha's song "You Can't Stop the Girl" (the inspiration for this book's title) accompanies the related recovery of villain-turned-hero Maleficent in the 2019 movie *Maleficent: Mistress of Evil*. We could, of course, avoid the word "bitch" altogether, eliminating it from our lexicon of insults. But using it while avoiding *negative* applications of the term has several potential advantages. As *Wordslut* author Amanda Montell writes, it's a "gradual process wherein one meaning slowly overlaps another, then eclipses it." It has the potential to change the underlying thinking behind the word, too. The word can become a means of self-empowerment, reframing and celebrating female strength. It's a two-part attack. And we need all the strategies we can get.

As we've seen throughout this book, the toxic labeling of women in music is everywhere. And it helps uphold a particular worldview, cementing for men the leading role. With ramifications for our present and generations in the future, words are then more than sticks and stones. As Sara Bareilles sings in the song "Brave," "Nothing's gonna hurt you the way that words do." Responding to criticism of her 2022 song "Grrrls," Lizzo similarly addressed the true impact of words when she announced that she was changing the song's lyrics to get rid of an ableist slur: "As a fat black woman in America, I've had many hateful words used against me so I understand the power words can have (whether intentionally or in my case unintentionally)." Ultimately, language is an issue of social justice, defining, confining, and punishing women. And words absolutely hurt us all, sometimes physically. I, for one, have certainly seen an ugly headline and then felt my pulse quicken or my chest tighten. I, like so many people, have felt many of the words in this book deeply and in different ways. But we can take our own action. We can upend some of this hurtful language before it ends us, limiting the possibilities and promise we seek to make real, whether in music or the fundamental performance of our everyday lives.

DEFINING BITCH

The specific insult, bitch, is a particular favorite in the punishment of women, especially those who break with established patterns. In the *Oxford English Dictionary*, the term originally had two meanings: female dog and "a lewd or sensual woman." The two definitions are related, because dogs can have many puppies. The dog is sexualized as is the woman. The negative use of the term existed as far back as the fifteenth century. In the twentieth century, however, "bitch" gained new meaning: "a malicious or treacherous woman." That more general definition, even then, was changing and adapting. In some ways, bitch was expanding. It became a catchall for a woman who is seen as "conceited," "self-absorbed," "competitive," "annoying," or "pushy."[2] Now, the word is remarkably imprecise. But, whatever the specifics, this woman has crossed a line limiting expected and accepted feminine behavior.

In the 1920s, general use of the term spread rapidly. As Arielle Pardes observes in *Vice*'s "The Evolution of the Bitch," at that time, just as women had earned the right to vote, men started calling women bitches in earnest. That was no coincidence. It was retribution and a forced reminder of a woman's supposed place when that place was actively changing. In fact, the public punishment of women can often be linked to gains in women's rights. Sociologist Carolyn Chernoff, for example, has connected harsh media scrutiny in the 1980s to feminist advancement, with more women then newly in positions of power.[3]

In this sort of pushback, "bitch" has been especially prevalent in the political realm. In 2020, Representative Ted Yoho called fellow Congress member Alexandria Ocasio-Cortez a "bitch" while speaking in front of the Capitol. Yoho issued a non-apology, describing himself as "passionate." Retaliation against Maines was explicitly political, too, as captured in the 2006 documentary *Shut Up & Sing*. On stage in London, Maines offered her statement calmly, almost quietly, after the group sang their popular song "Travelin' Soldier." The audience cheered. She smiled. No one seemed to expect the immediate eruption that followed back home, with fans protesting and country radio stations informally banning the group. Political pundit Bill O'Reilly proclaimed, "These are callow, foolish women who deserve to be slapped around." Physical abuse, as with Ono, was a casual, almost accepted response, as was the word "bitch."

Sure, the word is handy, given its adaptability in these contexts. But it was—and is—fun to say, too. Montell highlights the "phonetic delight" in saying words such as bitch and slut, any slur that is "short and plosive," with a hard consonant at the start and stop. With that attraction to the sound and saying of "bitch," it's no wonder that the insult has come to occupy such a significant place in music. Jazz trumpeter Miles Davis made the term central to his album released in 1970, *Bitches Brew*, playing with the power of the sound in alliteration. Elton John did something similar with his 1974 song "The Bitch Is Back." In "A Bitch Iz a Bitch" (1988), NWA riffed on the word in rhyme—"rich" and "pitch"—while arguing that "all women have a little bitch in 'em."

Of course, some musicians used the word without any special reverence for its sound. For Public Enemy, in "Sophisticated Bitch" (1987), it was all about the negative sentiment and a woman so awful that "people wonder" why she wasn't beaten "till she almost died." Almost a decade later, it was more of the same in Tupac Shakur's "Wonda Why They Call U Bitch," about a "slut" who is after money. She only finds "peace" once she's "deceased." In these songs, Love's "death wish" is bitch-specific.

At the same time, in 1996, Lisa Jervis and Andi Zeisler created *Bitch* magazine (a remarkable publication that shuttered in 2022). Zeisler observed, "It would be great to reclaim the word 'bitch' for strong, outspoken women, much the same way that 'queer' has been reclaimed by the gay community." Independently, women in music seemed to agree. At this point, there might even be something of a musical genre around women investing "bitch" with positive energy: Lil' Kim's "Queen Bitch," Nicki Minaj's "Baddest Bitch," Madonna's "Bitch I'm Madonna," Britney Spears's "Work Bitch," among many, many others. In her *SNL* monologue on April 16, 2022, host and musical guest Lizzo pledged with a big smile to break the existing record for the number of times a host says "bitch." And so "bitch" has become positive, even revelatory. As Ocasio-Cortez wrote on Twitter, in response to Yoho, "Bitches get stuff done."

REDEFINING BITCH

There are a few early examples of women appropriating bitch in song. Yoko Ono called herself a bitch in her 1974 song "Yes, I'm a Witch"; and the group Berlin similarly claimed the word in their song "Sex (I'm a . . .)" (1982), with the lead singer Terri Nunn declaring, "I'm a man—I'm a bitch." Some women used the term in performance. On stage, Courtney Love would refer to herself as a bitch. In fact, before she dove into the audience and was sexually assaulted in 1991, she chanted with the audience, "I'm a bitch."[4] The English group Huggy Bear performed with the words "slut" and "bitch" written on their bodies.[5] Trying to quell the furor after Maines's comment, the Chicks would do something similar for a cover shoot connected to an exclusive interview in *Entertainment Weekly*. In the published shot, all three members of the group appear naked with words people were calling them painted on their bodies: "Dixie Sluts," "Traitors," but also "brave" and "heroes."

The band Huggy Bear is associated with a particular moment of female empowerment, rebellion, and reclamation: Riot Grrrl. This movement, tied to the early 1990s, is difficult to define, with links to the punk scenes in Washington, D.C., and Olympia, Washington. It was, for many, "punk rock feminism" with "an added growl to replace the perceived passivity of 'girl.'"[6] Both music and language were central to the movement's activities, with the publication of zines, including the band Bikini Kill's pioneering *Riot Grrrl*. In its first issue, published July 1991, drummer Tobi Vail named Yoko Ono as hero and idol, "the first punk rock girl singer ever." Vail also recognized Ono's cultural treatment as reinforcing ideas of women as "outsiders" in popular music.[7] In contrast, Riot Grrrl celebrated women and grrrls as insiders, and they would not be silent. Quite the opposite. They would SCREAM!

Another band tied to Riot Grrrl was the all-women 7 Year Bitch, which Carrie Brownstein of the related band Sleater-Kinney recalls in her memoir as "the heroines of the Seattle scene in the '90s." The band name—a play on the title of the movie *The Seven Year Itch*, an iconic 1955 film starring Marilyn Monroe—was suggested to the group by a friend of the band, Ben London.[8]

These examples bravely exist. Though the phenomenon itself was generally subcultural, Riot Grrrl and the movement's powerful use of language did receive mainstream attention. And recent movies, such as Netflix's *Moxie* (2021), have carried it forward. Still, the term "bitch" only became widely popular in a positive sense in 1997, with the song "Bitch" by Peiken and Brooks. The song was everywhere then, and it was embraced despite the aggressive potential in the word. For the first time, girls were singing along with their radios as a pop star sang constructively about being a bitch. And the word wasn't hidden away in the song. It bluntly led the way as the song's title and central focus. With its popularity, including a Grammy nomination, the song was impossible to miss. And it opened up new possibilities for positive definition and reclamation of the word in a way that nothing else had. In the song, being a bitch wasn't so bad. It was, well, complicated, like women themselves.

THE STORY OF A SONG

In Peiken's telling, the song started with a bad day: "As the story goes, I was coming home from a session. I was in a really crappy mood. A lot of people say, 'Oh, it sounds like you had PMS.'" "I mean, let's be honest," she added, with a big laugh. But that wasn't the only reason, she told me: "I felt like everybody around me that had been in the business for as long as I had was having hit songs, finally. It worked for just about all them. And I was just feeling like, 'Why isn't it going well for me?'" That bad mood sparked an idea, and, ironically, her first big hit. Peiken wrote on her blog, "I stopped at a red light, blew a couple of smoke rings out the window and had this exact thought: *I hate the world today*. I was on my way home to a guy who loved me no matter what even though he knew sometimes I could be such a . . . bitch."

Peiken instantly knew that she had something, a central line—"I hate the world today"—and a core idea—"bitch." She revealed to me that the word "bitch" related to her "crappy mood," but it was also "a composite," "a word used for a roof under which all of these moods can live." "I realized it has a way broader meaning, and it could be offensive and vulgar if it's spoken with an intent that is hostile," she added. Her use of the word may have subconsciously related to an experience with the term she had had when she was very young, when "someone close to me," during an argument, "referred to me as a bitch." But, in the song, the word wasn't hostile, and that early experience had changed, too. Thinking about her particular handling of the term, she said, "Maybe I used it in a very productive way. So I thank that person."

With that beginning, Peiken immediately thought about next steps. She knew that it was "going to take a very unique co-writer, somebody that gets this, somebody that believes it." She had known Brooks for about six months. Brooks had been part of the band Sapphire and later The Graces but had signed with Capitol Records as a solo artist in 1995. "I just knew she was the girl to call," Peiken told me. Brooks has since described her own particular experience with the word "bitch." In a 2007 NPR interview with Madeline Brand, she described it as her "no": "I wasn't able to say no very well." "So it was my strength," she continued. "It's a power word."

After Peiken called, Brooks wasted no time: "She came over the next day," Peiken explained, and the two got to work with only Brooks's acoustic guitar. Peiken recalled, "All I had was that first line, which was 'I hate the world today.' And we just went at it back and forth. I often refer to it as analogous to a game [of] Ping Pong. Just she said a line, and it made me think of another line and made her think of another line." The song itself, with only guitar backing, showcases the lyrics: "I'm a bitch." The message is remarkably clear, and the chorus emphasizes all the many sides of a woman—"bitch," "lover," "child," "mother." Each role is weighted equally and showcased through the same melodic profile. In this way, none of the roles are treated as wrong. As the singer repeats, "You know I wouldn't want it any other way."

Peiken and Brooks wondered if radio stations would play the song, but they decided to push away that concern and just write the song. Once finished, it was their record label's turn to worry. Internationally, there was an early request for a title change, "Nothing in Between." Peiken told me, "It might have originated in Japan." There was also some talk about possible substitutes for the word "bitch" in the song itself: "The way I remember it is that they were going to try as best they could to get it on the radio." But, just in case, they asked the two women to think about alternate words or sounds. "And I don't think we could," Peiken revealed. "What were we going to do?" Any substitute—even a bleep or the "B-word"—would have changed the song completely. As Peiken maintained, "the song was all about I think the courage to use that word and not replace it with anything else." Thankfully, the issue was immaterial, because "one station had the audacity to play it, and everybody followed suit, and the rest is history."

A FEMINIST ANTHEM

In addition to the Grammy nomination, the song was second on the U.S. singles chart and stayed there for three weeks. Peiken reflected, "I think the universe rewarded us for standing our ground. I think people embrace it, you know?" It has even been called a "feminist anthem," something Brooks herself wasn't completely comfortable with at the time. In an interview in the *Buffalo News* (May 21, 1998), Dana Duffield asked, "Did you expect 'Bitch' to become a feminist anthem?" "Oh, God," Brooks said, "I hope it's not a feminist anthem. I hope it's a humanist anthem." In another interview, with *USA Today* in 1997, Brooks said, "The song is working because people are more evolved. Five years ago, it would have been considered only a feminist anthem. Now it can apply to anyone."[9]

Part of the song's feminist credentials had to do with its place in Lilith Fair history. Brooks herself was part of the all-women music festival, which toured 1997–1999, and the song was, too. As journalist Erica Palan wrote of "Bitch," "The Lilith Fair ladies ate it up with a spoon and the song became an anthem of female empowerment."[10] The tour set out to disprove the then myth that women are not commercially viable as musicians. The reigning notion was that organizers simply couldn't have more than one woman on the same concert roster. Even radio stations tried not to program one female singer after another. The plan to fight the prevailing wisdom by proving it wrong originated with Sarah McLachlan. In its three years of touring, the festival had more than 130 performances in North America, with about three hundred musical women, including Tracy Chapman, the Indigo Girls, Suzanne Vega, Meshell Ndegeocello, Patti Smith, Lisa Loeb, Missy Elliott, Erykah Badu, Dido, Nelly Furtado, Paula Cole, Christina Aguilera, and Meredith Brooks. And it did what it set out to do, bringing in more than $52 million, $10 million of it donated to women's charities.

Many performers and attendees enjoyed Lilith in a way that they hadn't enjoyed performances before. In *Vanity Fair*'s "Building a Mystery: An Oral History of Lilith Fair," performer Nelly Furtado said, "It was probably one of the first 'safe spaces' in the history of the entertainment history." Critic Ann Powers added, "I had been a working music critic for so many years by that time, and to go to a music festival when you're a young woman is to be harassed, or to deal with men leering at you or pinching your ass, or, conversely, being violent or rude in other ways. To be in a space where that just wasn't a factor was a huge relief."

Backlash followed, of course. In some ways, with so many women involved, Lilith was inevitably a target. To certain people, it was all a little "corny." As Powers revealed, "Lilith seemed uncool, not only because the music it featured wasn't edgy, but because especially in rock, to be a cool woman was to hang out with mostly guys." At the time, *SNL*, always ready to take a swipe at women, featured comedian Ana Gasteyer playing the character Cinder Calhoun, a supposed comic performer at Lilith Fair who is painfully self-important and prefers being called a "wordsmith." We are supposed to laugh at her as she openly questions labels and refers to her "platform," vegetarianism, and a "dream journal." Even Brooks wasn't sure about Lilith at first: "I turned it down the first time I got asked. I at first thought, I don't know if I want to do a folk festival."

The folk rep overlapped a diversity issue. But McLachlan insisted that she had tried to be as inclusive as possible: "The first year, it wasn't very diverse musically, ethnically, racially. We got a lot of flak for that. But we asked everybody. This is who said yes." The concert tour would be tied to these various issues—folk, white, women. Lilith itself became a label, and some Lilith performers struggled with the association. Paula Cole shared, "People started just kind of thinking of me as a 'Lilith Fair artist.' I just needed to have my own identity, so I needed to get away from that." Certain performers connected to Riot Grrrl similarly dealt with labels, especially "woman." As Brownstein wrote in her memoir, "there was always a sense we were going to have to defend and analyze what we were doing. Why are you in an all-female band?" An obvious double standard was at work in both settings: "I doubt in the history of rock journalism and writing any man has been asked, 'Why are you in an all-male band?'"

Despite the issues, Lilith Fair was revolutionary (as was Riot Grrrl), and it proved that women in music were just as significant commercially as men. To make its case, it flipped conventional wisdom, just as it flipped the figure of Lilith. Adam's first wife, Lilith, who would not do as she was told, was no longer an antihero. She was a role model. In this moment, women reappropriated the fallen woman just as Peiken and Brooks took back the term "bitch."[11] Shortly thereafter, many more women in song would power- fully call themselves bitches, redefining bitch as boss or queen but always a woman in charge of her own destiny.

"SHE'S A BITCH"

Inspired by her time at Lilith Fair, Missy Elliott did her Ladies First Tour in 2004, with Alicia Keys and Beyoncé. She would also add to a growing early chorus of those using the word "bitch" in a positive sense, as in her song "She's a Bitch," which was inspired by Whitney Houston. Elliott had worked with Houston and was impressed by her "take-charge attitude."[12] Elliott had—and has—a similar strength. She didn't let early criticism stop her—feedback that she was "too fat" to make it in music.[13] With her song "She's a Bitch," she showcased that power: "When I do my thing / Got the place on fire." And, in the accompanying video, she was all strength, too— in all black with spiked hair.

She told *Ms. Magazine*, "I became a bitch in power because when I walked in, I asked for what I wanted. And at the end of the day, if this is the way I want it, this is the way I'm going to have it." That assumption of power was and is important, especially for women in music. In a 2014 interview with Michael Musto in *Interview Magazine*, Elliott said, "Music is a male-dominated field. Women are not always taken as seriously as we should be, so sometimes we have to put our foot down. To other people that may come across as being a bitch, but it's just knowing what we want and being confident."

As with Peiken and Brooks's "Bitch," the popularity of Elliott and her song ensured widespread transformation. In 1999, Danyel Smith, then editor in chief of the magazine *Vibe*, explained, "If I was 21 . . . I would think that Missy is about the coolest chick in the universe. And I would think 'if she's using it and it's no big deal to her, then it's no big deal to me.'"[14] By the following year, the word "bitch" was everywhere; its positive use was widely accepted and repeated. In 2007, in her song "Gimme More," Britney Spears announced, "It's Britney, bitch!" And in 2013, she released her song "Work Bitch." Two years later, Madonna released her song "Bitch I'm Madonna." And, in 2018, Miley Cyrus released her cover version of Elton John's "The Bitch Is Back" on the album *Restoration: Reimagining the Songs of Elton John and Bernie Taupin*. Alongside this musical transformation, friends began calling each other "beyotches," with a bitch defined as "sexy," "bad," and "boss," from Trina's 1999 "Da Baddest Bitch" to Doja Cat's 2020 "Boss Bitch."

So pervasive now is the term in song that Peiken called it all a bit "redundant." But the evolution is significant, and Peiken and Brooks's song was a pivotal moment in that change. The song, after all, was a massive hit—and one with staying power. As Peiken recalled: "[I]t wasn't just . . . here today, gone tomorrow. It was talked about and written about and 25 years later, it's still carrying me. Because it was so novel and because it was so reso-nant, it's still being used as markers of that year and time in film and still being rerecorded in TV shows." In 2020, for example, recording artist Ruby Amanfu covered the song for Hulu's show *Little Fires Everywhere*. In this light, I suggested to Peiken that the song was the start of the word's posi-tive reclamation in music. Peiken insisted that she "never really thought of it that way." But, she said, "I am flattered, and I am honored, and I hope you're right."

Writers have pointed out specific issues with various "bitch" appro-priations and their context—the antifeminist bent of Spears's song "Work Bitch" (Caroline Linton's take in the *Daily Beast*) or Doja Cat's controver-sial work with Dr. Luke. Concerns also center on a "false power" in these seemingly positive uses of the word, with the negative association still very much present. That negative association has entered the vernacular in other applications, too: "bitch slap," a hit with an open palm; "to bitch," as in to complain; and bitch as an insult to men, meaning he's "girlish."[15] This latter evolution relates to wider use of words coded feminine to insult men. And the same strategy exists in music, with some men, such as Justin Bieber or boy-band members more generally, insulted as "wimpy" or "too femi-nine"—labels that insult women and the whole complex of gender identity at the same time.[16]

But we shouldn't necessarily be concerned, at least about the evolving misuse of "bitch." As Montell writes, "A word doesn't have to lose its nega-tive meanings completely to be considered reclaimed. The path to recla-mation is almost never smooth." Positive deployment of "bitch" clearly can help in the process. Obviously, awareness of the thinking behind negative uses of the word can, too. And it's that awareness that has been central to this book. By targeting language and the thinking that supports its destruc-tive use, I have attempted to strike at the core of misogyny. To some, it might seem like a weak approach. *Words will never hurt us.* But, like so much of our commonly held pseudo-wisdom, the idea that words can't hurt is misleading and fundamentally wrong. Sticks and stones aren't weapons without supporting belief and conviction established and created through language.

Epilogue
RACIST, SEXIST WORDS

While working on this book—learning and writing about the lives of women in music—I've also learned related truths about other women in other artistic fields. Sometimes I've stumbled upon these stories in research. Other times, it's been a conversation with friends or my kids, as with the story of Medusa. I'll mention something about one of the women featured in this book, and it will remind them of something they had heard about another woman outside of music. One story leads to another—all of them connected. It's a similar pattern, playing out over and over, swallowing women and their realities whole.

In this way, as I was working on the last chapter, I encountered the biography of Zelda Fitzgerald, who has been cast in popular imaginings as "crazy." But, as revealed in articles such as "How F. Scott Fitzgerald, Author of 'The Great Gatsby,' Plagiarized His Own Wife," she, in fact, contributed much to the writing of her husband's classic novel *The Great Gatsby*. Some believe F. Scott stole whole portions of *her* writing and published them as his own, as he did in the case of other writing projects, such as *The Beautiful and Damned*. In a review, she called him out, writing, "Mr. Fitzgerald—I believe that is how he spells his name—seems to believe that plagiarism begins at home."

Honestly, I'm no longer surprised—by the truth or the later spin in reception. At this point, I'm all too familiar with the pattern. The celebrity world, for women in the arts, is like a gilded cage—the glitzy world of *Gatsby* come to life, with all the sordid details and, of course, the tragic end, including Zelda's. But that doesn't mean I'm not angry. In fact, I fear I'll be mad forever.

In music, a web of interconnected words and toxic labeling links so many women, at the same time trapping them in story after story of bias and inequity. This trap was set long ago, but it's still active in new and old ways, baited by society's protection of the patriarchy and a related distrust of extraordinary women. In practice, it has devalued talented women in music for centuries. It has tied genius to toxic behavior—reserving both for men alone. It has privileged production and management as male enterprises. And all her work, whatever she's accomplished, is further discounted if the men around her fail or fall down.

Of course, many of the women treated in this way have recognized the odds stacked against them. In response, they have tried to keep the focus on their music rather than their personal lives. They have tried to control the narrative, avoiding interviews or photographs. They have even tried to play along or joke at their own expense. But those understandable efforts have been used against some of them, too.

The only escape from all of this isn't up, the proverbial high road. No, another escape is in careful attention to the language we use, now and in the future. Perhaps less flashy and certainly less clichéd, this escape relies on understanding the history of certain words. It also relies on recognizing certain patterns—the way words are consistently deployed to support beliefs and standards that tear down women in music while conditioning us to accept this cycle as the norm. Those patterns are hugely frustrating, confusing, and, yes, a source of anger—at least for me. But, at the same time, they can be a source of power. Witnesses can discount the testimony of one woman. But there is strength in numbers—the stories of so many women—when they repeat in basic contour and language. Every time I had to write "once more" or "again," which happened often in this book, I was reinforcing those patterns and those stories. Hopefully, the double standards and toxic attention are now undeniable.

With knowledge of these patterns of oppression, people might better understand the testimony of one woman in the future, as they could have in the case of Jennifer Lopez and her recent revelations in the 2022 Netflix documentary *Halftime*. In it, she complains about having to share the 2020 Super Bowl halftime show. That disclosure was ridiculed online, viewed as an insult to Shakira, her co-headliner (e.g., see *People*'s "Jennifer Lopez Slammed for Calling 2020 Super Bowl Halftime Performance with Shakira 'the Worst Idea'"). But as Lopez says in the documentary, historically, a single star has fronted that show. She saw the change, in her case, as an indictment of society's values. Because she was a woman and Latina, apparently those in power felt she wasn't enough. In light of this book, I have no doubt that her conclusion is valid. And the naysayers missed the point completely, opting once more to create a fictional narrative of feuding divas.

A recognition of these patterns in the treatment of women and the words involved, then, allows us to grasp in full the lives and work of women in music as well as their struggles. But, with that recognition, we can also change the thinking behind these words—thinking rooted in misogyny. Then we can represent and help create the world in which we want to live through language. If enough of us make that move, honesty and equality can become the new norm. As Lizzo told *People* in 2022, "What I'm doing is stepping into my confidence and my power to create my own beauty standard. And one day that will just be the standard."

Modeling the right use of words can help—both in writing and, as we saw in the previous chapter, in song. Singers have given us anthems of change, such as Christina Aguilera's "Can't Hold Us Down" (2002). And related hope rests in the musical resistance of new generations, such as the teen and preteen girls in the Los Angeles-based punk band the Linda Lindas. This group gave us the powerful 2021 viral hit "Racist, Sexist Boy," written in direct response to band member Mila's real-life experience dealing with a racist boy at her school. Performing in the LA public library for AAPI Heritage Month, they let loose their anger, singing, "you have racist, sexist joys," but "we rebuild what you destroy." Explaining the song, Mila told *The Guardian*, "We wanted to use our voice for people who don't have one."

Several women in music are also working to target the music industry itself. In 2018, Alicia Keys announced the establishment of the initiative She Is the Music. The nonprofit organization, according to its website, is dedicated to "increasing the number of women working in music—songwriters, engineers, producers, artists and industry professionals." Fundamental to its mission are recent statistics around the place of women in these areas of music: women represent only 2.6 percent of producers and engineers/mixers credited with top songs in 2019. In her acceptance speech for the Icon Songwriter in 2018, Keys explained that through this initiative, she is working with other powerful women in music to create "real opportunities" for women in these areas in order to ultimately "reshape the industry that we all love."

Songwriter and producer Linda Perry is working similarly through her project EqualizeHer, which aims to close the gender gap in "all aspects of the music industry, from recording studios to stages to board rooms." She certainly has the experience to back up her mission. Referencing her own work in music production, she told *The Guardian* in 2022, "There's not very many women [who] do what I do." And she had to push to make that move, from musician in the group 4 Non Blondes to producer. For a lot of female musicians, working with Perry as a producer was a welcome change: "It gave them a sense of ease, knowing I wasn't going to be hitting on them."

In country music, Amanda Shires is specifically targeting a localized gender imbalance, much as McLachlan did earlier in music more generally (at least in theory). As Shires observed, the musicians who perform country on the radio are overwhelmingly male, increasingly so. In musician Maren Morris's experience, as she explained in 2019 to the *New York Times*, "Everyone blames somebody else. It's the labels, it's the radio, it's the publishers that don't sign enough women." But the disparity seems to rely on conviction—one articulated in 2015 by a supposed expert on "music scheduling," radio consultant Keith Hill. Women, he said, are the "tomatoes" of the salad that is country music: "If you want to make ratings in country radio, take females out." Again, the very label "woman" was an issue.

This problem in country music made headlines then and again in 2020, including one in the *Washington Post*, when writer Chris Wilman joked on Twitter, "I turned on the 105.1 country station in L.A. just now, and they are playing the new song by Gabby Barrett, and then, without any pause or interruption at all, they went into a Kelsea Ballerini song. Can't they get fined for that?" The pointed barb about the unspoken practice of carefully spacing female musicians on country radio attracted confirmation from a station in Michigan: "We cannot play two females back to back . . . I applaud their courage."

Rather than a festival, Shires wanted to create a supergroup, like the 1980s Highwaymen, with Johnny Cash, Waylon Jennings, Kris Kristofferson, and

Willie Nelson. Her supergroup, however, would be women only, the High-women. With musicians Brandi Carlile, Natalie Hemby, and Morris, among others, they released their first album in 2019. In some ways, their song "Highwomen" plainly asserts and maintains their existence. And they'll "come back again and again and again." Unfortunately, country music needs that reminder.

Efforts such as these are encouraging. They represent the transformation we need, though change of this kind can be slow and stubborn. In April 2022, yet another negative Yoko reference appeared on film—in the Net-flix movie *Metal Lords*. The myths of the past clearly persist. Thankfully, efforts of reassessment are continuing, too, in journalistic criticism and on television. Hopefully, any new efforts will avoid the "temptation of the talk-ing penis," my phrase (via *Pam & Tommy*) for tawdry elements that work at cross-purposes with any educational aims. If they can do that, this reap-praisal is worthwhile, even if the education involved is sadly simplistic—as in the article "Nirvana's Former Soundman Says Courtney Love Was a 'Pretty Positive Presence' around the Band" (May 17, 2022). After all, it's all valuable if it's necessary.

I find myself committed to a similar sort of basic truth telling. And no doubt I'll continue to make parallel arguments, sometimes in surprising settings, as I did at a party in April 2022. The party featured the fantas-tic Sun Kings, a Beatles cover band, and guests were asked to dress in keeping with the theme of the event. In a sea of '70s tie-dye and colorful peace signs, I danced to hits such as "Here Comes the Sun" and "Let It Be" dressed in all black, big sunglasses, and a wide-brimmed white hat. Obviously, it was not the most original homage to Ono, instead a cheap mix of her witch costume and pictures I've seen of her in black and white. But it seemed only right that I make an attempt, at least, to assert her positive presence in the Beatles' story. The party was among friends and family, and yet someone with whom I wasn't previously acquainted assessed my outfit: "Oh, no," he said. "You're going to break up the party." I countered, "If anything is going to break up the party, it's that sort of misogyny."

I cushioned my response with a smile, as women often do. And I didn't mention the racism involved—a prejudice around Asians and Asian Ameri-cans only amplified in recent years. It wasn't my party, after all. In this book, of course, I can highlight all of that—the whole ugly history. And it is, indeed, ugly. I suppose, I can do that because this book is my party, though it's certainly a rather grim affair.

Still, I remain optimistic. With awareness and the efforts of so many extraordinary women in music, real revolution is possible—in how we see women in music in the past and present, and how we see ourselves. As the Linda Lindas sing, "we rebuild what you destroy." And, with that, women will be able to do and be even more. After all, women already have achieved so much in music, often through undeniable talent, work ethic, and creative subversion, as we've seen throughout this book. What could they do if the world around them supported their efforts completely? What could they do if they weren't held back by language?

Here comes the sun.

AFTERWORD

Amy Ray with Lily E. Hirsch

The power of language is such a huge topic, so I'm glad this book is addressing it. Because I think about it all the time. There are certain artists I really love, and I love how they use words. But words can be used against artists too. And it's on all of us—musicians, fans, people in the media—to make sure we don't develop unquestioned references, labels, or stereotypes about a musician's audience or their music. The alternative is obviously not constructive. It's lazy.

During my career in the Indigo Girls with Emily Saliers, I was aware of associations with listening to our music. And our fan base was talked about almost as much as our music. These white, male writers had a fascination or voyeurism when it came to us and they talked about us, about our audience, and how gay the audience was, or how they focused on our presentation as gay women, with constant references to our dress and what we looked like. It was a very monolithic sort of description. And it was always presented in a very derogatory way.

So I would meet people along the way, and they'd say, "Well, I'm a closet Indigo Girl fan." And I would say, "Well, you don't have to be in the closet about it." But if you were a straight guy of a certain ilk or age, that categorization and media presentation had an effect. You didn't want people to know you listened to the Indigo Girls.

There was also a lot of negative association with our songs, their confessional nature and a certain earnestness in our music. Of course, male musicians were treated differently. When you're emo and you're a white guy with a certain crowd, it's cool. But when you're a woman with an acoustic guitar, it isn't. That was what we carried. And it made us even hate ourselves sometimes.

Lilith Fair happened on the heels of a lot of that criticism. And there was this brief moment in time when people were forced to reckon with the economic power of all these women fronting bands and singer-songwriters. The tables were starting to turn a bit. But not long after that, it became derogatory again to be associated with Lilith Fair, as radio sort of shifted. Instead of having us on the show, even *Saturday Night Live* made comedic references to us that were a wink and a nod about lesbians. As Susan Faludi wrote in her book *Backlash*, with female advancement, there are antifeminist reactions in the media, corporate American, and political structures. And that's what we felt like was always happening in music.

We couldn't really let that get us down. Because if you're going to try to just do your thing and play music, which is what we wanted to do, you have to, as Meshell wrote, have your own world, in a way, and keep doing it. You have to be doing what you do, forcing everything else to change so that society accepts you. I don't know everybody else's journey, but I do know that one.

Now there is a generational change, and it does give you hope. Younger people are learning to navigate music media and the internet, experimenting in terms of musical taste. And they're free about gender and sexuality and race and socioeconomics; it's a beautiful thing. But it's on us all to do the same—to branch out, hear what's out there, poke around constantly, be fearless about your own sort of consuming of music and art. And that goes for musicians too and how they support one another. It's good to share gigs, share information, expanding the space to include other people. As a woman, you have to keep doing that.

It's also on us to think through the language and categorizations we use—all of which support our habits, listening and otherwise. Of course, language is complicated. I personally think about the word "bitch," negative uses of the word but also how my friend, the musician Bitch, also known as Capital B, wants to take it back, as other women have tried and are trying to do too. Then there's the words dark and light, their associations with good and bad.

It seems like a racial trope sometimes. And yet, it's popular. "Don't dwell in the darkness." It's an old biblical thing. And great writers, great singers, like Billie Holiday and Nina Simone, have used dark and light imagery in a way that can be really beautiful. There's a lot of layers because darkness is not light, and it can be scary to be in a place that doesn't have light.

I also think about the name Indigo Girls. We were so young. When we started, we were sixteen. When we came up with the name, we were, I believe, twenty-one. I called Emily, and we looked through the dictionary. I said, "How about the word indigo?" She said, "Oh, that's cool. Why don't we put girls with it because of the alliteration?" Indigo women or womyn just didn't have the same sound. But why the gender identifier, especially since we value gender fluidity? Girls is also a sort of submissive word. Now it's funny because we're old but we're still Girls.

Honestly, there's so many shifts in language; I don't always know what to do. But the words we use affect everything—the level of respect musicians receive as well as the self-respect of the people who consume those musicians. So, it's on us to not take the easy road, and to really try to think about language, from both sides of the equation, from the artist to the person that's talking about the artist. Then there can be change, fostered by the shared experience, friendship, and community created around music.

NOTES

INTRODUCTION

1. Andrew Von Hendy, *The Modern Construction of Myth* (Bloomington: Indiana University Press, 2002), 294 and 304.

2. Dominic Green called Alice an "inferior talent" and "the Yoko Ono of jazz" in "John Coltrane and the End of Jazz," *Washington Examiner*, August 26, 2018. See also Jimi Izrael, "Alice Coltrane, Wife of John, Left Her Own Mark," *NPR*, January 16, 2007.

3. Julie Zeveloff, "There's a Brilliant Reason Why Van Halen Asked for a Bowl of M&Ms with All the Brown Candies Removed before Every Show," *Insider*, September 6, 2016.

4. Kate Manne, *Down Girl: The Logic of Misogyny* (Oxford: Oxford University Press, 2018).

5. Paige Sweet, "The Sociology of Gaslighting," *American Sociological Review* 84, no. 5 (October 2019): 851–52.

6. Amanda Montell, *Wordslut: A Feminist Guide to Taking Back the English Language* (New York: Harper, 2019), 3.

7. Sally Anne Gross and George Musgrave, *Can Music Make You Sick? Measuring the Price of Musical Ambition* (London: University of Westminster Press, 2020), 87–92.

8. Mark Yarm, "The All-Female Band Fanny Made History. A New Doc Illuminates It," *New York Times*, May 25, 2022.

9. For a wonderfully complete discussion of the many wrongs in Alma Mahler's reception narrative, see Nancy Newman, "#AlmaToo: The Art of Being Believed," *Journal of the American Musicological Society* 75, no. 1 (2022): 39–79.

10. Alan Henry, "How to Succeed When You're Marginalized or Discriminated Against at Work," *New York Times*, October 1, 2019.

11. Komeil Soheili, "Grueling Gym Routines, Restrictive Diets, and No Dating: K-pop Stars Tell Us about the Dark Side of Their Industry," *Insider*, December 1, 2019.

12. Quoted in Katherine Ellis, "Female Pianists and Their Male Critics in Nineteenth-Century Paris," *Journal of the American Musicological Society* 50, nos. 2/3 (Summer–Autumn, 1997): 362. See also Ellis, 355. Friedrich Nietzsche wrote in similar terms, "The danger for artists, for geniuses . . . is woman: adoring women confront them with corruption. Hardly any of them have character enough not to be corrupted—or 'redeemed'—when they find themselves treated like gods: soon they condescend to the level of the women." Cited in Andreas Huyssen, *After the Great Divide: Modernism, Mass Culture, Postmodernism* (Ann Arbor: University of Michigan Press, 1986), 51.

13. Sarah McLachlan in Buffy Childerhose, *From Lilith to Lilith Fair* (New York: St. Martin's Griffin, 1998), xi.

14. Cited in Kimberly J. Stern, *The Social Life of Criticism: Gender, Critical Writing, and the Politics of Belonging* (Ann Arbor: University of Michigan Press, 2016), 1.

15. Kembrew McLeod, "Between Rock and a Hard Place: Gender and Rock Criticism," in *Pop Music and the Press*, ed. Steve Jones (Philadelphia: Temple University Press, 2002), 94.

16. For some great exceptions, see *Rock She Wrote: Women Write about Rock, Pop, and Rap*, ed. Evelyn McDonnell and Ann Powers (Medford, NJ: Plexus Publishing, 2014).

17. Brenda Johnson-Grau, "Sweet Nothings: Presentation of Women Musicians in Pop Journalism," in *Pop Music and the Press*, ed. Steve Jones (Philadelphia: Temple University Press, 2002), 205. See also Holly Kruse, "Abandoning the Absolute: Transcendence and Gender in Popular Music Discourse," in *Pop Music and the Press*, ed. Steve Jones (Philadelphia: Temple University Press, 2002), 135.

18. Cited in Johnson-Grau, "Sweet Nothings," 213–14.

19. Paula Wolfe, *Women in the Studio: Creativity, Control and Gender in Popular Music Production* (London: Routledge, 2020), 81.

20. Pierre Bourdieu, "The Social Space and the Genesis of Groups," *Theory and Society* 14, no. 6 (1985): 729.

21. J. L. Austin, *How to Do Things with Words* (Cambridge, MA: Harvard University Press, 1962), 6.

22. Erin A. Meyers, *Cupcakes, Pinterest, and Ladyporn: Feminized Popular Culture in the Early Twenty-First Century* (Urbana: University of Illinois Press, 2015), 72.

CHAPTER I

1. Jerry Hopkins, *Yoko Ono* (New York: Macmillan, 1986), 89.

2. David Frost, "Paul McCartney: Yoko Ono Didn't Break Up the Beatles," *Rolling Stone*, October 29, 2012.

3. Quoted in Chuck Arnold, "How 'The Ballad of John and Yoko' Changed the Music World," *New York Post*, March 19, 2019.

4. Kenneth Womack and Kit O'Toole, *Fandom and the Beatles: The Act You've Known for All These Years* (Oxford: Oxford University Press, 2021), 4–5.

5. "Beatle's Marriage on Rocks?," *Los Angeles Times*, June 25, 1968, F8.

6. "Lennon Sued for Divorce," *Los Angeles Times*, August 23, 1968.

7. SooJin Lee, "The Art of Artists' Personae: Yayoi Kusama, Yoko Ono, and Mariko Mori" (PhD diss., University of Illinois, 2014), 103.

8. "Mind Games," *Santa Barbara News-Press*, September 2, 1994.

9. Brigid Cohen, "Limits of National History: Yoko Ono, Stefan Wolpe, and Dilemmas of Cosmopolitanism," *Musical Quarterly* 97, no. 2 (Summer 2014): 181–237.

10. John Kuo Wei Tchen and Dylan Yeats, eds., *Yellow Peril! An Archive of Anti-Asian Fear* (London: Verso, 2014), 223.

11. Tchen and Yeats, introduction, *Yellow Peril!*, 16.

12. Rosalind S. Chou and Joe R. Feagin, *The Myth of the Model Minority: Asian Americans Facing Racism* (London: Routledge, 2016), 7–9.

13. Tamara Levitz, "Yoko Ono and the Unfinished Music of 'John & Yoko': Imagining Gender and Racial Equality in the Late 1960s," in *Impossible to Hold: Women and Culture in the 1960s*, ed. Avital H. Bloch and Lauri Umansky (New York: New York University Press, 2005), 220.

14. Jann S. Wenner, "The Beatles: One Guy Standing There, Shouting 'I'm Leaving,'" *Rolling Stone*, May 14, 1970.

15. Sheridan Prasso, *The Asian Mystique: Dragon Ladies, Geisha Girls, and Our Fantasies of the Exotic Orient* (New York: Public Affairs, 2005), 29–34.

16. Lee, "The Art of Artists' Personae."

17. Manne, *Down Girl*, 59. See also Tamura Lomax, *Jezebel Unhinged: Loosing the Black Female Body in Religion and Culture* (Durham, NC: Duke University Press, 2018).

18. Quoted in Levitz, "Yoko Ono."

19. Midori Yoshimoto and Kathy O'Dell have noted that, though women were a part of Fluxus, they are often overlooked in histories of the artistic movement in favor of men. See Lee, "The Art of Artists' Personae," 107.

20. Carolyn St. Stevens, "Yoko Ono: A Transgressive Diva," in *Diva Nation: Female Icons from Japanese Cultural History*, ed. Laura Miller and Rebecca Copeland (Berkeley: University of California Press, 2018), 120.

21. Manne, *Down Girl*, xxi.

22. Lili Zarzycki, "Interview with Christine Battersby," *Architectural Review*, March 26, 2020.

23. Quoted in Cynthia Haven, "Yoko Ono Reflects on Her Life, Work and Public Perception," *Stanford Report*, January 15, 2009.

CHAPTER 2

1. Eric Arias, "How Does Media Influence Social Norms? Experimental Evidence on the Role of Common Knowledge," *Political Science Research and Methods* 7, no. 3 (July 2019): 565.

2. See, for example, social norms theory, in the writing of Alan D. Berkowitz, editor and founder of "The Report on Social Norms."

3. Karl French and Michael McKean, "With an Introduction by Michael McKean," *The Guardian*, September 22, 2000.

4. Quoted in John Kenneth Muir, *This Is Spinal Tap* (Milwaukee, WI: Limelight Editions, 2010), 90.

5. Wolfe, *Women in the Studio*, 31.

6. Wolfe, *Women in the Studio*, 81.

7. Quoted in Muir, *This Is Spinal Tap*, 67.

8. Georgina Gregory, *Boy Bands and the Performance of Pop Masculinity* (New York: Routledge, 2019), 18.

9. Building tropes on top of tropes, Barenaked Ladies is responsible for a rendition of the theme song used on the show *The Big Bang Theory*, which also features the song "Be My Yoko Ono" in an episode making use of the "Yoko Oh No" trope as a plot point.

CHAPTER 3

1. See, for example, James Nye, "Courtney Love's Father Claims He Can Prove SHE Was Responsible for Kurt Cobain's Death," *Daily Mail*, May 1, 2014.

2. Wolfe, *Women in the Studio*, 13.

3. Charles R. Cross, *Heavier than Heaven: A Biography of Kurt Cobain* (New York: Hyperion, 2001), 211.

4. See Cross, *Heavier than Heaven*, 240–41.

5. "And One More Thing: Courtney Love Heard Enough Unflattering Comparisons between Her Marriage to Nirvana's Kurt Cobain and John Lennon and Yoko Ono's," *Los Angeles Times*, October 25, 1992.

6. Quoted in Amica Lane, "Asking for It: Giving Outspoken Women in Music a Bad Name," *The F Word*, May 27, 2013.

7. Robert Hilburn, "The Trials of Love," *Los Angeles Times*, April 10, 1994, G1.

8. Brian Donovan, *American Gold Digger: Marriage, Money, and the Law from the Ziegfeld Follies to Anna Nicole Smith* (Chapel Hill: University of North Carolina Press, 2020), 6.

9. See Anwen Crawford, *Live through This* (New York: Bloomsbury, 2015), 88.

10. *Hartford Courant*, April 14, 1994.

11. See Debra Kay Gorney, "Image Construction in Print and Internet Media: Analysis of the Controversial Courtney Love" (PhD diss., Wayne State University, 1999), 124.

12. Gorney, "Image Construction." 126.

13. Polk and Colicchio, quoted in Jessica Wakeman, "Flashback: Nancy Spungen Found Dead at Chelsea Hotel," *Rolling Stone*, October 12, 2017.

14. Manne, *Down Girl*, 14.

15. Quoted in Robin Murray, "Courtney Love Praises Yoko Ono," *Clash*, February 24, 2010.

16. Courtney Love, *Dirty Blonde* (London: Faber and Faber, 2006).

17. Quoted in Hannah Ewens, *Fangirls: Scenes from Modern Music Culture* (Austin: University of Texas Press, 2020), 221.

CHAPTER 4

1. Michel Foucault, *Madness and Civilization: A History of Insanity in the Age of Reason* (New York: Random House, 1988), 68.

2. Eleanor Morgan, *Hysterical: Why We Need to Talk about Women, Hormones, and Mental Health* (New York: Seal Press, 2019), 91.

3. Stephen Harper, *Madness, Power, and the Media: Class, Gender and Race in Popular Representations of Mental Distress* (London: Palgrave Macmillan, 2009), 5.

4. Harper, *Madness, Power, and the Media*, 117.

5. Susan McClary, *Feminine Endings* (Minneapolis: University of Minnesota Press, 1991).

6. "Sopranos Losing It on Stage—Here Are the 7 Best 'Mad Scenes' in Opera," *Classic FM*, November 3, 2015.

7. Melanie Lowe, "Colliding Feminism: Britney Spears, 'Tweens,' and the Politics of Reception," *Popular Music and Society* 26 (2003): 123–40.

8. Roger Friedman, "Britney Doesn't Know Yoko; Will Justin Go Solo?," *Fox News*, March 1, 2002.

9. Quoted in Jim Farber, "Teen Queen's Heavy Crown," *New York Daily News*, May 14, 2000.

10. A. J. Racy, "Domesticating Otherness: The Snake Charmer in American Popular Culture," *Ethnomusicology* 60, no. 2 (Spring/Summer 2016): 197–232.

11. Lowe, "Colliding Feminism," 124.

12. Meyers, *Cupcakes, Pinterest, and Ladyporn*, 74–76.

13. Sady Doyle, *Trainwreck: The Women We Love to Hate, Mock, and Fear . . . and Why* (Brooklyn, NY: Melville House, 2016), xiii.

14. Christopher R. Smit, *The Exile of Britney Spears: A Tale of 21st Century Consumption* (Bristol, UK: Intellect Books, 2011), 30.

15. John Dingwall, Karen Bale, and Beverley Lyons, "The Raz: Justin: Britney 'Is Crazy,'" *Daily Record* (Glasgow, UK), January 17, 2004, 21.

16. "Britney Spears' Record Label Accused of Calling her 'Crazy' in Secret Clash," *Daily Star* (Online) (London), October 4, 2019.

17. Lewis Corner, "Britney Spears, Ke$ha Responsible for 'Vocal Fry' Craze among Girls," *Digital Spy*, December 14, 2011. Nina Eidsheim also connects vocal fry to "gendered and generational dimensions." See Nina Eidsheim, *The Race of Sound: Listening, Timbre, and Vocality in African American Music* (Durham, NC: Duke University Press, 2019), 28.

18. Brittany Spanos, "#FreeBritney: Understanding the Fan-let Britney Spears Movement," *Rolling Stone*, February 8, 2021.

CHAPTER 5

1. Lomax, *Jezebel Unhinged*, 11, 21.

2. Moya Bailey, *Misogynoir Transformed: Black Women's Digital Resistance* (New York: New York University Press, 2021), 2.

3. Wulf D. Hund and Charles W. Mills, "Comparing Black People to Monkeys Has a Long, Dark Simian History," *The Conversation*, February 28, 2016.

4. Manne, *Down Girl*, 135–37.

5. See, for example, "Are Meghan Markle & Prince Harry Today's Yoko Ono & John Lennon?" *CNN*, August 28, 2020.

6. Quoted in Eric Harvey, "How Twitter Changed Music," *Pitchfork*, October 14, 2019.

7. Robin James, "Coincidental Consumption and the Thinkpiece Economy," *Society Pages*, November 15, 2013.

8. Lauren Aker, *Fan Phenomena: The Twilight Sage* (Bristol, UK: Intellect Books, 2016), 36.

9. Maggie Parke and Natalie Wilson, eds., *Theorizing Twilight: Critical Essays on What's at Stake in a Post-Vampire World* (Jefferson, NC: McFarland, 2011), 3.

10. Heather Anastasiu, "The Hero and the Id: A Psychoanalytic Inquiry into the Popularity of Twilight," in *Theorizing Twilight: Critical Essays on What's at Stake in a Post-Vampire World*, ed. Maggie Parke and Natalie Wilson (Jefferson, NC: McFarland, 2011), 51.

11. See Melissa Miller, "Maybe Edward Is the Most Dangerous Thing Out There," in *Theorizing Twilight: Critical Essays on What's at Stake in a Post-Vampire World*, ed. Maggie Parke and Natalie Wilson (Jefferson, NC: McFarland, 2011), 168–71.

12. Frankie Dunn, "FKA twigs Reveals the Meaning behind Every Track on 'Magdalene,'" *i-D*, November 8, 2019.

13. Dionne P. Stephens and Layli D. Phillips, "Freaks, Gold Diggers, Divas, and Dykes: The Sociohistorical Development of Adolescent African American Women's Sexual Scripts," *Sexuality & Culture* (Winter 2003): 5.

14. Bailey, *Misogynoir Transformed*, 2.

CHAPTER 6

1. Manne, *Down Girl*, xxi.

2. Ralph W. Hood and W. Paul Williamson, *Them That Believe: The Power and Meaning of the Christian Serpent-Handling Tradition* (Berkeley: University of California Press, 2008), 93 and 98.

3. Chloe Govan, *Taylor Swift: The Rise of the Nashville Teen* (London: Omnibus Press, 2012), 145.

4. For other examples, see Diadem Pambid, "Taylor Swift Getting Death Threats from 'Directioners,'" *IBT*, www.ibtimes.com.au, November 20, 2012.

5. Govan, *Taylor Swift*, 175.

6. Quoted in Govan, *Taylor Swift*, 185.

7. Nate Jones, "When Did the Media Turn against Taylor Swift," *Vulture*, July 21, 2016.

8. Shaun Cullen, "The Innocent and the Runaway: Kanye West, Taylor Swift, and the Cultural Politics of Racial Melodrama," *Journal of Popular Music Studies* 28, no. 1 (2016): 33–50.

9. Christobel Hastings, "The Timeless Myth of Medusa, a Rape Victim Turned into a Monster," *Vice*, April 9, 2018.

CHAPTER 7

1. Rachel Kadzi Ghanash, "Her Eyes Were Watching the Stars: How Missy Elliott Became an Icon," *Elle*, May 15, 2017.

2. Gerrick Kennedy, *Didn't We Almost Have It All: In Defense of Whitney Houston* (New York: Abrams, 2022), 88.

3. Quoted in Kennedy, *Didn't We Almost Have It All*, 89.

4. Quoted in Gross and Musgrave, *Can Music Make You Sick?*, 102.

5. Moira Donegan, "How Bertha Pappenheim Cured Herself," in Jessica Valenti and Jaclyn Friedman, eds., *Believe Me: How Trusting Women Can Change the World* (New York: Seal Press, 2020), 10.

6. In Jessica Valenti and Jaclyn Friedman, eds., *Believe Me: How Trusting Women Can Change the World* (New York: Seal Press, 2020).

7. See also Valenti and Friedman, *Believe Me*, 152.

8. Cass R. Sunstein, "#MeToo as a Revolutionary Cascade," in *The Routledge Handbook of the Politics of the #MeToo Movement*, ed. Giti Chandra and Irma Erlingsdóttir (New York: Routledge, 2021), 37.

9. Karen Boyle, "Of Moguls, Monsters, and Men," in *The Routledge Handbook of the Politics of the #MeToo Movement*, ed. Giti Chandra and Irma Erlingsdóttir (New York: Routledge, 2021), 188.

10. See also Valenti and Friedman, *Believe Me*, 152.

11. Robyn Autry, "Chris Brown Told the World Who He Was with Rihanna. We Didn't Listen," *NBC Think*, June 27, 2018.

CHAPTER 8

1. "Tardy to the Party: Performers Who've Been Late to the Stage," *CNN*, March 5, 2013.

2. Rachel Cowgill and Hilary Poriss, "Introduction," in *The Arts of the Prima Donna in the Long Nineteenth Century*, ed. Rachel Cowgill and Hilary Poriss (Oxford: Oxford University Press, 2012), xxxiii.

3. Susan Rutherford, *The Prima Donna and Opera, 1815–1930* (Cambridge: Cambridge University Press, 2006), 4; see also Beth L. Glixon, "Private Lives of Public Women: Prima Donnas in Mid-Seventeenth-Century Venice," *Music & Letters* 76, no. 4 (November 1995): 509–31.

4. Roberta Montemorra Marvin, "Idealizing the Prima Donna in Mid-Victorian London," in *The Arts of the Prima Donna in the Long Nineteenth Century*, ed. Rachel Cowgill and Hilary Poriss (Oxford: Oxford University Press, 2012), 23.

5. Karen Hensen, "Introduction," in *Technology and the Diva: Sopranos, Opera, and Media from Romanticism to the Digital Age*, ed. Karen Hensen (Cambridge: Cambridge University Press, 2016), 12

6. Stephens and Phillips, "Freaks, Gold Diggers, Divas, and Dykes," 15.

7. Mariah Carey, quoted in Emma Brockes, "Mariah Carey: 'I try not to be a jerk. I really do,'" *The Guardian*, October 2, 2009.

8. Quoted in John Soeder, "Whitney Houston Could Be a Daunting Diva, but That Amazing Voice of Hers Soared above Everything Else," *Cleveland.com*, February 12, 2002.

9. "Whitney Houston: Return of the Troubled Diva," *The Guardian*, September 19, 2009.

10. Robin James, *Resilience & Melancholy: Pop Music, Feminism Neoliberalism* (Winchester, UK: Zero Books, 2015), 116.

11. Quoted in Tim Teeman, "Why Jennifer Lopez Doesn't Want to Be Called a 'Diva,'" *Daily Beast*, April 13, 2017.

12. Quoted in Olivia Singh, "Jennifer Lopez Says She Was Unfairly Labeled as a 'Diva' because 'I was Latin, and I was a woman,'" *Insider*, November 18, 2019.

13. Sesali Bowen, "There Are Important Lessons in Mariah Carey's Diva Behavior," *Refinery29*, May 26, 2017.

14. She described the diva character as fun in an interview with Alex Frank, "Forever Mariah: An Interview with an Icon," *Pitchfork*, November 28, 2018.

15. "Mariah Carey Swims in Evening Gowns and Heels: 25 Things You Don't Know about Me," *Us Weekly*, July 1, 2015.

CHAPTER 9

1. Montell, *Wordslut*, 35.

2. Meredith Ralston, *Slut-Shaming, Whorephobia, and the Unfinished Sexual Revolution* (Montreal and Kingston: McGill-Queen's University Press, 2021), 26.

3. Jarune Uwujaren, "How Women Are Pressured into Being Sexy, but Punished for Being Sexual," everydayfeminism.com, January 12, 2015.

4. Quoted in Hannah Ewens, *Fangirls: Scenes from Modern Music Culture* (Austin: University of Texas Press, 2020), 179.

CHAPTER 10

1. Quoted in Elizabeth Goodman, "Dave Grohl Speaks Out about Kurt Cobain and Courtney-Love Inspired Track," *Rolling Stone*, September 17, 2007.

2. Beverly Gross, "Bitch," *Salmagundi* 103 (Summer 1994): 147–48.

3. See the discussion in Alexis Soloski's "Why the Sudden Urge to Reconsider Famous Women?," *New York Times*, March 31, 2022.

4. Gross, "Bitch," 129.

5. Karina Eileraas, "Witches, Bitches & Fluids: Girl Bands Performing Ugliness as Resistance," *TDR* 41, no. 3 (Autumn 1997): 123.

6. Jessica Rosenberg and Gitana Garofalo, "Riot Grrrl: Revolution from Within," *Signs* 23, no. 3 (Spring 1998): 809.

7. For more on Yoko Ono's connection to punk, see Shelina Louise Brown, "Yoko Ono's Experimental Vocality as Matrixial Borderspace: Theorizing Yoko Ono's Extended Vocal Technique and Her Contributions to the Development of Underground and Popular Vocal Repertoires, 1968–Present" (PhD diss., University of California, Los Angeles, 2018).

8. Ben London is credited for the name in a 7 Year Bitch Facebook post, January 22, 2016.

9. Edna Gundersen, "A Hit That Rhymes with Witch," *USA Today*, June 9, 1997.

10. Erica Palan, "Is the B-Word Still Insulting," phillymag.com, May 7, 2012.

11. Kalene Westmoreland, "'Bitch' and Lilith Fair: Resisting Anger, Celebrating Contradictions," *Popular Music & Society* 25, nos. 1–2 (2001): 218.

12. Priya Elan, "It's Time to Drop the 'Bitch' from Hip-Hop," *The Guardian*, September 19, 2012.

13. Ted Kessler, "Missy in Action," *The Guardian*, August 5, 2001.

14. Quoted in Vanessa Jones, "Whose Word Is It Anyway? Women, Some of Them, Co-opt 'Bitch,'" *Boston Globe*, July 7, 1999, D1.

15. Joanne Laucius, "Who Are You Calling a Bitch? The B-word Has Been Tamed, Reclaimed and Used to Sell stuff, from Wine to Empowerment," *Vancouver Sun*, April 21, 2012, C1.

16. For more on the policing of masculinity in pop music, see Kai Arne Hansen, *Pop Masculinities: The Politics of Gender in Twenty-First Century Popular Music* (Oxford: Oxford University Press, 2022).

SELECTED BIBLIOGRAPHY

Aker, Lauren. *Fan Phenomena: The Twilight Sage*. Bristol, UK: Intellect Books, 2016.

Arias, Eric. "How Does Media Influence Social Norms? Experimental Evidence on the Role of Common Knowledge." *Political Science Research and Methods* 7, no. 3 (July 2019): 561–78.

Austin, J. L. *How to Do Things with Words*. Cambridge, MA: Harvard University Press, 1962.

Bailey, Moya. *Misogynoir Transformed: Black Women's Digital Resistance*. New York: New York University Press, 2021.

Bourdieu, Pierre. "The Social Space and the Genesis of Groups." *Theory and Society* 14, no. 6 (1985): 723–44.

Brown, Shelina Louise. "Yoko Ono's Experimental Vocality as Matrixial Borderspace: Theorizing Yoko Ono's Extended Vocal Technique and Her Contributions to the Development of Underground and Popular Vocal Repertoires, 1968–Present." PhD diss., University of California, Los Angeles, 2018.

Carey, Mariah. *The Meaning of Mariah Carey*. New York: Andy Cohen Books, 2020.

Chandra, Giti, and Irma Erlingsdóttir, eds. *The Routledge Handbook of the Politics of the #MeToo Movement*. New York: Routledge, 2021.

Cheng, William. "So You've Been Musically Shamed." *Journal of Popular Music Studies* 30, no. 3 (2014): 63–98.

Childerhose, Buffy. *From Lilith to Lilith Fair*. New York: St. Martin's Griffin, 1998.

Chou, Rosalind S., and Joe R. Feagin. *The Myth of the Model Minority: Asian Americans Facing Racism.* London: Routledge, 2016.

Cohen, Brigid. "Limits of National History: Yoko Ono, Stefan Wolpe, and Dilemmas of Cosmopolitanism." *Musical Quarterly* 97, no. 2 (Summer 2014): 181–237.

Coluccia, Pina, Anette Paffrath, and Jean Pütz. *Belly Dancing: The Sensual Art of Energy and Spirit.* Randolph, VT: Park Street Press, 2005.

Copeland, Rebecca, and Laura Miller. *Diva Nation: Female Icons from Japanese Cultural History.* Berkeley: University of California Press, 2018.

Cowgill, Rachel, and Hilary Poriss, eds. *The Arts of the Prima Donna in the Long Nineteenth Century.* Oxford: Oxford University Press, 2012.

Crawford, Anwen. *Live through This.* New York: Bloomsbury, 2015.

Cross, Charles R. *Heavier than Heaven: A Biography of Kurt Cobain.* New York: Hyperion, 2001.

Cullen, Shaun. "The Innocent and the Runaway: Kanye West, Taylor Swift, and the Cultural Politics of Racial Melodrama." *Journal of Popular Music Studies* 28, no. 1 (2017): 33–50.

Donovan, Brian. *American Gold Digger: Marriage, Money, and the Law from the Ziegfeld Follies to Anna Nicole Smith.* Chapel Hill: University of North Carolina Press, 2020.

Doyle, Sady. *Trainwreck: The Women We Love to Hate, Mock, and Fear . . . and Why.* Brooklyn, NY: Melville House, 2016.

Eidsheim, Nina. *The Race of Sound: Listening, Timbre, and Vocality in African American Music.* Durham, NC: Duke University, 2019.

Eileraas, Karina. "Witches, Bitches & Fluids: Girl Bands Performing Ugliness as Resistance." *TDR* 41, no. 3 (Autumn 1997): 122–39.

Ellis, Katherine. "Female Pianists and Their Male Critics in Nineteenth-Century Paris." *Journal of the American Musicological Society* 50, nos. 2 and 3 (Summer–Autumn 1997): 353–85.

Ewens, Hannah. *Fangirls: Scenes from Modern Music Culture.* Austin: University of Texas Press, 2020.

Faithfull, Marianne. *Faithfull: An Autobiography.* Lanham, MD: Cooper Square Press, 2000.

Fink, Moritz. *The Simpsons: A Cultural History.* Lanham, MD: Rowman & Littlefield, 2019.

Foucault, Michel. *Madness and Civilization: A History of Insanity in the Age of Reason.* New York: Random House, 1988.

Glixon, Beth L. "Private Lives of Public Women: Prima Donnas in Mid-Seventeenth-Century Venice." *Music & Letters* 76, no. 4 (November 1995): 509–31.

Gorney, Debra Kay. "Image Construction in Print and Internet Media: Analysis of the Controversial Courtney Love." PhD diss., Wayne State University, 1999.

Govan, Chloe. *Taylor Swift: The Rise of the Nashville Teen*. London: Omnibus Press, 2012.

Gregory, Georgina. *Boy Bands and the Performance of Pop Masculinity*. New York: Routledge, 2019.

Gross, Beverly. "Bitch." *Salmagundi* 103 (Summer 1994): 147–48.

Gross, Sally Anne, and George Musgrave. *Can Music Make You Sick? Measuring the Price of Musical Ambition*. London: University of Westminster Press, 2020.

Hansen, Kai Arne. *Pop Masculinities: The Politics of Gender in Twenty-First Century Popular Music*. Oxford: Oxford University Press, 2022.

Hansen, Karen, ed. *Technology and the Diva: Sopranos, Opera, and Media from Romanticism to the Digital Age*. Cambridge: Cambridge University Press, 2016.

Harper, Stephen. *Madness, Power, and the Media: Class, Gender and Race in Popular Representations of Mental Distress*. London: Palgrave Macmillan, 2009.

Haven, Cynthia. "Yoko Ono Reflects on Her Life, Work and Public Perception." *Stanford Report*, January 15, 2009.

Hood, Ralph W., and W. Paul Williamson. *Them That Believe: The Power and Meaning of the Christian Serpent-Handling Tradition*. Berkeley: University of California Press, 2008.

Hopkins, Jerry. *Yoko Ono*. New York: Macmillan, 1986.

Huyssen, Andreas. *After the Great Divide: Modernism, Mass Culture, Postmodernism*. Ann Arbor: University of Michigan Press, 1986.

James, Robin. "Coincidental Consumption and the Thinkpiece Economy." *Society Pages*, November 15, 2013.

———. *Resilience & Melancholy: Pop Music, Feminism Neoliberalism*. Winchester, UK: Zero Books, 2015.

Johnson-Grau, Brenda. "Sweet Nothings: Presentation of Women Musicians in Pop Journalism." In *Pop Music and the Press*, edited by Steve Jones, 202–18. Philadelphia: Temple University Press, 2002.

Kennedy, Gerrick. *Didn't We Almost Have It All: In Defense of Whitney Houston*. New York: Abrams, 2022.

Kruse, Holly. "Abandoning the Absolute: Transcendence and Gender in Popular Music Discourse." In *Pop Music and the Press*, edited by Steve Jones, 134–55. Philadelphia: Temple University Press, 2002.

Lane, Amica. "Asking for It: Giving Outspoken Women in Music a Bad Name." *The F Word*, May 27, 2013.

Lee, SooJin. "The Art of Artists' Personae: Yayoi Kusama, Yoko Ono, and Mariko Mori." PhD diss., University of Illinois, 2014.

Levitz, Tamara. "Yoko Ono and the Unfinished Music of 'John & Yoko': Imagining Gender and Racial Equality in the Late 1960s." In *Impossible to Hold: Women and Culture in the 1960s*, edited by Avital H. Bloch and Lauri Umansky, 217–40. New York: New York University Press, 2005.

Lomax, Tamura. *Jezebel Unhinged: Loosing the Black Female Body in Religion and Culture*. Durham, NC: Duke University Press, 2018.

Love, Courtney. *Dirty Blonde*. London: Faber and Faber, 2006.

Lowe, Melanie. "Colliding Feminism: Britney Spears, 'Tweens,' and the Politics of Reception." *Popular Music and Society* 26 (2003): 123–40.

Manne, Kate. *Down Girl: The Logic of Misogyny*. Oxford: Oxford University Press, 2018.

McClary, Susan. *Feminine Endings*. Minneapolis: University of Minnesota Press, 1991.

McLeod, Kembrew. "Between Rock and a Hard Place: Gender and Rock Criticism." In *Pop Music and the Press*, edited by Steve Jones, 93–111. Philadelphia: Temple University Press, 2002.

Meyers, Erin A. *Cupcakes, Pinterest, and Ladyporn: Feminized Popular Culture in the Early Twenty-First Century*. Urbana: University of Illinois Press, 2015.

Mills, Richard. *The Beatles and Fandom: Sex, Death, and Progressive Nostalgia*. New York: Bloomsbury, 2019.

Montell, Amanda. *Wordslut: A Feminist Guide to Taking Back the English Language*. New York: Harper, 2019.

Morgan, Eleanor. *Hysterical: Why We Need to Talk about Women, Hormones, and Mental Health*. New York: Seal Press, 2019.

Muir, John Kenneth. *This Is Spinal Tap*. Milwaukee, WI: Limelight Editions, 2010.

Newman, Nancy. "#AlmaToo: The Art of Being Believed." *Journal of the American Musicological Society* 75, no. 1 (2022): 39–79.

Norman, Philip. *Shout! The Beatles in Their Generation*. New York: Simon & Schuster, 2005.

Parke, Maggie, and Natalie Wilson, eds. *Theorizing Twilight: Critical Essays on What's at Stake in a Post-Vampire World*. Jefferson, NC: McFarland, 2011.

Pearson, Tanya. *Why Marianne Faithfull Matters*. Austin: University of Texas Press, 2021.

Prasso, Sheridan. *The Asian Mystique: Dragon Ladies, Geisha Girls, and Our Fantasies of the Exotic Orient*. New York: Public Affairs, 2005.

Racy, A. J. "Domesticating Otherness: The Snake Charmer in American Popular Culture." *Ethnomusicology* 60, no. 2 (Spring/Summer 2016): 197–232.

Ralston, Meredith. *Slut-Shaming, Whorephobia, and the Unfinished Sexual Revolution*. Montreal and Kingston: McGill-Queen's University Press, 2021.

Rosenberg, Jessica, and Gitana Garofalo. "Riot Grrrl: Revolution from Within." *Signs* 23, no. 3 (Spring 1998): 809–41.

Rutherford, Susan. *The Prima Donna and Opera, 1815–1930.* Cambridge: Cambridge University Press, 2006.

Schearing, Linda S., and Valarie H. Ziegler. *Enticed by Eden: How Western Culture Uses, Confuses, (and Sometimes Abuses) Adam and Eve.* Waco: Baylor University Press, 2013.

Showalter, Elaine. *The Female Malady: Women, Madness and English Culture, 1830–1980.* London: Time Warner Books, 1987.

Skurnick, Lizzie, ed. *Pretty Bitches: On Being Called Crazy, Angry, Bossy, Frumpy, Feisty, and All the Other Words That Are Used to Undermine Women.* New York: Seal Press, 2020.

Smit, Christopher R. *The Exile of Britney Spears: A Tale of 21st Century Consumption.* Bristol, UK: Intellect, 2011.

Spears, Lynn. *Through the Storm.* Nashville: Thomas Nelson, 2010.

Stephens, Dionne P., and Layli D. Phillips. "Freaks, Gold Diggers, Divas, and Dykes: The Sociohistorical Development of Adolescent African American Women's Sexual Scripts." *Sexuality & Culture* (Winter 2003): 3–49.

Stern, Kimberly J. *The Social Life of Criticism: Gender, Critical Writing, and the Politics of Belonging.* Ann Arbor: University of Michigan Press, 2016.

St. Stevens, Carolyn. "Yoko Ono: A Transgressive Diva." In *Diva Nation: Female Icons from Japanese Cultural History,* edited by Laura Miller and Rebecca Copeland, 115–32. Berkeley: University of California Press, 2018.

Sweet, Paige. "The Sociology of Gaslighting." *American Sociological Review* 84, no. 5 (October 2019): 851–75.

Tchen, John Kuo Wei, and Dylan Yeats, eds. *Yellow Peril! An Archive of Anti-Asian Fear.* London: Verso, 2014.

Valenti, Jessica, and Jaclyn Friedman. *Believe Me: How Trusting Women Can Change the World.* New York: Seal Press, 2020.

Von Hendy, Andrew. *The Modern Construction of Myth.* Bloomington: Indiana University Press, 2002.

Westmoreland, Kalene. "'Bitch' and Lilith Fair: Resisting Anger, Celebrating Contradictions." *Popular Music & Society* 25, nos. 1–2 (2001): 205–20.

Whiteley, Sheila. *Women and Popular Music: Sexuality, Identity and Subjectivity.* London: Routledge, 2000.

Wolfe, Paula. *Women in the Studio: Creativity, Control and Gender in Popular Music Production.* London: Routledge, 2020.

Womack, Kenneth, and Kit O'Toole. *Fandom and the Beatles: The Act You've Known for All These Years.* Oxford: Oxford University Press, 2021.

Zarzycki, Lili. "Interview with Christine Battersby." *Architectural Review*, March 26, 2020.

Zimmerman, Jess. *Women and Other Monsters: Building a New Mythology*. Boston: Beacon Press, 2021.

INDEX

ABOUT THE AUTHOR

Lily E. Hirsch is a musicologist, book reviews editor for the *Journal of Musicological Research*, and visiting scholar at California State University, Bakersfield. She studied music history as an undergraduate at the University of the Pacific and earned her PhD in musicology from Duke University. She then taught as assistant professor of music at Cleveland State University.

She is the author of *A Jewish Orchestra in Nazi Germany: Musical Politics and the Berlin Jewish Culture League* (2010), *Music in American Crime Prevention and Punishment* (2012), *Anneliese Landau's Life in Music: Nazi Germany to Émigré California* (2019), and *Weird Al: Seriously* (2020; expanded edition, 2022); and coeditor of *Dislocated Memories: Jews, Music, and Postwar German Culture* (2014), winner of the American Musicological Society's Ruth A. Solie Award. In addition to chapters in books such as *You Shook Me All Campaign Long* and the *Cambridge Companion to Jewish Music*, she has published articles in musicological journals as well as newspapers and online sites, including the *Washington Post*, *The Guardian*, and *A Women's Thing*.

CPSIA information can be obtained
at www.ICGtesting.com
Printed in the USA
BVHW050552301122
653055BV00001B/1

9 781538 169063